# Foundations in Quantitative Business Techniques

# Foundations in Quantitative Business Techniques

G. Bancroft and G. O'Sullivan

McGraw-Hill Publishing Company
**London** · New York · Burr Ridge, IL · St Louis · San Francisco
Auckland · Bogota · Caracas · Lisbon · Madrid · Mexico
Milan · Montreal · New Delhi · Panama · Paris · San Juan
São Paulo · Singapore · Sydney · Tokyo · Toronto

Published by
**McGraw-Hill Publishing Company**
Shoppenhangers Road, Maidenhead, Berkshire, SL6 2QL, England
Telephone 01628 502500
Facsimile 01628 770224

**British Library Cataloguing in Publication Data**
A catalogue record for this book is available from the British Library

**Library of Congress Cataloging-in-publication Data**
A catalog record for this book is available from the Library of Congress

**Further information on this title is to be found at http://www.mcgraw-hill.co.uk/textbooks/bancroft**

Publisher: Andy Goss
Sponsoring Editor: Domenic Recaldin
Desk Editor: Alastair Lindsay
Produced by Steven Gardiner Limited
Cover designed by Simon Levy Associates

Printed and bound by Interprint Limited, Malta

ISBN 007 709468 9

# Contents

# *Preface*

There are ever increasing numbers of students entering Higher Education to study business, accounting and economics without relevant qualifications in mathematics. The authors of this text have previously written a more advanced text – *Quantitative Methods on Accounting and Business Studies* – which did not cover the numerical foundations needed in both everyday life and business, but did include additional topics normally delivered at a more advanced level in business courses. The authors therefore recognised a need for a text that assumed little background knowledge in numeracy and that delivered the material at a speed that was appropriate to readers who lacked confidence in handling numerical information. This text responds to that need. It describes and illustrates the core quantitative techniques required bot business decision-making. It is suitable for students on HND and undergraduate introductory modules.

Furthermore, the text has been developed to enable a student to work through it without supervision from a lecturer. The text includes numerous integrated examples and exercises and further exercises at the end of each chapter. To understand the chapter material fully, it is important that you attempt and complete these examples and exercises. Solutions to all the exercises are given in Appendix 1. Formulae sheets and tables are also provided in Appendix 2 and 3 respectively. The calculator is a valuable tool for performing calculations, particularly when these calculations are large and time-consuming. The use of a calculator is taught throughout the text. In addition, frequent reference to the use of spreadsheets, and EXCEL in particular, is made.

Gordon Bancroft
George O'Sullivan

# Acknowledgements

We are grateful to the many readers of the book, both students and colleagues.

Special thanks go to the reviewers:

Bernard Pearson, University of Exeter
John Flynn, University of Hull
Sidney Tyrell, University of Coventry
Les Oakshott, University of the West of England
Michael Wood, University of Portsmouth
Jean Swanson, London Guildhall University
Mark Cleary, Anglia Polytechnic University

The authors would like to express their particular gratitude to Paul Cockram, late of the University of Central Lancashire, who critically reviewed the entire manuscript and checked all the numerical examples. Any errors which may remain are, of course, the authors' responsibility.

We are also indebted to our wives, Anne and Eleanor, and Dominic Recaldin for their encouragement during the writing of the text.

# Numerical Techniques

## 1.1 Arithmetic Operations

In all aspects of life today—whether at work or at home—you really do
have to be able to handle **numbers**. In fact, it is as important to understand
and to perform basic arithmetic in today's society as it is to read and write.
In the first part of this chapter we are going to look at some absolutely
basic arithmetic techniques and apply them to real-life situations. We also
give you lots of examples, with answers, for you to practise until you feel
confident that you've got the idea.

First of all, try the calculation

$$21 - 8 \times 2$$

What answer did you get?   5?   26?   Something else?

The right answer is 5, but you could be forgiven for thinking it is 26. (If
you thought it was something else, have another go at it.)

The trouble is we don't know for certain in which order to do the calculation. Now if we had put **brackets** round part of the calculation it would
have made it much clearer, because expressions in brackets are done first.
**An essential rule in mathematics, not just arithmetic, is that expressions
within brackets are evaluated first.**

So, if we put brackets round the multiplication part, like this, we get:

$$21 - (8 \times 2) = 21 - 16 = 5$$

But if we had put brackets round the other part of the calculation, like this,
we get:

$$(21 - 8) \times 2 = 13 \times 2 = 26$$

If we look at the following calculation, however:

$$(15 \times 5) - (12 \times 4) = 75 - 48 = 27$$

there is no argument about the answer because you have to do the parts in brackets first.

Let's go back to our first problem, $21 - 8 \times 2$, and see how a calculator copes with it. The following key sequence

$$[21] \ [-] \ [8] \ [\times] \ [2] \ [=]$$

on most good calculators will give you the answer 5, because the calculator will do the multiplication before the subtraction. **This is a basic rule in mathematics: do multiplications and divisions BEFORE additions and subtractions.**

That is why the right answer to:

$$21 - 8 \times 2$$

is 5 and not 26. It gives the same answer as if brackets were put round the multiplication part. Unfortunately some calculators do work out the expression from left to right giving the answer of 26. Therefore it is a sensible idea to become familiar with the way that your calculator works.

From now on perform the multiplication (or division) operation before addition (or subtraction). Are you comfortable about that? Try the questions in Example 1.1.1 and see if you get the same answers.

## Example 1.1.1

Use your calculator to get answers to the following questions. Check that your calculator is carrying out the operations in the correct order.

    **a**  $42 \div 7 + 4$
    **b**  $3 + 5 \times 2$
    **c**  $4 - (9 \div 3)$
    **d**  $8 \times 5 - 4 \times 9$

## *Solution to Example 1.1.1*

The answers that you should get are:

    **a**  $42 \div 7 + 4$    $= 6 + 4$    $= 10$
    **b**  $3 + 5 \times 2$    $= 3 + 10$    $= 13$
    **c**  $4 - (9 \div 3)$    $= 4 - 3$    $= 1$
    **d**  $8 \times 5 - 4 \times 9$    $= 40 - 36$    $= 4$

**If a problem contains only pluses or minuses (or only multiplications and divisions)** there is not usually any confusion as **you should work through the problem from left to right**. For example

$$15 + 8 - 14 + 2$$
$$= 23 - 14 + 2$$
$$= 9 + 2$$
$$= 11$$

These key rules of arithmetic are illustrated in two examples that describe situations in everyday life.

## Example 1.1.2

Table 1.1 shows the daily cost of hiring four cars from U HIRE plc. The total car hire charge includes a daily rate charge and an excess mileage charge for each mile over the daily free mileage allowance.

**Table 1.1. Car hire charges**

| Car | Daily rate | Free miles per day | Excess mileage charge |
| --- | --- | --- | --- |
| Nissan Micra | £28 | 50 | 9p |
| Toyota Corolla | £36 | 100 | 19p |
| Ford Mondeo | £61 | 150 | 35p |
| Audi Quattro | £93 | 50 | 50p |

**a** Anne hires an Audi Quattro for a day and drives 134 miles. What is the hire charge?

**b** Navinder, living in Manchester, hires a Mondeo, and drives to London for a business meeting. What is the hire charge if Navinder does the return journey in one day? Manchester is 204 miles from London.

**c** Stephen hires a Nissan Micra for two days and pays £83. How many miles has he done in the two days?

**d** Claire, who lives in London, hires a Corolla to take a computer to Glasgow. The journey from London to Glasgow is 412 miles each way. How much will she save by doing the return journey in one day rather than in two days?

### Solution to Example 1.1.2

**a**  Anne's cost will include the daily charge of £93 plus 84 excess miles at 50p per mile. As we have a mixture of units it is best to perform all calculations in pence.

Anne's total cost  $= $ hire charge $+$ excess mileage charge
$$= 9300 + 84 \times 50$$
$$= 9300 + 4200$$
$$= 13\,500\,\text{p} \qquad = £135$$

Clearly it would be wrong to do the calculations in the order they are written, ignoring the key rule that multiplications should be done before additions as it would give the incorrect answer of £4692.

**b**  Navinder drives $2 \times 204 = 408$ miles in the day, which is $408 - 150 = 258$ excess miles.

Navinder's cost  $= 6100 + 258 \times 35$
$$= 6100 + 9030$$
$$= 15\,130\,\text{p} \qquad = £151.30\text{p}$$

**c**  Stephen pays $2 \times £28 = £56$ for the daily rate charge of the Nissan Micra, which means that the remaining $83 - 56 = £27$ (or 2700 pence) is for excess mileage. His excess mileage is therefore $2700 \div 9 = 300$ miles.

  As he also received $2 \times 50 = 100$ free miles for the two days, then, in total, Stephen must have travelled $300 + 100 = 400$ miles.

**d**  Claire's cost (for two days) involving $2 \times 412 - 2 \times 100 = 824 - 200 = 624$ excess miles would be

$2 \times 3600 + 624 \times 19$
$= 7200 + 11\,856$
$= 19\,056\,\text{p} \qquad = £190.56\text{p}$

In one day the excess mileage would be $2 \times 412 - 100 = 724$ miles, and the total cost would be

$3600 + 724 \times 19\,\text{p}$
$= 3600 + 13\,756$
$= 17\,356\,\text{p} \qquad = £173.56\text{p}$

This is a saving of £17.

## Example 1.1.3

Jason needs a personal loan of £6800 to enable him to purchase a new car. His bank supplies him with Table 1.2, which gives the monthly repayments for differing amounts and lengths of loans.

**Table 1.2. Monthly repayments**

| Amount borrowed | 24 months Monthly payment With insurance (£) | 24 months Monthly payment Without insurance (£) | 30 months Monthly payment With insurance (£) | 30 months Monthly payment Without insurance (£) | 36 months Monthly payment With insurance (£) | 36 months Monthly payment Without insurance (£) | 48 months Monthly payment With insurance (£) | 48 months Monthly payment Without insurance (£) |
|---|---|---|---|---|---|---|---|---|
| £50 | 2.82 | 2.54 | 2.39 | 2.13 | 2.10 | 1.85 | 1.74 | 1.50 |
| £100 | 5.63 | 5.08 | 4.77 | 4.25 | 4.21 | 3.69 | 3.48 | 3.00 |
| £500 | 28.15 | 25.42 | 23.86 | 21.25 | 21.04 | 18.47 | 17.39 | 15.00 |
| £1000 | 56.30 | 50.83 | 47.72 | 42.50 | 42.07 | 36.94 | 34.79 | 30.00 |
| £5000 | 281.50 | 254.15 | 238.60 | 212.50 | 210.36 | 184.70 | 173.94 | 150.00 |
| £10 000 | 563.00 | 508.30 | 477.20 | 425.00 | 420.70 | 369.40 | 347.90 | 300.00 |
|  | (APR = 21.7%) | | (APR = 21.6%) | | (APR = 21.4%) | | (APR = 20.9%) | |

Jason decides to repay over the loan period of 48 months. Obtain his monthly repayment if

**a**  he decides to pay no insurance
**b**  he decides to pay the insurance

Calculate the total cost of the insurance over the 48 months.

## *Solution to Example 1.1.3*

In the table there is no reference to the £6800 down the left-hand side, so it will be necessary to make up this amount from the other amounts included.

As 6800 = 5000 + 1000 + 500 + 3 × 100 the monthly payment will be obtained from adding the appropriate £5000 payment to the £1000, then adding the £500 payment and finally adding the £100 payment three times. In practice, this is what a bank manager would do to find the monthly repayment.

**a**  Without insurance the monthly payment will be

$$£150 + £30 + £15 + 3 \times £3$$
$$= £150 + £30 + £15 + £9$$
$$= £204$$

**b**   With insurance the monthly payment will be

£173.94 + £34.79 + £17.39 + 3 × £3.48
= £173.94 + £34.79 + £17.39 + £10.44 = £236.56

This is an increase of £236.56 − £204 = £32.56 each month over the 48 months. The total cost of the insurance over the 48 months is 32.56 × 48 = £1562.88

In this example you might think that you would get the same answer if you multiplied the £100 value in the table by 68. Try this with the insurance element included. You get

68 × £3.48 = £236.64

This is different, albeit slightly, to the answer obtained in part (b). Why do you think this is?

It is because all the figures in the table are rounded to the nearest penny and your answer tends to be more accurate if you build up to the amount borrowed by adding amounts close to the total in the way that we did, rather than taking a small amount and multiplying by a large number. If you have a small rounding error and multiply it by 68, say, it might become a large rounding error.

We get further complications if some of the numbers are **negative**. A daily weather report might give a maximum daytime temperature of 16 °C and a minimum temperature on that day of −3 °C. The difference between the two numbers is found by subtracting the smaller number from the larger one; here

16 − (−3)

The answer is 19 °C; that is, there is 19° difference between 16 °C and −3 °C.

This shows clearly the rule that **subtracting a negative number is the same as adding a positive number**.

$$\text{Temperature difference} = 16 - (-3)$$
$$= 16 + 3$$
$$= 19$$

An everyday situation where both positive and negative numbers are used is the operation of a bank account. Here the value of a credit can be treated as a positive number whereas the amount of a cheque or withdrawal is the negative number.

## Example 1.1.4

On 1 January John Price had a balance of £476 in his account. During January he paid in amounts of £53 and £72 and wrote cheques to the value of £167, £96 and a further three cheques to the value of £150. What is the balance of his account at the end of January? How much must John pay into his account at the end of January to pay off his overdraft?

### Solution to Example 1.1.4

As the values of the cheques are treated as negative numbers, the balance, in £, at the end of January is

$$476 + (53) + (72) + (-167) + (-96) + 3 \times (-150)$$

The [+/−] button on your calculator changes the sign of the number displayed and is therefore useful when inputting negative numbers. The key sequence

[476] [+] [53] [+] [72] [+] [167] [+/–] [+] [96] [+/–] [+] [3] [×] [150] [+/–] [=]

gives the balance of John's account. The answer displayed is −112, indicating that John Price is £112 overdrawn at the end of January.

Another way of doing this is to note that the **addition of a negative number is equivalent to subtracting a positive number**. Therefore John's bank balance could be found directly from

| Opening balance | +credit total | − cheque total |
|---|---|---|
| = 476 | +(53 + 72) | − (167 + 96+3 × (150)) |
| = 476 | +125 | − 713 |
| = −112 | | |

In order to pay off his overdraft he must add £112 to his account.

## Example 1.1.5

A rock climber started climbing in the morning at 430 metres below base camp and ended up at the end of the day 90 metres above base camp. What distance did the rock climber achieve during the day?

### Solution to Example 1.1.5

The climber had to climb 430 metres to reach base camp, and a further 90 metres to reach his finishing point, making a total of 520 metres during the day.

Looking at this mathematically,

$$\text{Distance climbed} = \text{finishing point} - \text{starting point}$$

Using the base camp as the datum point,

$$\text{Distance climbed} = 90 - (-430)$$

This points again to the rule that **subtracting a negative number is the same as adding the positive number**.

$$
\begin{aligned}
\text{Distance climbed} \ &= 90 - (-430) \\
&= 90 + 430 \\
&= 520 \text{ m}
\end{aligned}
$$

Care needs to be taken when multiplying with negative numbers. On a calculator it is usual to input a negative number, as before, by using the [+/−] key after entering the equivalent positive number. So, you find the answer to

$$7 \times (-5)$$

using the key sequence

$$[7]\,[\times]\,[5]\,[+/-]\,[=]$$

The answer is $-35$. Also

$$(-6) \times (-2)$$

using the key sequence on a calculator

$$[6]\,[+/-]\,[\times]\,[2]\,[+/-]\,[=]$$

has an answer of 12.

From these examples you see that the following rules apply to multiplication using negative numbers:

$$\textbf{(positive number)} \times \textbf{(negative number)} = \textbf{(negative number)}$$

and

$$\textbf{(negative number)} \times \textbf{(negative number)} = \textbf{(positive number)}$$

These rules apply for both multiplication and division. Perhaps the second of these rules is difficult to comprehend, but in speech a double negative statement, such as not unusual, may imply a positive statement, such as usual. You should try the questions in Example 1.1.6, if possible without using a calculator.

## Example 1.1.6

For each of the following expressions, work out the answer

**a** $5 \times (-8)$     **b** $(-4) \times (-7)$     **c** $(-9) \div (-3)$     **d** $(72) \div (-8)$

## *Solution to Example 1.1.6*

**a** As $5 \times 8 = 40$ and multiplication here is between a positive number and a negative number, we have

$$5 \times (-8) = -40$$

**b** Multiplication of two negative numbers gives a positive answer

$$(-4) \times (-7) = 28$$

**c** Division of two negative numbers also gives a positive answer.

$$(-9) \div (-3) = 9 \div 3 = 3$$

**d** Here        $(72) \div (-8) = -(72 \div 8) = -9$

A further useful skill when dealing with numbers is that of **rounding** a number to the degree of accuracy appropriate to the situation in hand. Often this has the additional advantage of making the general size of the number more comprehensible. For example, you may have a large win in a competition which amounts to £161 731. It is quite likely that this figure will be reported in the local press as £160 000. From the reader's point of view the published figure gives a good idea of the size of the win and is easy to remember. This type of approximation is often carried out with large numbers, or with numbers that have a lot of digits, 532.957 435 32, say. In the competition example the win has been rounded to the nearest ten thousand pounds, or correct to two **significant figures** (as there are two digits to the left of the zeros).

There are many situations where it is more sensible to estimate the value of a quantity, rather than use its exact value. For example, you may wish to know approximately how long it would take to journey from York to London by car. Using the AA recommended route the distance by road is 211 miles but it is unlikely that you are travelling from the centre of York to the centre of London so it may be sensible to round the distance to the nearest ten miles. As 211 miles is nearer to 210 miles than 220 miles, the distance between the two cities is 210 miles to the nearest ten miles.

## Example 1.1.7

Table 1.3 shows the distance, in miles, between cities within Great Britain. The distances are given to the nearest mile and are measured along the normal AA recommended route.

**Table 1.3. Mileage chart for certain cities**

| London | | | | |
|---|---|---|---|---|
| 545 | Aberdeen | | | |
| 77 | 587 | Dover | | |
| 143 | 387 | 220 | Lincoln | |
| 310 | 697 | 356 | 396 | Penzance |

a    Determine the distance between the following pairs of cities rounded to the nearest 10 miles.
  • Lincoln and London
  • Dover and London
  • London and Aberdeen
b    What is the distance between Penzance and Aberdeen to the nearest 100 miles?

## Solution to Example 1.1.7

a   • The distance between Lincoln and London is 143 miles which is nearer to 140 miles than 150 miles, so the answer is 140 miles.
  • 77 miles is closer to 80 miles than 70 miles, so the answer is 80 miles.
  • The distance between London and Aberdeen is 545 miles, which is exactly halfway between 540 miles and 550 miles. Convention states that if this happens then the number should be rounded up rather than down. This gives an answer of 550 miles.
b   697 miles is nearer to 700 miles than 600 miles, so choose 700 miles.

1   A quarterly electricity bill includes both a standing charge of £8.30 plus a further charge of 7p per kWh. Provide an arithmetic expression for the total bill if 1240 kWhs are used in the quarter and evaluate this total bill.

2   Juanita's current account was £128 overdrawn at the start of a day. During the day an amount was paid into the account giving a new balance of £64. How much was this amount?

3   You read in a daily newspaper that a major company had made an annual profit of £54 754 273. What would this be to the nearest

   **a** hundred pounds
   **b** thousand pounds
   **c** million pounds?

4   The population of a city in 1995 was seven hundred and thirteen thousand five hundred and thirty.

   **a** Write fully in figures the 1995 population.
   **b** Write the 1995 population in figures correct to the nearest thousand.

5   Beverley and Robert decide to purchase a house costing £82 000. They pay a deposit of £21 000 and obtain a mortgage from a building society for the remainder. The building society gives them a table showing the monthly repayments on a mortgage of £1000 for different numbers of years of repayment and different interest rates.

| Interest rate (%) | 15 years (£) | 20 years (£) | 25 years (£) | 30 years (£) |
| --- | --- | --- | --- | --- |
| 9.0 | 8.93 | 7.74 | 6.91 | 6.47 |
| 9.5 | 9.19 | 7.97 | 7.15 | 6.71 |
| 10.0 | 9.38 | 8.20 | 7.39 | 6.89 |
| 10.5 | 9.58 | 8.43 | 7.64 | 7.11 |
| 11.0 | 9.80 | 8.68 | 7.89 | 7.36 |
| 11.5 | 10.01 | 9.91 | 8.14 | 7.59 |

Beverley and Robert are charged an interest rate of 9.5 per cent and they decide to pay back the mortgage over 20 years. What is their monthly repayment?

## 1.2 Fractions

In the previous section we generally restricted our attention to arithmetic operations involving whole numbers. However a glance at any newspaper may reveal, say, that the exchange rate is 9.75 French francs to the pound, or that one-quarter of the UK population is aged over 60. Each of these pieces of information contains numbers that are part of a whole. It is important to be able to manipulate numbers that are of this type. One way of writing a number which is only 'part of a whole' is as a fraction.

A *fraction* is a number written like $^2/_5$, where the number above the line is called the **numerator** and the number below the line is called the **denominator**. The fraction $^2/_5$ can be envisaged by splitting the whole into five equal parts and taking two of these parts (see Fig.1.1).

$\frac{2}{5}$ Two-fifths

**Figure 1.1** Representation of Two-fifths

By considering similar diagrams (see Fig.1.2) you can see that the fractions $^2/_4$ and $^1/_2$ are the same. You can see clearly that $^2/_4 = {^1/_2}$. In fact there are many different ways of writing one-half:

$$\frac{1}{2} = \frac{2}{4} = \frac{3}{6} = \frac{4}{8} = \frac{5}{10} = \frac{8}{16}$$

These are all **equal (or equivalent) fractions** and can be formed by multiplying both the numerator and denominator of the fraction by the same constant. It is usual to write a fraction in its simplest form. To do this, divide both the numerator and denominator by the same whole number. When no number other than one will divide into both the numbers, the fraction is in its **lowest form**. The following example shows how to find fractions in their lowest form.

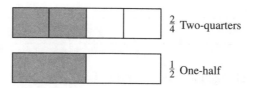

$\frac{2}{4}$ Two-quarters

$\frac{1}{2}$ One-half

**Figure 1.2** Representation of One-half

## Example 1.2.1

Convert the following fractions to their lowest form.

**a** $^4/_{12}$   **b** $^{16}/_{24}$   **c** $^7/_8$

## *Solution to Example 1.2.1*

**a**   $^4/_{12} = {}^1/_3$ as both the numerator and denominator of the original fraction can be divided by 4.
**b**   $^{16}/_{24} = {}^2/_3$. Both numbers can be divided by 8.
**c**   $^7/_8$ is in its lowest form. Although the denominator can be divided by 2 and 4 the numerator cannot. Hence it is in its lowest form.

In order to **add or subtract two or more fractions they must have the same denominator**. Therefore the first step when carrying out this operation is to find the common denominator of all the fractions.

## Example 1.2.2

Evaluate

**a** $^1/_7 + {}^4/_7$   **b** $^1/_2 + {}^2/_3 - {}^5/_6$   **c** $^3/_4 + {}^3/_8$

## *Solution to Example 1.2.2*

**a**   $^1/_7$ and $^4/_7$ both have a denominator equal to 7. Therefore these fractions can be added immediately.

$$\frac{1}{7} + \frac{4}{7} = \frac{1+4}{7} = \frac{5}{7}$$

**b**   The smallest number divisible by 2, 3 and 6 is 6 so the fractions are converted to equivalent fractions with denominator equal to 6.

$$\frac{1}{2} + \frac{2}{3} - \frac{5}{6} = \frac{3}{6} + \frac{4}{6} - \frac{5}{6} = \frac{3+4-5}{6} = \frac{2}{6}$$

In its lowest form the answer is $^1/_3$.

**c**   $^3/_4$ and $^3/_8$ have denominators equal to 4 and 8 respectively. The smallest number divisible by both 4 and 8 is 8. The two fractions need to be rewritten so that they are equivalent fractions with denominator equal to 8.

$$\frac{3}{4} = \frac{6}{8} \qquad \text{so} \qquad \frac{3}{4} + \frac{3}{8} = \frac{6}{8} + \frac{3}{8} = \frac{9}{8}$$

The answer $\frac{9}{8}$ is an **improper fraction** (as the numerator is greater than the denominator) and can be written as the mixed number, $1\frac{1}{8}$. A **mixed number** is a combination of a whole number and a fraction.

## Example 1.2.3

A small company consists of 60 employees. 25 of the employees are female, 24 are aged under 30 and 48 work in the production department. Express as fractions:

**a**   the proportion of production workers
**b**   the proportion of male workers
**c**   the proportion aged under 30.

## *Solution to Example 1.2.3*

**a**   48 out of the 60 employees are in the production department. Consequently the required fraction is

$$\frac{48}{60} \text{ which in its simplest form is } \frac{4}{5}.$$

as both 48 and 60 can be divided by 12.

**b**   As 25 of the employees are female, the remainder $60 - 25 = 35$ are male. The proportion of male workers is

$$\frac{35}{60} = \frac{7}{12}$$

**c**   The proportion aged under 30 is

$$\frac{24}{60} \text{ or in its lowest form, } \frac{2}{5}$$

Many calculators are capable of performing calculations directly. This involves using the [a$\frac{b}{c}$] button. For example, $\frac{3}{4} - \frac{1}{6}$ can be worked out by using the key sequence:

$$[3] \text{ [a}\tfrac{b}{c}\text{] } [4] [-] [1] \text{ [a}\tfrac{b}{c}\text{] } [6] [=]$$

The answer is $\frac{7}{12}$, given as 7⌋12, on most calculators.

In a similar way,

$$2^1/_4 + 1^7/_8$$

is worked out by using the key sequence

[2] [a$\frac{b}{c}$] [1] [a$\frac{b}{c}$] [4] [+] [1] [a$\frac{b}{c}$] [7] [a$\frac{b}{c}$] [8] [=]

giving an answer of $4^1/_8$ ( given as 4⌋1⌋8 on the calculator).

To multiply fractions there is *no* need to rewrite the fractions so that they have the same denominator. All you need to do is **multiply the numerators together and multiply the denominators together**. The resulting fraction then needs to be written in its lowest form

$$\frac{9}{16} \times \frac{4}{15} = \frac{9 \times 4}{16 \times 15} = \frac{36}{240} = \frac{3}{20}$$

To **divide one fraction by another, the second fraction (the *divisor*) is turned 'upside down'** (the numerator becomes the denominator and the denominator becomes the numerator) **and the two fractions are then multiplied together**. For example

$$\frac{8}{9} \div \frac{2}{3} = \frac{8}{9} \times \frac{3}{2} = \frac{8 \times 3}{9 \times 2} = \frac{24}{18} = \frac{4}{3} = 1\frac{1}{3}$$

In this example $^2/_3$ is turned 'upside down' to give $^3/_2$ which is then multiplied by $^8/_9$, giving $1^1/_3$ as the answer. In the same way

$$9 : \frac{3}{5} = \frac{9 \times 5}{1 \times 3} = \frac{45}{3} = \frac{15}{1} = 15$$

Now try these in Example 1.2.4 to see if you have understood how to perform arithmetic on fractions.

## Example 1.2.4

Evaluate the following expressions involving manipulation of fractions.

**a** $\dfrac{3}{10} \times \dfrac{5}{6}$  **b** $\dfrac{4}{15} \div \dfrac{2}{5}$  **c** $\dfrac{3}{5} + \dfrac{2}{3} - \dfrac{4}{5}$  **d** $1\dfrac{3}{5} \times 1\dfrac{1}{2}$  **e** $3\dfrac{1}{8} - 1\dfrac{1}{4}$

## Solution to Example 1.2.4

**a**   The calculation can be carried out directly on most calculators using the key sequence:

[3] [a$\frac{b}{c}$] [10] [×] [5] [a$\frac{b}{c}$] [6] [=]

to give an answer of $\frac{1}{4}$. Alternatively, the calculation can be done without a calculator

$$\frac{3}{10} \times \frac{5}{6} = \frac{15}{60}, \text{ which is } \frac{1}{4} \text{ in its lowest form.}$$

b    $$\frac{4}{15} \div \frac{2}{5} = \frac{4}{15} \times \frac{5}{2} = \frac{20}{30} = \frac{2}{3}$$

which could also have been obtained more directly from the key sequence:

[4] [a$\frac{b}{c}$] [15] [÷] [2] [a$\frac{b}{c}$] [5] [=]

c    $$\frac{3}{5} + \frac{2}{3} - \frac{4}{5} = \frac{9}{15} + \frac{10}{15} - \frac{12}{15} = \frac{7}{15}$$

Using the calculator

[3] [a$\frac{b}{c}$] [5] [+] [2] [a$\frac{b}{c}$] [3] [–] [4] [a$\frac{b}{c}$] [5] [=]

gives the same answer.

d    $$1\frac{3}{5} \times 1\frac{1}{2} = \frac{8}{5} \times \frac{3}{2} = \frac{24}{10} = 2\frac{2}{5} \text{ or}$$

[1] [a$\frac{b}{c}$] [3] [a$\frac{b}{c}$] [5] [×] [1] [a$\frac{b}{c}$] [1] [a$\frac{b}{c}$] [2] [=]

gives the same answer, $2\frac{2}{5}$.

e    $$3\frac{1}{8} - 1\frac{1}{4} = \frac{25}{8} - \frac{10}{8} = \frac{15}{8} = 1\frac{7}{8}.$$

## Example 1.2.5

In a survey of a group of 1200 employees it was found that 450 travelled to work by train, 240 travelled to work by car, $\frac{3}{10}$ of the group walked to work and the remainder travelled by bus. Calculate what fraction of the group travelled to work by bus.

## Solution to Example 1.2.5

The number walking to work is $\frac{3}{10} \times 1200 = 360$.

The number travelling by bus is $1200 - (450 + 240 + 360) = 150$

The fraction travelling by bus is $\dfrac{150}{1200} = \dfrac{1}{8}$

1   A person spends $\frac{1}{3}$ of a 24-hour day asleep, $\frac{3}{8}$ at work, $\frac{1}{16}$ travelling, and the remainder is free time. What fraction of the day is free time?

2   On Monday John worked $6\frac{3}{4}$ hours, on Tuesday he worked $7\frac{3}{4}$ hours, on Wednesday and Thursday he worked $7\frac{1}{2}$ hours, and on Friday, $6\frac{1}{4}$ hours. Express the total time worked that week as a fraction. Determine his pay for the week if he is paid at £4.26 per hour.

3   John Worth wished to buy a house and needs to take out a mortgage to help purchase the house. A large bank will allow Mr Worth to borrow $2\frac{3}{4}$ times his annual salary, whereas his local building society will only lend him $2\frac{1}{2}$ times his salary. If Mr Worth's annual salary is £16 500 determine the size of loan that each institution will give him.

4   Write 400 metres as a fraction of 20 kilometres.

5   Evaluate

    **a** $\dfrac{2}{5} + \dfrac{1}{4}$    **b** $\dfrac{2}{5} - \dfrac{1}{4}$    **c** $\dfrac{2}{5} \times \dfrac{1}{4}$    **d** $\dfrac{2}{5} \div \dfrac{1}{4}$

## 1.3 Decimals

*Decimals* are fractions expressed in tenths, hundredths, thousandths, etc., and as normal counting takes place in tens, decimals are easier to work with than common fractions. To identify where the whole number ends and the fractional part begins, a decimal point is used, thus 3.7 is equivalent to $3\frac{7}{10}$ or 0.29 is equivalent to $\frac{29}{100}$.

As well as being more commonly used nowadays, decimal fractions have the advantage over common fractions that arithmetic is somewhat easier. For example, addition (and subtraction) of decimals is exactly the same as the addition (and subtraction) of whole numbers if a calculator is being used. For example,

$$7.23 + 15.8 + 0.576 = 23.606$$

If you carry out this calculation by hand you must keep the decimal points in a vertical line.

$$
\begin{array}{r}
7.23 \\
15.8 \\
\underline{0.576} \\
\underline{23.606}
\end{array}
$$

Again multiplication of (or division between) two decimal numbers is similar to that between whole numbers, but you must be careful to make sure that the decimal point is in the correct position.

The answer to the problem $8.23 \times 6.1 = 50.203$ has three digits to the right of the decimal point which is the same as the total number of digits to the right of the decimal point in the two numbers 8.23 and 6.1. However, be careful as some of the digits may be zeros.

**To avoid making very large errors it is safer to estimate the answer when multiplying or dividing decimals**. For example, $8.91 \div 7.26$ is just a little more than 1 so if you get the answer to 12.27 you would know you were wrong (1.227 is the correct answer).

The following four examples each involve the use of decimal numbers in a practical business context. Try each of these four examples using a calculator. In general the main problem is to identify what calculations need to be done and to interpret the final answer. Always check that your answer is a sensible one. It is very easy to multiply two numbers when really one should be divided by another, or alternatively it is easy to write down a number with the wrong number of decimal places. Is the answer you get within the range of answers you would expect using common sense?

## Example 1.3.1

A school-leaver when looking for employment in a Job Centre notices three situations that appeal to her. The jobs and associated pay are shown in Table 1.4. In order to compare the pay determine the weekly pay of each of the jobs.

| Table 1.4. Pay description of three jobs | |
| --- | --- |
| Job | Pay |
| VDU operative | £646.84 per month |
| Sales assistant | £8685.00 per annum |
| Accounts clerk | £4.15 per hour (40 hour week) |

## Solution to Example 1.3.1

*VDU operative*: There are 12 months in a year so the annual pay is

$$646.84 \times 12 = £7762.08$$

The weekly pay is equal to the annual salary divided by 52, giving

$$7762.08 \div 52 = £149.27$$

rounded to the nearest penny. You should note that it is not safe to assume that there are four weeks in a month, this would give a different, and incorrect, answer.

*Sales assistant*: The weekly pay is

$$8685 \div 52 = £167.02.$$

*Accounts clerk*: The weekly pay is

$$4.15 \times 40 = £166.00$$

In terms of weekly pay the sales assistant job is preferable (just!).

## Example 1.3.2

A plane flies from London to Naples at an average speed of 500 miles per hour. The distance is 1400 miles. Find the time taken in hours and minutes.

## Solution to Example 1.3.2

Time = distance ÷ speed, so the time taken in hours is $1400 \div 500 = 2.8$ hours, in decimals. As there are 60 minutes in one hour, 0.8 h is $0.8 \times 60 = 48$ minutes.

The time taken would be 2 hours 48 minutes.

## Example 1.3.3

A bank in England quotes two rates of exchange for French francs. The bank sells French francs at 9.18 Ffrs to the £1. The bank buys French francs at 9.85 Ffrs to the £1.

A business traveller changed £800 to francs at the bank before the journey, spent 6200 Ffrs while in France, then changed the remaining francs back to £ sterling at the bank on returning to England. The bank does not charge commission. How much does the traveller receive in £ sterling?

### Solution to Example 1.3.3

On changing £800 the business traveller would receive

$$800 \times 9.18 = 7344 \text{ Ffrs}$$

After spending 6200 Ffrs, the traveller requires 1144 Ffrs to be changed back.

$$1144 \div 9.85 = £116.14$$

## Example 1.3.4

A company has a small van that travels 35 miles on 1 gallon of petrol. A van driver travels a distance of 840 kilometres in the van and can buy petrol at 74 p per litre. Using the information that 1 kilometre is 0.625 miles and that 1 gallon is 4.54 litres, calculate the cost of petrol used on the journey.

### Solution to Example 1.3.4

The distance of 840 kilometres is the same as

$$840 \times 0.625 = 525 \text{ miles}$$

The journey will require $525 \div 35 = 15$ gallons of petrol, which is equivalent to

$$15 \times 4.54 = 68.1 \text{ litres}$$

The cost of the petrol is $68.1 \times 0.74 = £50.39$.

**Exercises 1.3**    1    The national rate for the cost of sending parcels within the United Kingdom is given in Table 1.5. A company wishes to send 8 parcels.

**Table 1.5. Inland postal rate**

| Weight not over (kg) | Rate (£) | Weight not over (kg) | Rate (£) |
|---|---|---|---|
| 1 | 2.70 | 8 | 6.30 |
| 2 | 3.35 | 10 | 7.30 |
| 4 | 4.90 | 30 | 8.55 |
| 6 | 5.50 | | |

The weight of each of these parcels is 0.95 kilogram, 1.75 kilogram, 2.30 kilogram, 2.74 kilogram, 5.61 kilogram, 5.75 kilogram, 7.40 kilogram and 11.40 kilogram. Calculate the total cost of sending these eight parcels.

2. Julian travels to the United States on a business trip. He changes £950 into dollars at a rate of exchange of £1 = $1.64. He spends $900 dollars during his stay in the States. He decides to return via Italy, and converts his remaining dollars into euros (€) at a rate of €1 = $1.15. On leaving Italy he has €200 left (rounded to the nearest euro). How much, in euros, did he spend in Italy?

3 Abdul and Bernadette receive their pay in different ways. Abdul earns a steady salary of £13 000 per annum. Bernadette earns £6 per hour. In one week Bernadette works 37 hours at standard rate, plus 8 hours overtime at time-and-a-half. Which of the two earned more in that week?

4 Peter calculates that he has used 693 units of electricity and he knows that electricity costs 7.53p per unit. Calculate the cost of the electricity to the nearest penny.

5 Richard is paid £4.70 per hour for his basic 37 hour week. In one week Richard also works overtime at time-and-a-half. His total pay is £195.05. How many hours overtime does Richard work?

6 James and Mary drive their car from Calais to Frejus in the South of France. The distance is 735 miles each way. The cost of petrol in France is 5.32 francs per litre. The exchange rate is 10.3 francs to the £ and 4.55 litres are equivalent to one gallon.

  a Find the cost of petrol in France in £s per gallon.

  b Their car averages 42 miles per gallon. What is the cost in £s of the petrol for the return journey?

  c James realizes that they will need to pay tolls for the journey, which amount to 310 francs each way. Mary remembers that a night's accommodation will be needed on both journeys, and they estimate that this will cost £27 per person per night. What is the total cost of the journey?

## Further Exercises

1 A typist finds that she can get 14 words in one line and 42 lines of typing on one page. If she types a manuscript consisting of 37 044 words, how many pages will she type?

    A. 59     B. 61     C. 63     D. 67

2  You have £48 left in your bank account. However, the bank has just informed you that you owe £60 in bank charges and has deducted this from your account. How much is left in your account?

   A. −£12      B. £12          C. £108          D. £188

3  The deepest place in the Pacific Ocean is 36 000 feet below sea level in the Marianas Trench near Guam. The highest mountain in the Himalayas is Mount Everest at 29 000 feet above sea level. What is the difference in their heights (in feet)?

   A. 7000        B. 36 000      C. 58 000      D. 65 000

4  The annual profit of a small business is £25 000. It is shared between three partners, Alex receives $2/5$, Betty receives $3/10$, and Colin receives the rest. How much money does Colin receive?

   A. £5000       B. £7500       C. £10 000     D. £12 500

5  Mr Richardson insures his house for £81 000 and its contents for £17 000. The premiums for the insurance are: buildings—18p per annum for every £100 of cover; contents—93p per annum for every £100 of cover.
   What is the total cost of Mr Richardson's insurance this year?

   A. £303.90   B. £305.80   C. £323.70    D. £345.20

6  Kate wishes to redecorate her hall. She calculates the area of the walls to be painted as 28.75 square metres. Two coats of paint are needed. One litre of paint covers 9 square metres with one coat. The paint can be bought in 1 litre tins costing £6.50 and 2.5 litre tins costing £14.50. Assuming Kate buys the cheapest combination of tins necessary, what is the cost of the paint required for two coats?

7  John pays a hotel bill of 5285 Ffrs in France for one week's holiday for his family, with his credit card. The exchange rate is 9.75 Ffrs to the £. What is the cost of the hotel bill in £? When the credit card company receives the bill some weeks later, the exchange rate has become 10.14 Ffrs to the £. How much is the hotel bill as charged to John by the credit card company?

8  **a** The train from London to Manchester takes 2 hours 30 minutes. This train travels at an average speed of 80 miles per hour. What is the distance from London to Manchester?
   **b** The railway company is going to buy some faster trains. These

new trains will have an average speed of 100 miles per hour. How much time will be saved on the journey from London to Manchester?

9  A tourist drives a car which travels 35 miles on one gallon of petrol.

   a  How many kilometres will this car travel on one gallon of petrol? (Take 5 miles to be equal to 8 kilometres.)
   b  This tourist drives a distance of 840 kilometres. Calculate the number of litres of petrol used on this journey. (Take 1 gallon to be equal to 4.55 litres.)

10  The table shows the distances, in kilometres, between six places in Canada.

| Town | Banff | Calgary | Edmonton | Jasper | Medicine Hat | Peace River |
|------|-------|---------|----------|--------|--------------|-------------|
| Banff |  | 128 | 401 | 287 | 419 | 809 |
| Calgary | 128 |  | 294 | 412 | 293 | 749 |
| Edmonton | 401 | 294 |  | 366 | 526 | 484 |
| Jasper | 287 | 412 | 366 |  | 703 | 578 |
| Medicine Hat | 419 | 293 | 526 | 703 |  | 1010 |
| Peace River | 809 | 749 | 484 | 578 | 1010 |  |

   a  Val drives from Calgary to Banff then on to Jasper. How far is this to the nearest 10 kilometres?
   b  Val drives from Edmonton to Jasper. What is this distance
      • to the nearest 10 kilometres?
      • to the nearest 100 kilometres?
   c  To estimate the number of miles, Val uses a rough rule of thumb:
      *Round off to the nearest 10 kilometres. Cross off the zero. Multiply by 6.*
      Use this rule to estimate the number of miles in 164 kilometres.
   d  A more accurate rule linking kilometres and miles is
      *8 kilometres = 5 miles*
      How many miles are there in 164 kilometres using this rule?
      What is the difference, in miles, between your answers to **c** and **d**?

11  a  A television, priced at £428.64, can be bought free of interest by payment of 12 equal monthly instalments. Calculate the amount of each instalment.
    b  A used van is priced at £13 680. A customer agrees to pay a deposit of one-quarter of the price and pays the rest in 36

monthly instalments. If he is not charged interest calculate the value of the deposit and the monthly instalments.

12  On 1 January 1998, Gary purchased a car. During the year, he travelled 10 580 miles. The car averaged 46 miles per gallon and the petrol cost on average £2.85 per gallon. He had to replace the exhaust system at a cost of £145 and 2 tyres at a cost of £48 each. He also needed 2 services at £155 each. Other repair bills cost £265. His road fund licence cost £150 and insurance £625.

a  How much did Gary pay for petrol during the year?
b  Find the total cost of running his car.
c  Find the cost per mile of running the car, correct to the nearest penny.

# Commercial Applications

## 2.1 Percentages

You will frequently see references to percentages in everyday, and particularly business, situations. For example, an item of furniture may be advertised as

**20% off,**

indicating that the price has been reduced by 20%, or a national newspaper may have the headline

**Annual Inflation down to 2.7%**

This would indicate that prices, though increasing by 2.7% per annum, are increasing at a lower rate than previously. As well, it is almost certain that you have met percentages when receiving a mark for a piece of coursework. For example, you may have received a mark of 58% for an essay.

Percentages are used to indicate the relative size of one number when compared with another. For example, we may want to compare a student's performance at two tests. This student may have achieved a mark of 26 out of 40 in test A, and 28 out of 50 in test B. It is difficult, at the moment, to compare the relative performance of the student in these two tests as the total mark for each test is different. This section will identify ways of comparing the performances in these two tests.

In a business context you are likely to meet percentages when calculating values involving VAT, mortgage rates, National Insurance, discounts and commission. All of these require you to be able to calculate a given percentage of an amount. For example, VAT is a tax the UK government receives from the sale of most retail goods, and is currently set at 17.5%, so the UK government receives 17.5% of the sale value of most items sold in shops.

**Percentages** are used to represent the proportion of one number compared with another. Basically, percentages can be considered to be fractions with a denominator of 100, where the numerator appears alone with % after it. For example $\frac{1}{2}$ can be written as $^{50}/_{100} = 50\%$. Similarly $\frac{2}{5} = {}^{40}/_{100} = 40\%$ and $1 = 100\%$.

## Example 2.1.1

A workforce can be classified into managerial, skilled and unskilled as in Table 2.1.

**Table 2.1. Company staff profile**

| Class | Number of employees |
|-------|---------------------|
| Managerial | 50 |
| Skilled | 175 |
| Unskilled | 275 |

Express the number of employees in each class as a percentage of the total workforce.

## *Solution to Example 2.1.1*

The total workforce is $50 + 175 + 275 = 500$.
The percentage of employees is:

$$\text{in the managerial class} = \frac{50}{500} = \frac{1}{10} = 10\%$$

$$\text{in the skilled class} = \frac{175}{500} = \frac{35}{100} = 35\% \text{ and}$$

$$\text{in the unskilled class} = \frac{275}{500} = \frac{55}{100} = 55\%$$

Note that $10\% + 35\% + 55\% = 100\%$, as these categories include the whole workforce.

Percentages have many practical applications in everyday life. For example, in the car, double-glazing and insurance industries, salespeople are often paid on the basis of their success at selling, and receive a **commission**, which is a percentage of their sales income. A further important application of percentages involves the idea of discount. In order to stimulate sales a retailer may decide to offer his goods at a price less than its normal price. A **discount** is the monetary amount by which the normal price is reduced expressed as a percentage of the normal price. In addition to these applications, interest rates and investments are normally expressed in percentage form.

## Example 2.1.2

How much money does a salesperson earn on a £2400 sale if his commission is 20%?

## *Solution to Example 2.1.2*

Salesperson's commission is 20% of £2400

$$= \frac{20}{100} \times 2400 = £480$$

## Example 2.1.3

A computer initially costs £850 but then has VAT added at 17.5%. The retailer then offers a discount of 20%. Determine the selling price of the computer. Does the order of calculating the tax and discount influence the price of the computer?

## *Solution to Example 2.1.3*

The VAT on the computer is 17.5% of £850

$$= \frac{17.5}{100} \times 850 = £148.75$$

So the cost of the computer including VAT but before discount is

$$£850 + £148.75 = £998.75$$

The reduction in price due to the discount is 20% of £998.75

$$= \frac{20}{100} \times 998.75 = £199.75$$

Hence the price of the computer is £998.75 − 199.75 = £799.

What would happen if the price after discount is found first and then the tax is added? Would the answer be the same?

If the computer costs £850, then the discount would be 20% of £850

$$= \frac{20}{100} \times 850 = £170$$

This gives a price after discount but before tax is added of £850 − £170 = £680.

The tax can then be computed to be 17.5% of £680

$$= \frac{17.5}{100} \times 680 = £119$$

When this amount is added to £680 it gives a selling price for the computer of £799, thus agreeing with the previous answer.

Under most conditions, if a problem involves two percentages it does not matter in which order the percentage calculations are performed.

## Example 2.1.4

Brian has a number of deductions from his gross monthly wage. Of this wage, 9% goes in National Insurance contributions, 6% goes in pension contributions and 19% goes in tax. If his gross monthly wage is £500, determine the amount he pays towards National Insurance, his pension, and tax, together with his net monthly wage.

### Solution to Example 2.1.4

| | | |
|---|---|---|
| Gross monthly wage | | £500 |
| National Insurance 9/100 × £500 | £45 | |
| Pension contribution 6/100 × £500 | £30 | |
| Tax payment 19/100 × £500 | £95 | |
| Total contribution | £170 | |
| Net monthly wage | | £330 |

## Example 2.1.5

A shopkeeper bought 100 pairs of trousers from a manufacturer. The shopkeeper paid £27.50 for each pair and sold them to make a profit of 60% per pair on the cost price.

**a** Calculate the selling price of a pair of trousers.

When 70 pairs had been sold, the shopkeeper reduced the selling price to £30 per pair.

**b** Calculate the total profit made by the shopkeeper when all the trousers are sold.

**c** Calculate the total profit as a percentage of initial outlay.

## *Solution to Example 2.1.5*

**a** 60% of £27.50 is £16.50 ($60 \div 100 \times 27.5$) so the selling price of a pair of trousers is

$$27.50 + 16.50 = £44.$$

**b** 70 pairs of trousers are sold at £44 each, with the remaining 30 pairs sold at £30 each.
The total sales revenue = $(70 \times 44) + (30 \times 30) = £3980$
The initial cost of buying the trousers was $100 \times 27.50 = £2750$, giving a profit of

$$3980 - 2750 = £1230$$

**c** The percentage profit is

$$\frac{1230}{2750} \times 100 = 44.7\%$$

## Example 2.1.6

National Insurance contributions are calculated according to the following table.

| Weekly earning (£) | Rate of National Insurance contributions |
|---|---|
| 0–45.99 | NIL |
| 46–350 | 2% of £46 plus 7% of remainder |
| Above 350 | 2% of £46 plus 7% of £304 |

Ken earns £316 per week. How much is his weekly National Insurance contribution?

### Solution to Example 2.1.6

As Ken earns £316 per week, he will pay 2% of £46 plus 7% of the remainder

$$= (0.02 \times 46) + (0.07 \times 270)$$

$$= £0.92 + £18.90 = £19.82 \text{ each week in NI contributions.}$$

**Exercises 2.1**

1 The costs of the four departments in a company are

| | | | |
|---|---|---|---|
| Department A | £32 000 | Department B | £50 000 |
| Department C | £48 000 | Department D | £70 000 |

Find the percentage of all company costs for each department.

2 A meal for two costs £29.50, but then has VAT added at 17.5%, and a service charge at 10%. Obtain the final cost of the meal.

3 A student scores 26 out of 40 in test A and 28 out of 50 in test B. Calculate the student's percentage score for each test and decide which test gave the higher percentage score.

4 a Calculate 65% of £54 320
  b Calculate 5.72% of £978. Give your answer to the nearest penny.

5 An American tourist in England changed US$800 to £ sterling at an exchange rate of US$1.63 to the £. The bank charged a commission of 3% of the transaction.

  Calculate, correct to the nearest penny, the amount in £ sterling received by the tourist.

6 While on holiday in the United States, Gary finds jeans on sale at $24 a pair. The exchange rate is US$1.60 to the £.
  a Calculate the price of a pair of jeans in £.
  b Gary buys 80 pairs of jeans to sell in England. He has to pay 10% duty on them when they arrive back in England.
    • Calculate the total cost of the jeans including duty.
    • He sells 80% of the jeans at £29 per pair. How much does he receive from this sale.
    • Gary sells the remainder of the jeans at £5 per pair. What is the total amount of money he receives from the sale of all 80 pairs of jeans.

- Express the profit made as a percentage of the total expenditure.

7  In a sale everything is reduced by 20% of the marked price. Baljinder pays the sale price of £36 for a personal stereo. How much does she save?

8  In order to increase sales a DIY shop sells pine furniture at a discount of 30%. As a further promotion the shop has a one-day offer of a reduction of 20% of all current prices. What percentage discount can be obtained on the pine furniture on sale that day?

9  In shop A a computer costs £975 plus VAT at 17.5%. In shop B, the same computer costs £1250, including VAT, but it is offered with an 8% discount. In which of the two shops is the computer cheaper?

10  A special type of plug is guaranteed to cut photocopier electricity costs by 15%.
   a  The average cost of the electricity needed to run a photocopier for one year is £65. Calculate the annual saving from using this special plug.
   b  The price of a plug is £23.95. How long will it take before the money spent on buying this plug is recovered by the saving in electricity? Give your answer to a sensible degree of accuracy.

## 2.2 Ratios

It is often of interest in everyday activities to compare two or sometimes more numbers; for example, in a work group there may be 24 apprentices together with four qualified technicians. In this situation we can say that the ratio of apprentices to technicians is 24 : 4. However, as in the case of fractions, it is more usual to express this in its lowest terms, or simplest form. Here 24 and 4 are both divisible by 4 so in its lowest terms the ratio 24 : 4 is 6 : 1 or 6 apprentices for each qualified technician. A specific feature of a ratio is that it gives no indication of size; it is merely used as a basis for comparison. In the above example a ratio of 6:1 is not only appropriate for 24 apprentices to 4 technicians but the same ratio could be used for 12 apprentices to 2 technicians or 48 apprentices to 8 technicians.

Suppose, as a prospective student you are considering attendance at one of two universities, Exford University or Wyemouth University. The decision as to which of these two universities you attend may be dependent on two ratios, the male-to-female ratio and the student-staff ratio. The relevant information is provided in Table 2.2.

**Table 2.2. Staff and student numbers**

|                          | Exford | Wyemouth |
| ------------------------ | ------ | -------- |
| Number of staff          | 150    | 200      |
| Number of male students  | 1600   | 1800     |
| Number of female students| 800    | 1200     |

At Exford University the ratio of male students to female students is

$$1600:800$$

or, in lowest terms,    $2:1$

At Wyemouth University the ratio of male students to female students is

$$1800:1200 \text{ or } 3:2$$

(This might be put in the form $1.5:1$ when making comparisons)

Thus the ratio of males to females is greater at Exford University; that is, there are more males per female at this university even though there are more males at Wyemouth University.

The total number of students at Exford is 2400, giving a student-staff ratio of

$$2400:150 \text{ or } 16:1$$

Similarly the student-staff ratio at Wyemouth is

$$3000:200 \text{ or } 15:1$$

On the basis of this information you can expect slightly more personal tuition at Wyemouth as the number of students per staff member is 15 compared with 16 at Exford.

## Example 2.2.1

An opinion poll on election party preferences was conducted, with replies received from 1000 interviewees. It was found that 480 favoured the Conservatives, 360 favoured the Labour Party, 120 preferred the Liberal Democrats, and the remaining 40 were undecided. Determine

**a**    the ratio of decided to undecided,
**b**    the ratio of Conservatives to Labour,

## Solution to Example 2.2.1

**a**  Altogether there are 960 interviewees with specified party preferences compared with 40 who do not specify a preference.
The ratio of decided to undecided is $960:40$ or $24:1$.

**b**  The ratio of Conservatives to Labour is $480:360$ or, in lowest terms, $4:3$.

## Example 2.2.2

**a**  A firm has a workforce of 640 employees, of whom 400 are men. Calculate the ratio of men to women in lowest terms.

**b**  The workforce is divided into production staff and support staff in the ratio of $7:3$. How many of the workers are defined as production staff?

**c**  The hourly rates for production staff and support staff are in the ratio $3:2$. The hourly rate of pay for production workers is £5.82. Calculate how much a support staff member will earn in 37.5 hours.

## Solution to Example 2.2.2

**a**  If 400 of the 640 employees are men, then the remaining 240 are women. The ratio of men to women is

$$400:240$$

Both are divisible by 80, so in lowest terms this is

$$5:3$$

**b**  If the ratio of production workers to support workers is $7:3$ then

$$\frac{7}{10} \text{ are production workers and } \frac{3}{10} \text{ are support workers}$$

The number of workers defined as production staff is

$$\frac{7}{10} \times 640 = 448$$

**c**  The hourly rate of pay for support staff is

$$\frac{2}{3} \times £5.82 = £3.88$$

For a 37.5 hour week the support staff member will earn

$$37.5 \times £3.88 = £145.50$$

## Example 2.2.3

Anne and Ben are partners in a business with capital invested in the ratio 3 : 1. Anne, the major partner, invested capital of £12 000. With Ben's agreement, Anne withdraws £4000 of her capital.

a    Calculate the new ratio of their investment, in its lowest terms.

b    Anne and Ben decide to take £3000 of their profits as a dividend. They share this in proportion to their capital investments.
  • Calculate Anne's share of these profits.
  • How much more would she have received if she had not withdrawn part of her original investment?

## Solution to Example 2.2.3

a    Ben's initial investment was one-third that of Anne's, so his investment was £4000. When Anne withdraws £4000 of her investment she is left with £8000 invested. The ratio is now

  8000 : 4000 or, in lowest terms, 2 : 1

b    • Anne takes two-thirds of the dividend, which is £2000.
  • If she had not withdrawn part of her original investment she would have received three-quarters of the £3000, or £2250.
  She would have received an extra £250.

The principles of ratios and percentages can be applied to income tax situations, where, for example, an employee may have to pay tax at 20p in the £ on his taxable income. Thus, for every £ that this employee earns over and above his tax allowance he has to pay 20p to the Inland Revenue. In this case the ratio of the amount paid to the Inland Revenue to the amount the employee earns above his tax allowance is 20 : 100 or 1 : 5. Alternatively, you can think of this as 20% of the employees earnings above his tax allowance going to the Inland Revenue.

## Example 2.2.4

John earns £240 per week gross and has an annual tax allowance of £3580. Julie earns £2920 per month gross and has an annual tax allowance of £4250. The current UK tax rates are:

  10p in the £ for the first £1500 of taxable income
  23p in the £ between £1500 and £28 000 of taxable income
  40p in the £ above £28 000

Calculate how much tax John and Julie pay each year and hence find John's weekly income and Julie's monthly income net of tax.

### Solution to Example 2.2.4

John's annual gross income is

$$52 \times 240 = £12\,480$$

His taxable income is his gross annual income minus his tax allowance,

$$£12\,480 - £3580 = £8900$$

He pays tax, therefore, at 10p in the £ for his first £1500 of taxable income and 23p in the £ on the remaining £7400.

$$\begin{aligned} \text{Annual tax } &= £(1500 \times 0.10) + (7400 \times 0.23) \\ &= £150 + £1702 \\ &= £1852 \text{ (or } 1852 \div 52 = £35.62 \text{ per week)} \end{aligned}$$

His net weekly income is £240 − £35.62 = £204.38.

Julie's annual gross income is

$$12 \times 2920 = £35\,040$$

Her taxable income is

$$£35\,040 - £4250 = £30\,790$$

She pays tax at 10p in the £ on the first £1500, but as her taxable income is above the higher rate threshold she then pays tax at 23p in the £ on the next £26 500 (the difference between £1500 and £28 000) and 40p in the £ on the final £2790.

$$\begin{aligned} \text{Her annual tax } &= £(1500 \times 0.10) + (26\,500 \times 0.23) + (2790 \times 0.40) \\ &= £7361 \end{aligned}$$

and hence her monthly tax is

$$£7361 \div 12 = £613.42$$

Her net monthly income is then £2920 − £613.42 = £2306.58.

**Exercises 2.2**

1   A sum of money, £12 000, is divided between three partners of a company in the ratio 3 : 4 : 5. Determine the sum that each partner receives.

2   A college has 3120 students, of whom 1680 are male.
   a   State, in lowest terms, the ratio of the number of male students to the number of female students.
   b   The ratio of the number of students to the number of lecturers is 16 : 1. How many lecturers work at the college?
   c   The college day starts at 0830 and finishes at 1700. Each day is split into lecture time, laboratory work and free time in the ratio 8 : 5 : 4. Calculate how much time is spent on each.

3   Three friends start up a minicab service and agree to divide their income in the ratio of the distance that each of them drives. In one week, Alan drives 350 miles, Brian drives 280 miles and Carl drives 210 miles. Their week's income is £1360.80. How much does each person receive?

4   Mushtaq has an income of £1720 per month. He has a tax allowance of £3765.
   a   What is his taxable income?
   b   The rates of income tax are
      10% of the first £1500
      20% of the next £2700
      22% of any remaining taxable income
   Calculate how much income tax Mushtaq pays per year.

5   Gerdip and Sharon bought a house costing £23 000. Gerdip contributed £4000 and Sharon £19 000. They sell the house for £49 450, and agree to divide the sale price in the proportion in which they invested money. How much money does Sharon receive?

6   Four friends split the initial costs, totalling £920, of starting a new business. John paid £75, Alan £270, Barbara £310 and Caroline paid the remainder of the cost. They decide to split the first year profits of £2300 in the ratio of their contributions. How much does each receive?

## 2.3 Powers and Roots

So far in this book you have carried out a number of examples involving only addition, subtraction, multiplication and division. More difficult calculations are required time and time again in finance and can be made simpler by using powers and roots. Indeed, such financial problems would be very difficult to perform without an understanding of powers and roots. You will see this more clearly when you get to chapter 4 of this text.

Carry out the calculation

$$3 \times 3 \times 3 \times 3$$

You can do this on your calculator using the key sequence

[3] [×] [3] [×] [3] [×] [3] [=]

and find the answer 81. A shorthand way of writing this is $3^4$, where 3 is the **base** and 4 is the **power**, and is called 'three raised to the power four'. In the same way

$$2 \times 2 \times 2 \times 2 \times 2 = 2^5 = 32$$

If your calculator possesses a $[x^y]$ key or a $[y^x]$ key then $2^5$ can be computed on your calculator directly using the key sequence

[2] $[x^y]$ [5] [=]

Try this one: $5^3$. This is shorthand for $5 \times 5 \times 5$ and you can get the answer directly using the key sequence

5 $[x^y]$ 3 =

to get the displayed answer of 125.

Note that when the base is ten, the product is easy to find,

$$10^2 = 10(10) = 100$$
$$10^3 = 10(10)(10) = 1000$$
$$10^4 = 10(10)(10)(10) = 10\,000$$

because the power is always exactly equal to the number of zeros in the answer. Check this on your calculator. It follows that $10^1 = 10$ and $10^0 = 1$. In general any number to the power of 1 is equal to itself and any number to the power of 0 is equal to 1. Thus

$$2^1 = 2 \qquad 2^0 = 1$$
$$5^1 = 5 \qquad 5^0 = 1$$

Now try the questions in Example 2.3.1 using your calculator.

## Example 2.3.1

Use the $[x^y]$ key on your calculator to evaluate

**a** $6^3$          **d** $7^0$
**b** $8^1$          **e** $10^{-1}$
**c** $(-2)^5$       **f** $5^{-2}$

### Solution to Example 2.3.1

**a**   $6^3 = 216$
**b**   $8^1 = 8$
**c**   $(-2)^5 = -32$

Some calculators display an error message when using the $[x^y]$ key for negative values of $x$. If this is the case evaluate $2^5$ and change the sign of the answer if the power is odd, as is the case here. This is because you are multiplying a negative number by itself an odd number of times.

**d**   $7^0 = 1$
**e**   As $10^3 = 1000$, $10^2 = 100$, $10^1 = 10$, $10^0 = 1$, it would seem sensible for $10^{-1} = 0.1$ or $^1/_{10}$ This is, in fact, true as a negative power is the reciprocal of the equivalent positive power.

$$10^{-1} = \frac{1}{10} = 0.1$$

**f**   $$5^{-2} = \frac{1}{5^2} = \frac{1}{25}$$

The inverse of raising to a power is finding the **root** of a number. For example

$$\sqrt{49} = \text{square root of } 49 = 7 \text{ since } 7^2 = 49$$
$$\sqrt[3]{64} = \text{cube root of } 64 = 4 \text{ since } 4^3 = 64$$
$$\sqrt[4]{81} = \text{fourth root of } 81 = 3 \text{ since } 3^4 = 81$$

A calculator can be used to evaluate fractional powers, such as $49^{1/2}$, $64^{1/3}$, $81^{1/4}$, using the $[x^y]$ key.

The answers are, as above, 7, 4 and 3 . For example

$$[81] \, [x^y] \, [0.25] \, [=]$$

gives the answer 3.

You should note from these examples that a **fractional power is the same as a root**; for example

$$\sqrt{25} = \text{square root of } 25 = 25^{1/2} = 5$$
$$\sqrt[4]{81} = \text{fourth root of } 81 = 81^{1/4} = 3$$

An alternative way of obtaining this last answer is to use the $x^{1/y}$ key.

$$[81] \, [x^{1/y}] \, [4] \, [=]$$

This finds the fourth root of 81 (and displays the answer 3).

You can solve a number of practical problems involving money using powers of numbers. An example of this is the calculation of compound interest when money has been invested in a bank account or savings account (see Chapter 4). For example, if £500 is invested for 2½ years at 7.8% per annum then the final amount is obtained from the calculation

$$\left(1+\frac{7.8}{100}\right)^{2.5} \times 500$$

You can first work out the value in the brackets as 1.078 and then rewrite this as

$$1.078^{2.5} \times 500$$

The answer can be found from the key sequence

$$[1.078]\,[x^y]\,[2.5]\,[=]\,[\times]\,[500]\,[=]$$

and you get the answer £603.28.

## Example 2.3.2

A married couple take out a loan. They agree to make monthly repayments given by the following expression

$$\frac{50\,000 \times 0.06 \times (1.06)^{25}}{12 \times (1.06^{25} - 1)}$$

Find the size of these monthly repayments.

### *Solution to Example 2.3.2*

You first need to evaluate $1.06^{25}$, which is 4.291 870 72. You should write out this number in full (or better still, put it into your calculator memory) to avoid rounding errors. As $(1.06^{25} - 1) = 3.291\,870\,72$ the calculation simplifies to

$$\frac{50\,000 \times 0.06 \times 4.291\,870\,72}{12 \times 3.291\,870\,72} = £325.94$$

Finally in this section, properties of numbers written in scientific notation are described. A number is written in *scientific notation* (or *standard form*) when it is expressed as a number between 1 and 10 together with some power of 10. For example, you can write 250 as $2.5 \times 10^2$ or 0.36 as

$3.6 \times 10^{-1}$. The main advantage of this notation is that you can write very large or very small numbers more compactly.

$$486\,000 = 4.86 \times 10^5$$

Most calculators use this notation when giving answers that are very large or small. For example, carry out the following calculation

$$0.0000023 \times 0.00006$$

It is likely that the calculator will display 1.38 –10, indicating that the answer is $1.38 \times 10^{-10}$, the power of $-10$ moving the decimal point 10 places to the left

$$1.38 \times 10^{-10} = 0.000\,000\,000\,138$$

Now try the calculation

$$583\,000 \times 12\,135\,467 = 7.075 \times 10^{12}$$

$$= 7\,075\,000\,000\,000 \text{ correct to 4 significant figures}$$

## Example 2.3.3

Last year the population of the United Kingdom was approximately $5.3 \times 10^7$.

a    An average of £680 per person was spent on food last year in the United Kingdom. What was the *total* amount spent on food last year in the United Kingdom? Give your answer in standard form.

b    Last year there were $1.4 \times 10^7$ car drivers in the United Kingdom. They spent a total of £$1.5 \times 10^{10}$ on their cars. What was the *average* amount spent by each car driver? Give your answer to a suitable degree of accuracy.

## Solution to Example 2.3.3

a    If each of the $5.3 \times 10^7$ persons in the United Kingdom spent £680 on food then the total food spend (in £) is

$$5.3 \times 10^7 \times 680$$

You can enter $5.3 \times 10^7$ directly on your calculator by using the key sequence

[5.3] [EXP] [7]      or      [5.3] [EE] [7]

depending on the make of your calculator. Multiplying this number by 680 gives the answer on your calculator as

$£3.604 \times 10^{10}$

in standard form (or just over £36 billion).

**b**   You calculate the average amount spent for each car driver by dividing the total amount spent by the number of drivers:

$$\frac{1.5 \times 10^{10}}{1.4 \times 10^{7}}$$

Using the key sequence

[1.5]  [EXP][10]  [÷]  [1.4]  [EXP][7]  [=]

gives the answer £1071.43. Given that the accuracy of the original numbers was only given to two significant figures, it would clearly be wrong for you to give a final answer to the nearest penny (using six significant figures). It would be more sensible to give your answer to a similar degree of accuracy as the original information. Here a suitable degree of accuracy here would be £1100.

**Exercises 2.3**

1   Compute

   **a** $4^2 \times 3^3$     **b** $2^4 \times 10^2$     **c** $3^{-2}$     **d** $16^{1/2}$

2   Evaluate          $\left(1 + \dfrac{6.25}{100}\right)^5 \times £100$

3   Subtract $8.7 \times 10^{-1}$ from $2.624 \times 10^2$ and give the answer in scientific notation.

4   In 1992 the population of the United Kingdom was 58 million.

   **a**   Write 58 million in standard form.
   **b**   The National Debt of the United Kingdom in 1992 was £1.86 $\times$ $10^{11}$.
   • Calculate the National Debt per person giving your answer in standard form.
   • What would be a sensible rounded value for this figure?

5   Evaluate the following:

   **a** $4^2 \times 4^3$          **c** $8.975 \times 10^3$
   **b** $5^4 \times 5^5 \div 5^1$     **d** $6.57 \times 10^4$

6   In the United Kingdom 26 billion pots of tea are made each year. If there are 20 million homes in the United Kingdom how many pots of tea are made, on average, per week in a UK home?

## Further Exercises

1   A car costs £8000 new. It depreciates in value by 15% during the first year, and depreciates by a further 12% during the second year. What is the value of the car after two years?

     A. £1840     B. £5840     C. £5984     D. £6300

2   A father earns £400 per week and his son earns £250 per week. What is the ratio of their earnings?

     A. $2:1$     B. $7:5$     C. $8:1$     D. $8:5$

3   A householder takes out a loan and agrees to make monthly repayments given by:

$$\frac{15\,000 \times 0.08 \times (1.08^6)}{12 \times (1.08^6 - 1)}$$

Determine the size of the monthly repayment.

     A. £270.39     B. £279.85     C. £287.43     D. £297.54

4   A machine normally sells for £5500 plus VAT (at 17.5%). A company is offered a discount of 25% on this price. Find the discounted price of this machine (to the nearest £).

     A. £4837     B. £4847     C. £4915     D. £5183

5   Ling has an income of £420 per week. She has a tax allowance of £3445. The rates of tax are

    20p in the £ on the first £2900 of taxable income
    23p in the £ on any remaining income

How much tax does Ling pay per week?

     A. £71.48     B. £75.87     C. £79.69     D. £84.32

6   A shopkeeper buys 60 pre-recorded video tapes for £400 and sells 36 of them for £15 each. He then reduces the selling price of the remaining stock by 30%. The shopkeeper sells the remaining video

tapes at this price. Express the profit as a percentage of the cost price.

7    A car is offered for sale at £9200. If Neil pays cash he is offered a discount of 14%. If Neil cannot pay cash, he can buy the car on credit. This consists of a deposit of 20% (of £9200) and 36 monthly payments of £230. What is the extra amount paid for credit compared with paying cash?

8    Jenny receives £674 gross per week. There are a number of deductions from her weekly wage. She pays National Insurance at 9% on the first £600 of her weekly wage. She pays 3% of her total wage into a pension scheme (which is not regarded as taxable income). She pays £7.50 each week towards union subscriptions. Finally she pays tax—her tax allowance is £4250. If tax is charged at

> 20p in the £ up to £4100 of taxable income
> 23p in the £ between £4100 and £27 500 of taxable income
> 40p in the £ above £27 500 of taxable income.

   a    Find how much Jenny actually receives each week (assuming 52 weeks in a year).
   b    She takes a pay cut for a whole tax year to £610 gross per week. Find her new weekly wage.

9    Kate buys 300 bikinis for her boutique at £20 each and sells them at £35 each. In the middle of August, Kate finds that one-quarter of the bikinis are still not sold. She reduces the selling price by 40%.

   a    Find the new selling price of a bikini.
   b    Kate throws away the last 10 unsold bikinis as they are badly shop-soiled. Find the total amount Kate receives from selling bikinis.
   c    What percentage profit does Kate make on her original outlay?

10   Ron drives his coach from Spain to England. He fills up with fuel with 600 litres of diesel. The diesel costs 88.3 pesetas per litre. The exchange rate is 220 pesetas to £1.

   a    How much, in £s, does Ron pay for the diesel?
   b    Each of the coach's two fuel tanks can hold 180 gallons. What percentage of the coach's total fuel capacity does Ron buy in Spain? One gallon is 4.55 litres.

11  Jim buys 160 computer games and sells 60% of them for £6 each.

   a  How much money does he receive?
   b  Jim then reduces the price of the computer game by 40%. What is the new price?
   c  He sells 75% of the remaining stock at this new price and gives the rest to charity. What is the total amount of money Jim receives from the sale of the computer games?
   d  Jim paid £480 for the 160 computer games. Express his profit as a percentage of the cost price.

12  a  A supermarket manager, paid £17 000 per year, is awarded a 3.5% increase in salary. Calculate his new monthly salary.
   b  The supermarket manager also receives an end of year bonus of 1.5% of the value of sales for the year in excess of £1 500 000. Calculate the manager's bonus when sales for the year are valued at £1 542 800.

13  Last year a College had 1500 students and 125 lecturers.

   a  Give the ratio of students to lecturers in lowest terms.
   b  This year the number of students has increased by 180. How many more lecturers are required for the ratio of students to lecturers to remain constant?

14  Give the values of:

   a  $5^2 \div 2^5$    b  $25^{1/2}$    c  $\left(\dfrac{8}{27}\right)^{-1/3}$

15  In 1992–93, the British government collected a total of £2.019 × 10¹¹ from taxes. Of this total, £7.349 × 10¹⁰ was collected from income tax.

   How much was collected from other taxes? Give your answer in standard form.

16  a  Calculate 7.5% of £25 000
   b  Calculate, to the nearest penny, 5.8% of £753.

## Chapter Three

# *Equations and Graphs*

## 3.1 Spreadsheets and Coordinates

Figure 3.1 shows a grid formed by five rows labelled 1 to 5 and eight columns labelled A to H. Any cell in the grid can be identified by stating its letter, which tells us its column, and its number, which tells us its row. Thus, for example, the cell highlighted in Fig. 3.1 is cell E3. The expression E3 is referred to as the address of the cell. This idea has application both in the operation of spreadsheet software on computers and in the drawing of graphs, with which this chapter is principally concerned.

When you switch on any piece of spreadsheet software you will be presented with an initial screen having great similarity to the grid in Fig 3.1. In this book we shall be referring to the particular spreadsheet called EXCEL. This has been developed by Microsoft to utilize the facilities offered by the WINDOWS operating environment and it has many very powerful features.

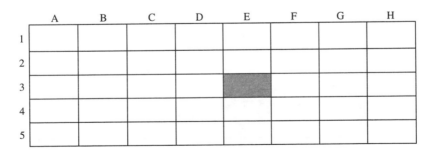

**Figure 3.1**

| | A | B | C | D | E | F | G | H |
|---|---|---|---|---|---|---|---|---|
| 1 | | | | | | | | |
| 2 | | | | | | | | |
| 3 | | | | | | | | |
| 4 | | | | | | | | |
| 5 | | | | | | | | |

**Figure 3.2**

Figure 3.2 is a print out of part of an initial screen in EXCEL, and its similarities with Fig. 3.1 will be immediately clear. It must be emphasized that what is seen on the computer screen at any time is only a tiny segment of the whole spreadsheet, which has many rows and many columns. Spreadsheets are a very important software tool and something you are highly likely to need to use in your current or future working situation.

It is not the purpose of this book to lead you into a detailed understanding of EXCEL. There are many excellent books available for this purpose, including the documentation published by Microsoft to accompany the software. In this book we shall be referring to EXCEL as a means for doing various types of quantitative work, and EXCEL screens will be presented from time to time. The concepts needed for doing basic work with spreadsheets are helpful in motivating algebraic ideas, and in this chapter in particular we shall see something of the graphical capabilities of EXCEL.

The concept of a graph is based very much on the idea of identifying a point by means of an indicator of its horizontal position combined with an indicator of its vertical position, just as we saw cell E3 identified in Fig. 3.1. However, in a graph numbers are used for both indicators, rather than having a letter for the horizontal combined with a number for the vertical. Also the convention in a graph is for the numbers in the vertical direction to increase upwards rather than downwards. Thus in the layout for a graph the

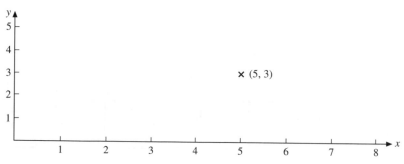

**Figure 3.3**

situation in Fig. 3.1 would be replaced by that shown in Fig. 3.3, using A = 1, B = 2, etc.

The equivalent of cell E3 in Fig. 3.1 would be the point indicated by a cross in Fig. 3.3 and would be denoted (5, 3). The separating comma is needed here to make clear where one number ends and the next begins. The values 5 and 3 are called the coordinates of the point concerned. The lines on which the values are shown are called the axes of the graph, with the horizontal axis being designated the $x$-axis and the vertical axis the $y$-axis. The value 5 is referred to as the $x$ coordinate of the point and the value 3 as the $y$ coordinate.

A further difference between the row and column labels of a spreadsheet and the axes of a graph is that points on a graph can have negative coordinates as well as positive ones. Figure 3.4 below is an extension of Fig. 3.3 showing sections of both axes with negative values.

On this graph in addition to the point (5, 3) of Fig. 3.3 are shown points (−3, 2), (−2, −2) and (4, −3). The four sections into which the graph is divided by the axes are called the 'quadrants', with the top right-hand corner being called the 'first quadrant'.

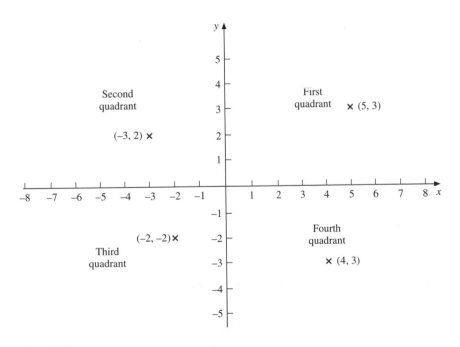

**Figure 3.4**

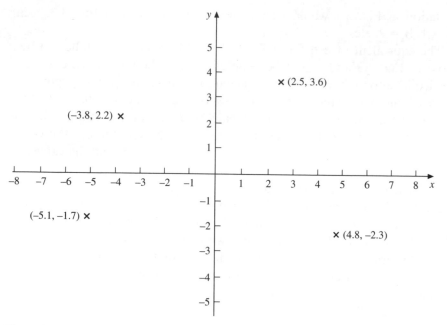

**Figure 3.5**

Another difference to be noted between the address of a cell in a spread-sheet and the coordinates of a point on a graph is that the latter can involve use of numbers other than whole numbers (or 'integers'). Figure 3.5 shows points plotted which have non-integer coordinates.

## Example 3.1.1

The times taken to produce six different size batches of an item were recorded and are shown below.

| Batch | 1 | 2 | 3 | 4 | 5 | 6 |
|---|---|---|---|---|---|---|
| No. of items | 100 | 180 | 300 | 500 | 560 | 700 |
| Time (minutes) | 240 | 350 | 400 | 450 | 470 | 510 |

Plot a graph showing the number of items in the batch on the horizontal axis and the time taken to produce the batch on the vertical axis.

## Solution to Example 3.1.1

The required graph is shown as Fig. 3.6.

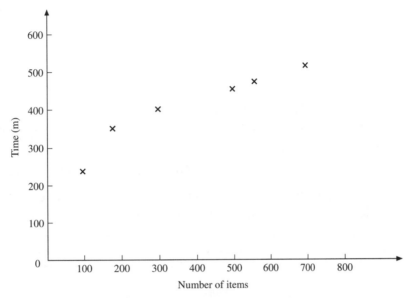

**Figure 3.6** Graph of production time against number of items in a batch

1    A marketing department wishes to investigate the relationship between sales of the company's main product and the amount of television advertising spent on it in the last quarter. Figures for 10 television regions for this quarter are shown below.

| Region | A | B | C | D | E | F | G | H | I | J |
|---|---|---|---|---|---|---|---|---|---|---|
| Sales (units) | 630 | 175 | 315 | 70 | 420 | 140 | 525 | 770 | 910 | 105 |
| Advertising (in £000 000s) | 5 | 2 | 3 | 1 | 4 | 2 | 4 | 5 | 6 | 1 |

As a first step in the investigation you are required to plot a graph showing number of units sold on the vertical axis and advertising expenditure on the horizontal axis.

2    As part of a manpower planning exercise the data given below have been collected on numbers of units of output and numbers of man-hours used for each of the last 12 months.

| Units output | 90 | 9 | 18 | 102 | 81 | 56 | 45 | 36 | 60 | 39 | 30 | 48 |
|---|---|---|---|---|---|---|---|---|---|---|---|---|
| Manhours | 900 | 378 | 390 | 990 | 756 | 720 | 546 | 360 | 600 | 480 | 480 | 720 |

Plot a graph showing numbers of units of output on the horizontal axis and number of manhours used on the vertical axis.

## 3.2 Straight Lines

Suppose that quarterly electricity payments are made up of a quarterly fixed charge of £50 plus a further charge of 10p per unit of electricity consumed. Then

Total quarterly bill = £50 + £0.1 × number of units consumed

If we imagine 0, 100, 200, 300, 400 and 500 units being consumed, we can calculate the corresponding bill in each case as follows.

| Number of units consumed | 0 | 100 | 200 | 300 | 400 | 500 |
|---|---|---|---|---|---|---|
| 0.1 × units consumed | 0 | 10 | 20 | 30 | 40 | 50 |
| Fixed charge | 50 | 50 | 50 | 50 | 50 | 50 |
| Total bill for quarter (£) | 50 | 60 | 70 | 80 | 90 | 100 |

The calculations for the second and fourth rows in the final column, for example, would be carried out on a calculator as follows.

Line 2:  [0.1] [×] [500] [=]
Line 4:  [50] [+] [50]  [=]

The points (0, 50), (100, 60), (200, 70), (300, 80), (400, 90), (500, 100) could now be plotted on a graph, as in Sec. 3.1, having the number of units consumed on the $x$-axis and total bill on the $y$-axis. The result of doing this is shown in Fig. 3.7.

It is clear from the graph that if the plotted points were joined together, the result would be a straight line. So if we use the letter $y$ to represent 'total bill' and the letter $x$ to represent 'number of units consumed' then the statement

$$y = 50 + 0.1x$$

is seen to represent a straight line on the graph.

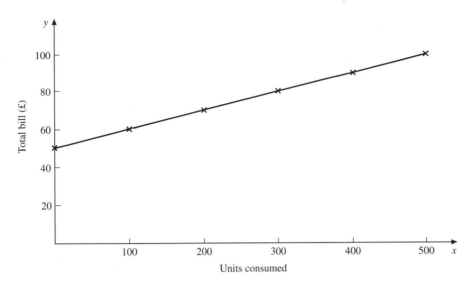

**Figure 3.7** Graph of total electricity bill against number of units consumed

This can also be appreciated in an EXCEL spreadsheet if we proceed as follows:

> Enter the value 50 in cell A1
> Enter the value 0.1 in cell B1

Enter the values 0, 100, 200, 300, 400, 500 in cells C1, C2, C3, C4, C5 and C6 respectively. Then in cell D1 enter the formula

> =A$1 + B$1*C1

This will result in the value 50 in cell D1, and if the formula is then copied down to cells D2 to D6 the values 60, 70, 80, 90, 100 will appear. Then highlight the block of cells from C1 to D6 and call up the Chart Wizard. The Chart Wizard menus can then be used to plot a line graph of column D against column C, giving the result shown in Fig. 3.8. This is essentially the same plot as Fig. 3.7, but the points have now been joined together to show the line. The issue is that the numbers of units for which the calculations were made were only examples. If any intermediate numbers of units had been considered they would have led to other points on the line.

If the EXCEL spreadsheet has been set up as described above, we can now explore the effect on the line of changes in the cost figures given by changing the numbers in cells A1 and B1.

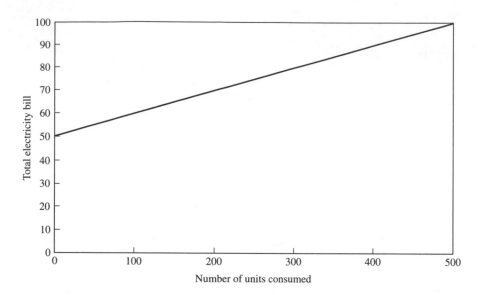

**Figure 3.8** Graph of total electricity bill against number of units consumed

If the fixed charge were changed to £60 by replacing the 50 in A1 by 60, the whole line would move upwards, with all $y$ values being increased by 10. In particular, the crossing point on the $y$-axis is seen to change to 60 instead of 50. Similarly, if the number in A1 were changed to 45, every $y$ value would be reduced by 5 relative to the original situation, and the crossing point on the $y$-axis would become 45. Thus the fixed charge item, represented by A\$1 in our spreadsheet formula, tells us the value of $y$ where the line crosses the $y$-axis and it is called the intercept on the $y$-axis.

Next, with the value in cell A1 held at 50, change the value in cell B1 to 0.2. The effect of this will be seen to be a line which goes up twice as steeply as the original line. If the figure in cell B1 is changed to 0.05, this line will go up only half as steeply as the original line. The charge per unit, represented by B\$1 in our spreadsheet formula is telling us the amount by which the total bill goes up when there is one extra unit consumed and is seen from the effect of changes on the graph to represent the gradient of the line.

When representing a straight line in mathematical notation, the A\$1 of our spreadsheet formula is replaced by $a$ and the B\$1 by $b$, giving the statement

$$y = a + bx$$

as the **general equation of a straight line**.

Just as 50 was the intercept on the $y$-axis in our example, $y = a$ will be the intercept in the general case.

In the same way as 0.1 was the gradient of the line in our example, $b$ will be the value of the gradient in the general case. The gradient of the line is the change in $y$ when there is an increase of one unit in the value of $x$. Note that if $b$ were a negative number, the value of $y$ would be decreasing as $x$ increased and so the line on the graph would be sloping downwards.

Examples 3.2.1 and 3.2.2 below are included as very simple examples to illustrate the appearance of lines with different values for $a$ and $b$. Although we have for purposes of explanation used six points to plot the line in the example above, only *two* points are strictly needed to plot a line in practice. However, using a third point is always a good idea to provide a check. If all three lie on a line, there is a fair chance you have got it right. In most of the straight line plots in the remainder of this chapter we shall use three points.

## Example 3.2.1

A supply function relates quantity supplied of an item, $Q$, to its price, $P$.

Plot the graph of the supply function

$$P = 6 + 2Q$$

with $Q$ on the horizontal axis and $P$ on the vertical axis, using $Q$ values 4, 8 and 12. Identify from your graph the intercept on the $P$-axis and identify the gradient of the line by ascertaining the change in $P$ as $Q$ increases from 0 to 1.

### Solution to Example 3.2.1

| $Q$ | 4 | 8 | 12 |
|---|---|---|---|
| $2Q$ | 8 | 16 | 24 |
| 6 | 6 | 6 | 6 |
| $P = 6 + 2Q$ | 14 | 22 | 30 |

The graph is plotted in Fig. 3.9.

We see from the graph that the intercept on the $P$-axis is at $P = 6$. This corresponds to the value of the $a$ term in the equation of this particular line being 6. As $Q$ increases from 0 to 1 we see from the graph that $P$ changes from 6 to 8, an increase of two units. Because the line is straight, it follows that any increase of 1 in $Q$ will lead to an increase of 2 in $P$, and so the line is seen to have a gradient of 2. This corresponds to the value of the $b$ term for this particular line being 2.

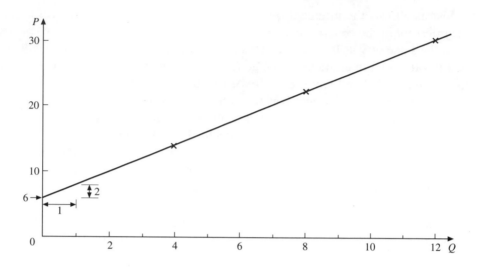

**Figure 3.9** Graph of the supply function $P = 6 + 2Q$

## Example 3.2.2

A demand function relates quantity demanded of an item, $Q$, to its price, $P$.
Plot the graph of the demand function

$$P = 20 - 4Q$$

using $Q$ values 2, 3 and 4. Identify from your graph the intercept on the $P$-axis and identify the gradient of the line by ascertaining the change in $P$ as $Q$ increases from 0 to 1.

### Solution to Example 3.2.2

| $Q$ | 2 | 3 | 4 |
|---|---|---|---|
| $-4Q$ | $-8$ | $-12$ | $-16$ |
| $20$ | 20 | 20 | 20 |
| $P = 20 - 4Q$ | 12 | 8 | 4 |

The graph is plotted in Fig. 3.10.

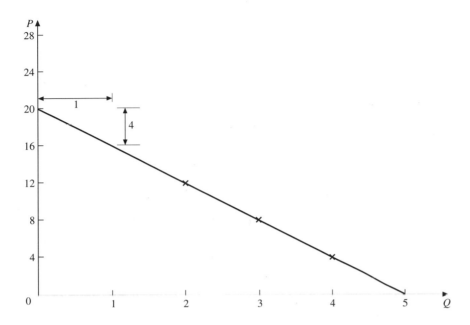

**Figure 3.10** Graph of the demand function $P = 20 - 4Q$

We see from the graph that the intercept on the *P*-axis is at $P = 20$. This corresponds to the value of the *a* term in the equation of this particular line being 20. As *Q* increases from 0 to 1 we see from the graph that *P* changes from 20 to 16, a decrease of four units. Because the line is straight, it follows that any increase of 1 in *Q* will lead to a decrease of 4 in *P*, and so the line is seen to have a gradient of $-4$. This corresponds to the value of the *b* term for this particular line being $-4$.

## Example 3.2.3

A company producing a particular item made the numbers shown in four quarters of a year and incurred the associated total costs shown below.

| Period | Q1 | Q2 | Q3 | Q4 |
|---|---|---|---|---|
| Number produced | 100 | 200 | 300 | 400 |
| Total cost (£000s) | 15 | 18 | 21 | 24 |

a    Plot a graph showing cost on the vertical axis plotted against number of items produced.

b    For the line obtained by joining the plotted points find the intercept and gradient and interpret them as different types of cost.

### Solution to Example 3.2.3

The required graph is shown as Fig. 3.11.

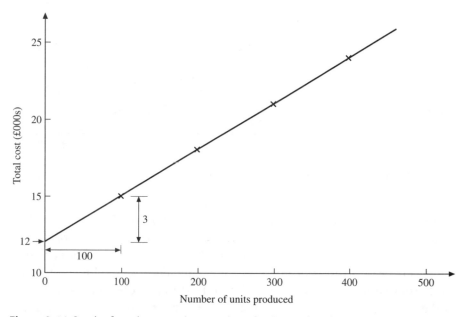

**Figure 3.11** Graph of total cost against number of units produced

From the graph we see that the intercept of the line on the vertical axis is at the value 12. This tells us that the company's fixed cost is £12 000.

We see also from the graph that an increase of 100 in the value of $x$ leads to an increase of 3 in the value of $y$. Hence the gradient of the line is $3/100$ = 0.03. As the units of the variable y are thousands of pounds, it follows that the company's variable cost is £3000/100 = £30 per unit produced.

**Exercises 3.2**    1    A car hire company publishes the following as examples of total charges that will be made for different numbers of miles travelled in a hired car in a month.

| Miles travelled | 500 | 1500 | 2500 |
| --- | --- | --- | --- |
| Total charge (£) | 210 | 290 | 370 |

   **a** Plot these pairs of values on a graph having miles travelled on the $x$-axis and total charge on the $y$-axis.

   **b** Join the points together to obtain a straight line and extend this line back to the $y$-axis.

   **c** Evaluate the intercept and the gradient of your graph and hence state the monthly fixed cost of hiring one of these cars, and the charge being made per mile driven.

2 Plot the following three pairs of numbers on a graph and then by examination of the gradient of the graph and its intercept on the $P$-axis determine the values of $a$ and $b$ in the equation

$$P = a + bQ \quad \text{which relates } P \text{ and } Q.$$

| $Q$: | 2 | 4 | 6 |
| --- | --- | --- | --- |
| $P$: | 12 | 8 | 4 |

   Is this equation more likely to represent a supply function or a demand function?

## 3.3 Linear Equations

Tables and chairs are to be made from a supply of wood, of which there are 100 kilograms available at the beginning of a particular week. Each table requires 4 kilograms of wood while each chair requires 1 kilogram. This means that if $x$ tables and $y$ chairs are made, the total number of kilograms of wood that will be needed is $y$ lots of 1 kilogram plus $x$ lots of 4 kilograms, giving $y + 4x$ kilograms in all. Since there are 100 kilograms of wood available for the week, the numbers of tables and chairs that can be made are determined by the requirement that

$$y + 4x = 100.$$

If tables have priority and wood can be used for chairs only after that needed for tables has been made available, the number of chairs that can be made can be expressed as $y = 100 - 4x$, which is a linear function of the type seen in Sec. 3.2. The graph of this function can be plotted as in the examples seen there.

| Number, $x$, of tables to be made | 0 | 10 | 20 |
|---|---|---|---|
| $(-4)x$ | 0 | $-40$ | $-80$ |
| Raw material available (100) | 100 | 100 | 100 |
| Number, $y$, of chairs that can be made | 100 | 60 | 20 |

The calculator steps for the second and fourth rows in the final column would be as follows:

Line 2: [4]  [+/−] [x] [20]  [=]
Line 4: [80] [+/−] [+]  [100] [=]

The graph could also be produced in EXCEL using the procedure set out in Sec. 3.2 by putting 100 in cell A1, −4 in cell B1 and the values 0, 10, 20 in cells C1 to C3 with the formula A\$1 + B\$1*C1 in cell D1 and copied down as far as D3. The graph as produced by EXCEL is shown in Fig. 3.12.

It will be noted from the graph, that $y$ takes the value zero when $x = 25$. That is to say, the number of tables required that will mean no chairs can be produced is 25. This value $x = 25$ is thus the solution to the linear equation

$$100 - 4x = 0.$$

So if we are given any linear equation $a + bx = 0$, one way to solve it

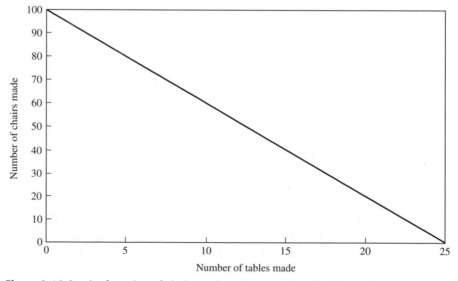

**Figure 3.12** Graph of number of chairs made against number of tables made

would be to plot the line $y = a + bx$ and find the value of $x$ at the point where it crosses the $x$-axis. This would, however, be a very inefficient way of going about things, as such an equation can be solved very simply without graphs so long as we bear in mind that there are just *two* things which it is permissible to do with an equation without changing its meaning:

1   **The same thing can be added to or subtracted from both sides of the equation.**
2   **Both sides of the equation can be multiplied or divided by the same thing.**

Let us apply these rules to the equation $100 - 4x = 0$

First, add $4x$ to both sides of the equation      $100 = 4x$
Second, divide both sides by 4                      $100/4 = x$

Thus we see that x $= 100/4 = 25$, as we saw from the graph.
    The same ideas could be applied to the general linear equation $a + bx = 0$

First, subtract $a$ from both sides of the equation   $bx = -a$
Second, divide both sides by $b$:                     $x = -a/b$

## Example 3.3.1

Solve the linear equation $6x - 24 = 0$.

## *Solution to Example 3.3.1*

$$6x - 24 = 0$$
Add 24 to both sides                $6x = 24$
Divide both sides by 6               $x = 4$

1   Solve the linear equation $7x - 56 = 0$
2   Solve the linear equation $8x + 34 = 0$
3   Solve the linear equation $6x - 27 = 0$
4   Solve the linear equation $9x + 54 = 0$

**Exercises 3.3**

## 3.4 Simultaneous Equations

Consider now a different situation where chairs and tables are being made. The construction process this time means that each of them needs inputs of plastic and metal. Suppose each chair requires 2 kilograms of plastic and 4 kilograms of metal while each table requires 5 kilograms of plastic and 4 kilograms of metal. Suppose also that the quantities available of the two resources are 150 kilograms of plastic and 180 kilograms of metal.

If $x$ chairs are made and $y$ tables, then the amount of plastic required is $x$ lots of 2 kilograms and $y$ lots of 5 kilograms, making a total of $2x + 5y$ kilograms. So availability of plastic imposes a limitation on the numbers of units that can be made which is

$$2x + 5y = 150 \qquad\qquad (3.1)$$

In the same way, the amount of metal being used is $x$ lots of 4 kilograms and $y$ lots of 4 kilograms, making a total of $4x + 4y$ kilograms. So availability of metal imposes on the values of $x$ and $y$ the limitation

$$4x + 4y = 180 \qquad\qquad (3.2)$$

To find the numbers of chairs and tables that can be made so that the two resource limitations are met then means looking for a pair of values for $x$ and $y$ which makes Eqs (3.1) and (3.2) true at the same time, or *simultaneously*. Hence equations of this kind are referred to as 'simultaneous equations'.

One way to go about finding the required pair of values for $x$ and $y$ would be to begin by rearranging the equations into the standard form of linear functions as seen earlier. In (3.1) we could first subtract $2x$ from both sides to obtain

$$5y = 150 - 2x$$

Then divide both sides by 5 to obtain

$$y = 30 - 0.4x$$

In (3.2) we could first subtract $4x$ from both sides to obtain

$$4y = 180 - 4x$$

Then divide both sides by 4 to obtain

$$y = 45 - x$$

We could then plot these two lines on the same graph and identify the point where they cross. The pair of values for $x$ and $y$ at this point satisfies both the relationships and so constitutes the solution to our pair of simultaneous equations.

Possible tables of values for the two graphs would be as follows:

| $x$ | 0 | 20 | 40 |
|---|---|---|---|
| $-0.4x$ | 0 | $-8$ | $-16$ |
| 30 | 30 | 30 | 30 |
| $y$ | 30 | 22 | 14 |

and

| $x$ | 0 | 20 | 40 |
|---|---|---|---|
| $-x$ | 0 | $-20$ | $-40$ |
| 45 | 45 | 45 | 45 |
| $y$ | 45 | 25 | 5 |

The calculator steps needed for obtaining the second and fourth lines of each of these tables are similar to those shown for a single line in Sec. 3.2.

The lines plotted from these two tables of values are shown in Fig. 3.13. You should carry out the plotting yourself, confirming the correctness of Fig. 3.13, and read off from your graph the values for $x$ and $y$ which solve the pair of simultaneous equations.

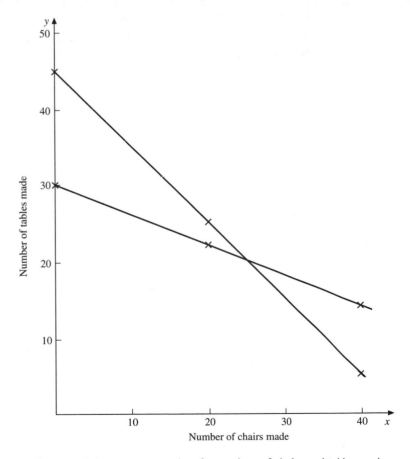

**Figure 3.13** Resource constraints for numbers of chairs and tables made

The relevant parts of the lines can also be plotted on a single graph in EXCEL by extending the procedure explained in Sec. 3.2 for a single line.

Enter the values 30 in cell A1 and 45 in cell A2
Enter the values −0.4 in cell B1 and −1 in cell B2
Enter the values 0, 20, 40 in cells C1, C2, C3 respectively

Then in cell D1 enter the formula

= A$1 + B$1*C1

This will result in the value 30 in cell D1, and if the formula is then copied down to cells D2 to D3 the values 22 and 14 will appear.

In cell E1 enter the formula

= A$2 + B$2*C1

This will result in the value 45 in cell E1, and if the formula is then copied down to cells E2 to E3 the values 25 and 5 will appear. Then highlight the block of cells from C1 to E3 and call up the Chart Wizard. The Chart Wizard menus can then be used to plot a line graph of columns D and E both against column C, giving the result shown in Fig. 3.14. However, as in the case of solving linear equations, it is usually more efficient to solve simultaneous equations without using graphs but by instead employing the two rules for operating on equations set out in Sec. 3.3.

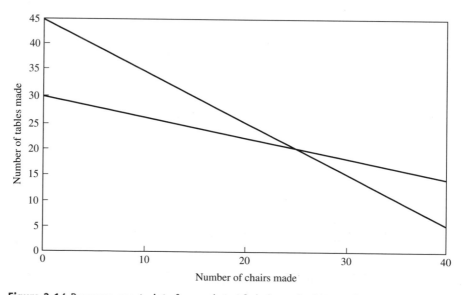

**Figure 3.14** Resource constraints for numbers of chairs and tables made

Consider again the pair of equations to be solved here

$$2x + 5y = 150 \qquad\qquad (3.3)$$

$$4x + 4y = 180 \qquad\qquad (3.4)$$

The first requirement is to get either $x$ or $y$ having the same multiplier in both equations. There are many ways this could be done, but the most obvious thing to do here is to multiply the first equation by 2 in order to change the $x$ multiplier 2 into a 4, which is the multiplier that $x$ has in Eq. (3.4).

$$\text{Write } 2 \times (3.3)\text{: } 4x + 10y = 300 \qquad\qquad (3.5)$$

The second step is then to subtract $4x + 4y$ from the left-hand side of Eq. (3.5) and 180 from the right-hand side of (3.5). This is allowed because Eq. (3.4) says these two things are equal and so we are subtracting the same thing from both sides of Eq. (3.5).

$$\text{Write } (3.5) - (3.4)\text{: } (4x + 10y) - (4x + 4y) = 300 - 180$$

The $4x$ terms cancel, which was the point of making $x$ have the same multiplier in both equations, giving

$$10y - 4y = 120$$

Hence $\qquad\qquad 6y = 120$

So $\qquad\qquad y = 20$

Using this $y$ value in Eq. (1) we have

$$2x + 5 \times 20 = 150$$

So $\qquad\qquad 2x = 150 - 100 = 50$

and hence $\qquad\qquad x = 25$

This is saying that it is possible to make 25 chairs and 20 tables by making use of all the plastic and metal available. Compare the values found in your graphical solution with these algebraically determined solutions.

## Example 3.4.1

Solve the following pair of simultaneous equations algebraically and draw a graph to illustrate the solution:

$$7x + y = 16$$

$$3x + 2y = 10$$

## Solution to Example 3.4.1

$$7x + y = 16 \tag{3.6}$$

$$3x + 2y = 10 \tag{3.7}$$

$2 \times (3.6)$:   $14x + 2y = 32$   (3.8)

$(3.8) - (3.7)$:   $11x = 22$

Divide through by 11:   $x = 2$

Substitute $x = 2$ in (3.6):   $7 \times 2 + y = 16$

Hence   $y = 16 - 14 = 2$

The solutions are $x = 2$ and $y = 2$

This answer is illustrated by the crossing of the lines in Fig. 3.15. The equations for plotting the lines are obtained as follows:

Subtracting $7x$ from both sides of Eq. (3.6):   $y = 16 - 7x$

Subtracting $3x$ from both sides of Eq. (3.7):   $2y = 10 - 3x$

so   $y = 5 - 1.5x$

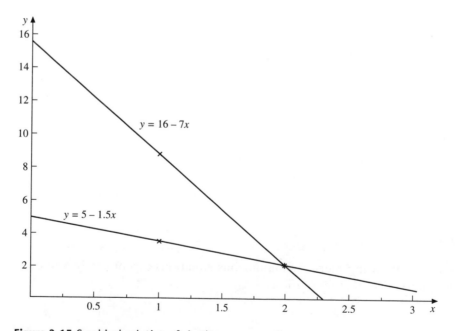

**Figure 3.15** Graphical solution of simultaneous equations

Then possible tables of values for the two graphs would be as follows:

| $x$ | 0 | 1 | 2 |
|---|---|---|---|
| $-7x$ | 0 | $-7$ | $-14$ |
| 16 | 16 | 16 | 16 |
| $y$ | 16 | 9 | 2 |

| $x$ | 0 | 1 | 2 |
|---|---|---|---|
| $-1.5x$ | 0 | $-1.5$ | $-3$ |
| 5 | 5 | 5 | 5 |
| $y$ | 5 | 3.5 | 2 |

**Exercises 3.4**

1  Solve the simultaneous equations

$$2x + y = 4$$

and

$$4x - 3y = 3$$

   a  by drawing a suitable graph
   b  by means of a graph on an EXCEL spreadsheet
   c  algebraically

2  A company makes its product at a variable cost of £8 per unit and sells it for £12 per unit. The company's fixed costs are £16 000 per month. The number of units produced and sold each month is to be denoted by $x$.

   a  Explain why the total monthly revenue is £12$x$ and the total monthly cost is £(16 000 + 8$x$).
   b  Draw a graph having $x$ on the horizontal axis and showing both the total revenue and total cost functions plotted against $x$
      • manually
      • using an EXCEL spreadsheet.
   c  Find the value of $x$ where the two lines on your graph cross
      • by reading off the value from your graph
      • by solving  $y = 12x$
                   $y = 16 000 + 8x$ as simultaneous equations.
   (This value of $x$ which makes *total revenue* = *total cost* is called the 'break-even quantity'.)
   d  State the value of total revenue and the value of total cost for the $x$ value found in answer to part **c**.

## 3.5 Quadratic Equations

Although linear functions and linear equations are important, there are very many functions that are not linear, and these lead us to non-linear equations. In most cases non-linear equations cannot be solved algebraically.

In this section we are concerned with a particular type of non-linear function called a 'quadratic function'. Its basic form is not dissimilar to that of the linear function

$$y = a + bx$$

but it has an additional term which is a constant multiplied by the square of $x$, that is, $x$ multiplied by itself, denoted $x^2$.

The way a quadratic function is most usually written is to have $a$ as the constant multiplying the $x^2$ term, $b$ multiplying the $x$ (as in the linear function case) and $c$ as the constant term. Thus the general form is

$$y = ax^2 + bx + c$$

To illustrate what the graph of this sort of function looks like, we shall consider a production situation where a maker of specialist cars has a revenue function

$$R = 20x - 2x^2$$

where $R$ is the revenue received, in tens of thousands of pounds, in a year when $x$ cars are produced and sold.

The cost function for this car maker, also in tens of thousands of pounds, is

$$C = 15 + 7x$$

The annual profit made by this car manufacturer is the difference between revenue and cost, which is

$$y = R - C = (20x - 2x^2) - (15 + 7x) = -2x^2 + 13x - 15$$

This is a particular case of the general form for a quadratic function given above where $a = -2$, $b = 13$ and $c = -15$.

We shall now plot the graph of this quadratic profit function

$$y = -2x^2 + 13x - 15$$

The graph for this type of function can be drawn using the same principles as for the linear functions seen earlier. We take a selection of values of $x$, calculate the corresponding values of $y$, plot the points and join them together. Note that for non-linear functions more than three points will be needed in order to make clear the shape of the graph, and it is most important that the points plotted are joined together by a *smooth curve* and not by straight lines. It is the smooth curve which will represent the points that have not been actually plotted.

For this case we have:

| $x$ | 0 | 1 | 2 | 3 | 4 | 5 | 6 | 7 |
|---|---|---|---|---|---|---|---|---|
| $x^2$ | 0 | 1 | 4 | 9 | 16 | 25 | 36 | 49 |
| $-2x^2$ | 0 | $-2$ | $-8$ | $-18$ | $-32$ | $-50$ | $-72$ | $-98$ |
| $13x$ | 0 | 13 | 26 | 39 | 52 | 65 | 78 | 91 |
| $-15$ | $-15$ | $-15$ | $-15$ | $-15$ | $-15$ | $-15$ | $-15$ | $-15$ |
| $y$ | $-15$ | $-4$ | 3 | 6 | 5 | 0 | $-9$ | $-22$ |

Calculator steps which will be appropriate for dealing with the calculations needed for lines 2, 3, 4 and 6 of this table are illustrated using the final column:

Line 2: [7] [$x^2$]
Line 3: [2] [+/–] [×] [49] [=]
Line 4: [13] [×] [7] [=]
Line 6: [−98] [+] [91] [−] [15] [=]

The graph of $y = -2x^2 + 13x - 15$ is shown in Fig. 3.16. Note that the value of $y$ when $x = 0$ is $y = -15$, reflecting the fact that the intercept on the $y$-axis of the general quadratic function $y = ax^2 + bx + c$ is $c$. This is clear as $c$ is the value taken by $y$ when $x$ is given the value zero in the quadratic function.

Note also from the graph that $y = 0$ when $x = 1.5$ or $x = 5$. These are the break-even quantities for this car manufacturer. They make the profit function equal to zero, indicating that the total revenue and total quantity are equal.

These two values are the solutions of the quadratic equation

$$-2x^2 + 13x - 15 = 0.$$

Such equations will be considered more generally below.

The quadratic function can be plotted in EXCEL by appropriate extension of the procedure explained in Sec. 3.2 for straight lines.

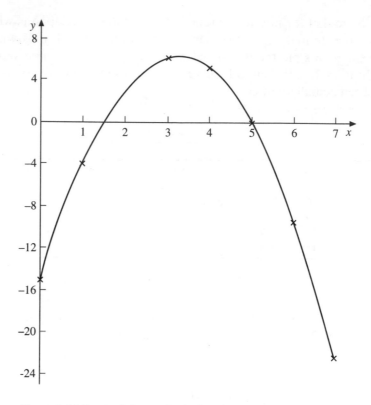

**Figure 3.16** Graph of the quadratic function $y = -2x^2 + 13x - 15$

Enter the value $-2$ in cell A1, 13 in cell B1 and $-15$ in cell C1.
Enter the values 0, 1, 2, 3, 4, 5, 6, 7 in cells D1, D2, D3, D4, D5, D6, D7 and D8 respectively.
Then in cell E1 enter the formula: =A\$1*D1^2 + B\$1*D1 + C\$1

This will result in the value $-15$ in cell E1, and if the formula is then copied down to cells E2 to E5 the values $-4$, 3, 6, 5, 0, $-9$ and $-22$ will appear. Highlight the block of cells from D1 to E8 and call up the Chart Wizard. Then use the Chart Wizard to plot a line graph of column E against column D. Be careful to use the option which specifies smooth joining of the points rather than joining by straight lines. The graph as drawn by EXCEL is shown in Fig. 3.17.

It will be noted from the graph of a quadratic function that it would be possible for such a function to have 0, 1 or 2 points where it cuts the $x$-axis (see Fig. 3.18). Thus a quadratic equation $ax^2 + bx + c = 0$ could have 0, 1 or 2 solutions. As in the cases of linear and simultaneous equations, these solutions

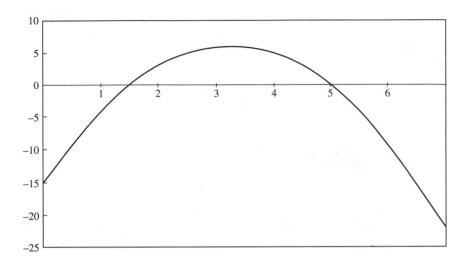

**Figure 3.17** Graph of a quadratic function

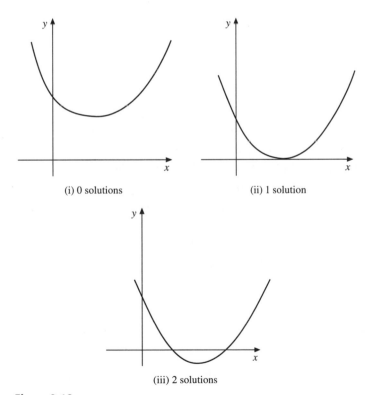

(i) 0 solutions

(ii) 1 solution

(iii) 2 solutions

**Figure 3.18**

would normally be found algebraically rather than by actually drawing the graph of the quadratic function and reading off the points where it cuts the $x$-axis. The algebraic method in this case involves evaluation of a formula which says that the solutions to the equation $ax^2 + bx + c = 0$ are found as

$$x = \frac{-b \pm \sqrt{\{b^2 - 4ac\}}}{2a}$$

It will be noted that this formula could generate 0, 1 or 2 solutions for $x$ corresponding to the three cases shown graphically in Fig. 3.18.

　　If $b^2 < 4ac$　then there will be no solutions as a negative number does not have a square root

　　If $b^2 = 4ac$　then there will be one solution, $x = -b/2a$.

　　If $b^2 > 4ac$　then there will be two solutions, one based on the positive square root of $b^2 - 4ac$ and one on the negative square root.

For the equation $-2x^2 + 13x - 15 = 0$ we have

$$x = \frac{-13 \pm \sqrt{\{13^2 - 4 \times (-2) \times (-15)\}}}{2x(-2)} = \frac{-13 \pm \sqrt{\{169 - 120\}}}{-4}$$

$$= \frac{-13 \pm 7}{-4}$$

　　Hence $x = -6/-4 = 1.5$　　or　　$x = -20/-4 = 5$

These correspond to the crossing points in Figs 3.16 and 3.17.

　　Evaluation of the above formula on a calculator requires use of a memory and we shall assume throughout the book the use of a calculator with one memory to which the following operations relate

　　[M+]　means add into the memory
　　[M−]　means subtract from the memory
　　[MR]　means read the memory
　　[MC]　means clear the memory

First the square root part of the formula can be found as follows and put into the memory:

　　[13] [$x^2$] [M+] [4] [×] [2] [+/–] [×] [15] [+/–] [=] [M−] [MR] [MC] [√] [M+]

With the square root in the memory, the two solutions can now be found as follows:

　　[13] [+/–] [+] [MR] [=] [÷] [4] [+/–] [=]

　　[13] [+/–] [−] [MR] [=] [÷] [4] [+/–] [=]

## Example 3.5.1

Solve the quadratic equation $2x^2 - 7x + 6 = 0$ and illustrate the solution by drawing a suitable graph.

### *Solution to Example 3.5.1*

For the quadratic equation $2x^2 - 7x + 6 = 0$ we have

$$x = \frac{7 \pm \sqrt{\{7^2 - 4 \times 2 \times 6\}}}{2 \times 2} = \frac{7 \pm \sqrt{\{49 - 48\}}}{4} = \frac{7 \pm 1}{4}$$

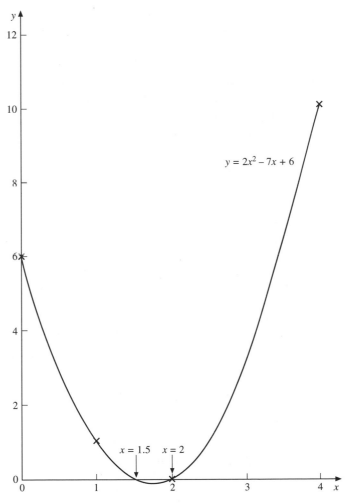

$$y = 2x^2 - 7x + 6$$

$$x = 1.5 \quad x = 2$$

**Figure 3.19** Graphical illustration of solutions to a quadratic equation

Hence   $x = 8/4 = 2$     or     $x = 6/4 = 1.5$

Figure 3.19 shows the graph of the quadratic function $y = 2x^2 - 7x + 6$ and we see that this graph crosses the horizontal axis at the points where $x = 2$ and $x = 1.5$, illustrating the solutions found above.

**Exercises 3.5**   1   A person producing and selling knitted garments of a particular kind has monthly revenue (in £s) given by

$$R = 84x - x^2$$

where $x$ is the number of garments sold in the month.
The monthly cost function is

$$C = 840 + 2x$$

The maximum number of garments which can be produced in a month is 50, and it may be assumed that all production is sold.
a   Plot the monthly revenue and cost functions on a single graph with the same scale and axes, using $x$ values 0, 10, 20, 30, 40 and 50.
b   Use your graph to estimate the break-even value of $x$.
c   Obtain a more precise value for the break-even quantity by calculation, and evaluate the total revenue and total cost for this value of $x$.
2   A firm is contemplating beginning the production of an item for which it predicts that the total weekly cost (in £s) will be

$$TC = 400 + x^2$$

where $x$ is the number of units produced per week.
The market is believed to be such that the selling price of the item will need to be set at £40. At this price it may be assumed that all production will be sold.
a   Explain why the revenue function for this product is $TR = 40x$.
b   Plot the weekly revenue and cost functions on a single graph with the same scale and axes, using $x$ values 0, 5, 10, 20, 25 and 30.
c   Use your graph to estimate the break-even value of $x$.
d   Confirm your value found in the answer to part c by solving the quadratic equation resulting from setting $TR$ equal to $TC$.
e   State with reasons whether you believe the company should go ahead with production of this item.

## Further Exercises

1. A company has fixed costs of £12 000 per month and produces its product at a variable cost of £3 per unit. If the break-even quantity for the product is 6000 units, which of the following is the selling price per unit?

    A. £4            B. £5            C. £6            D. £7

2 Which of the following pairs of values solves the following simultaneous equations?

   $5x + 3y = 3$
   $4x - 2y = 9$

    A. $x = 3$,    $y = -4$        B. $x = 1.8$, $y = -2$
    C. $x = 0.9$, $y = -0.5$       D. $x = 1.5$, $y = -1.5$

3 Which of the following pairs of values solves the simultaneous equations?

   $4x + 5y = 20$
   $6x - 2y = 11$

    A. $x = 1.25$, $y = 3.00$      B. $x = 2.00$, $y = 2.40$
    C. $x = 2.50$, $y = 2.00$      D. $x = 3.00$, $y = 1.60$

4 How many different values of $x$ make the following equation true?

   $4x^2 - 12x + 9 = 0$

    A. 0            B. 1            C. 2            D. 3

5 Which of the following cannot be the number of solutions possessed by a quadratic equation?

    A. 0            B. 1            C. 2            D. 3

6 Which one of the following quadratic equations has two positive solutions?

    A. $x^2 + 7x + 10 = 0$         B. $x^2 - 7x - 10 = 0$
    C. $x^2 + 7x - 10 = 0$         D. $x^2 - 7x + 10 = 0$

7  Which of the following pairs of numbers are the solutions to the quadratic equation?

$$x^2 + 5x - 14 = 0$$

A. $x = 2$ and $x = 7$      B. $x = -2$ and $x = 7$
C. $x = 2$ and $x = -7$     D. $x = -2$ and $x = -7$

8. A company has a choice of three tariffs for its electricity:

Tariff 1 involves a fixed cost of £1000 per quarter and a charge of 9p per unit of electricity consumed.
Tariff 2 involves a fixed cost of £2000 per quarter and a charge of 8p per unit of electricity consumed.
Tariff 3 involves a fixed cost of £5000 per quarter and a charge of 6p per unit of electricity consumed.

**a**  Denoting the number of units consumed per quarter by $x$, write down an expression in terms of $x$ for the total quarterly cost, $C$, of electricity under each of the three tariffs.
**b**  Plot on the same scale and axes, graphs of the total cost $C$ against units consumed $x$ for each of the three tariffs, using the expressions found in your answer to part **a**. (Consider in each case electricity usage up to 200 000 units.)
**c**  Estimate from your graph drawn in answer to part **b** the ranges of units for which each of the three tariffs gives the lowest total cost.
**d**  Calculate from your expressions found in answer to part **a**, and by reference to your graph drawn in answer to part **b**, the numbers of units $x$ at which it becomes advisable to transfer from one tariff to another.
State in each case the total cost $C$ at the cross-over point.

9  A firm making specialist cars has a revenue function of the form

$$y = ax - bx^2$$

where $x$ is the number of cars produced and sold per year
    $y$ is the total annual revenue in thousands of pounds
    $a$ is a constant
    $b$ is a constant

**a**  Accounting records show that in a year when $x = 5$ cars were sold, the total revenue was $y = 250$, while in a year when $x = 10$

cars were sold, the total revenue generated was $y = 400$. Show by solving appropriate simultaneous equations that $a = 60$ and $b = 2$.

b  Using your values for $a$ and $b$ found in answer to part **a**, plot a graph of $y$ against $x$ using $x$ values 0, 2, 4, 6, 8, 10 and 12 where 12 is the annual production capacity.

c  Annual fixed costs, in thousands of pounds, are 120 and the variable cost per car produced, in thousands of pounds, is 14. Express total cost $y$, in thousands of pounds, as a function of the number, $x$, of cars produced.

d  Plot the total cost function on the same scale and axes on the same graph as the revenue function plotted in answer to part **b**, and use your graph to estimate the number of cars that need to be produced and sold in order to break-even.

e  Confirm your answer to part **d** by solving an appropriate quadratic equation.

10. A firm's monthly revenue function, in pounds, for a certain product is

$$R = 200x - 5x^2$$

where $x$ is the number of units sold, in hundreds. The corresponding monthly cost function is

$$C = 375 + 100x.$$

a  Plot the two functions on a single graph with the same scale and axes, using $x$ values 0, 2, 4, 6, 8, 10, 12, 14 and 16.

b  Deduce an expression in terms of $x$ for the profit function, which is the difference between the revenue function and the cost function.

c  Use the profit function found in answer to part **b** to calculate two values of $x$ for which the profit function is zero, and therefore total revenue is exactly equal to total cost, giving a break-even situation.

d  Indicate on your graph drawn in answer to part **b** the break-even values of $x$.

## Chapter Four

# Financial Arithmetic

## 4.1 Simple and Compound Interest

National Savings sell Income Bonds. People make an **investment** of a sum of money and, in return, have a specified amount of money (called **interest**) paid to them each month. Similar products are available from banks, building societies and insurance companies. The interest earned from Income Bonds is called **simple interest** because, as long as the interest rate remains unchanged, the amount of interest each month is the same. This interest, which constitutes the **financial return** on the investment, is easy to calculate.

## Example 4.1.1

You invest £10 000 in an Income Bond at a rate of interest of 0.6% per month. How much interest would you earn in two years?

## *Solution to Example 4.1.1*

The interest earned each month is 0.6% of £10 000 which is

$$(0.6/100) \times £10\,000 = £60$$

Hence, over two years the amount you earn would be $24 \times £60 = £1440$.

Suppose we call the initial investment $P$ and the interest rate per period $r$%. Then the amount of interest earned each period is

$$(r/100) \times P = rP/100$$

So, over $n$ periods, the total amount of interest earned would be:

$$n \times (rP/100) = nrP/100$$

We usually use the letter $i$ instead of $r/100$ because it is simpler.

Using this notation, we see that the simple interest earned on investment $P$ over $n$ periods will be $niP$

In a National Savings *Capital* Bond, a sum of money is invested for a specified time and nothing at all is paid back to the investor until the end of that time. Interest is credited from time to time and is added to the investment itself. Thus, the amount on which interest is paid gets larger each period. Interest calculated in this way is called **compound** interest.

To explain the calculation of compound interest let's consider a sum of £30 000 invested for four years at an interest rate of 7% per year, paid annually. Here, $r = 7$ and so $i = 7/100 = 0.07$.

The interest earned in the first year, as it is with simple interest, will be:

$$0.07 \times £30\,000 = £2100$$

In the second year the situation will differ from that under simple interest because the interest in the second year will be earned not on an investment of £30 000 but on £30 000 + £2100 = £32 100. Hence, the interest earned in the second year will be:

$$0.07 \times £32\,100 = £2247$$

This, in turn, will be added into the investment so that the sum on which interest is earned in the *third* year will be £32 100 + £2247 = £34 347. Hence, the interest earned in the third year will be

$$0.07 \times £34\,347 = £2404.29.$$

This will now be added into the investment for the fourth and final year so that interest in that year will be on a total investment of

$$£34\,347 + £2404.29 = £36\,751.29$$

Hence, the interest earned in the fourth and final year will be

$$0.07 \times £36\,751.29 = £2572.59$$

So, the final value of the investment is £36 751.29 + £2572.59 = £39 323.88. The total interest earned over the four year life of the investment is £39 323.88 − £30 000 = £9323.88. Simple interest would have yielded only:

$$niP = 4 \times 0.07 \times £30\,000 = £8400.$$

The extra £923.88 comes from interest earned on interest!

Although compound interest problems can be solved in the way we have just seen, it is an inefficient method, especially if the number of periods involved is large. Imagine calculating compound interest using this method over a hundred years! Isn't there a better way?

There is. We shall explain it using the example above.

We saw that the interest earned in year 1 was $0.07 \times £30\,000$, so the investment going into year 2 was $£30\,000 + 0.07 \times £30\,000$. This can be written more conveniently as

$$(1 + 0.07) \times £30\,000$$

You can work this out on a calculator using

[1] [+] [0.07] [=] [×] [30 000] [=]

to get the value £32 100 which we had above.

Then the interest earned in the second year is $0.07 \times £32\,100$ so the investment going into the third year is $£32\,100 + 0.07 \times £32\,100$, or $(1 + 0.07) \times £32\,100$.

But you have already seen that the £32 000 is $(1 + 0.07) \times £30\,000$ so this investment going into the third year can be written as

$$(1 + 0.07) \times \{(1 + 0.07) \times £30\,000\}$$

which reduces to $(1 + 0.07)^2 £30\,000$. This can be worked out on a calculator using:

[1] [+] [0.07] [=] [$x^y$] [2] [=] [×] [30 000] [=]

to obtain the value £34 347 which we saw earlier.

As an exercise verify by going through the same steps that the investment going into the fourth year can be expressed in the form

$$(1 + 0.07)^3 £30\,000.$$

This can be worked out on a calculator using

[1] [+] [0.07] [=] [$x^y$] [3] [=] [×] [30 000] [=]

to confirm the value £36 751.29 seen in the earlier solution. Then, applying the same steps for a final time will lead to the investment at the end of the fourth year in the form $(1 + 0.07)^4 £30\,000$. This can be worked out on a calculator using

[1] [+] [0.07] [=] [$x^y$] [4] [=] [×] [30 000] [=]

to confirm the value £39 323.88.

The advantage of this approach is that we can use it to find the size of the investment at the end of any number of periods. Suppose we wanted to know the value at the end of 12 years. Finding this would involve an immense amount of calculation using the original method, but we can now see that the value at the end of 12 years is:

$$(1 + 0.07)^{12} \, £30\,000.$$

This can be worked out on a calculator using

$$[1]\,[+]\,[0.07]\,[=]\,[x^y]\,[12]\,[=]\,[\times]\,[30\,000]\,[=]$$

to obtain the value £67 565.75.

In fact, the formula can be very easily generalized not only for any number of periods, but also for any value of $i$ and any investment $P$. The usual notation is to denote the initial investment as $P_0$ and the size of the investment at the end of $n$ periods as $P_n$ so that the general compound interest formula appears as:

$$P_n = (1 + i)^n \, P_0$$

## Example 4.1.2

You invest £25 000 for 7 years at an interest rate of 6% per year paid annually. What is the final value of your investment?

### Solution to Example 4.1.2

The value of the investment at the end of 7 years is

$$(1 + 0.06)^n \times £25\,000 = 1.5036 \times £25\,000 = £37\,590.$$

Appendix 3 contains a table of *compound interest factors* obtained by calculating $(1 + r/100)^n$ for the selection of $n$ and $r$ values shown. If the table had been used to answer Example 4.1.2 , the factor obtained for the $n = 7$ row and the $r = 6$ column would have been 1.5036, giving rise to an answer of $1.5036 \times £25\,000 = £37\,590$, as found above using the calculator method.

We can rearrange the compound interest formula to calculate any of $P_0$, $i$ or $n$ in terms of the other three items. The first of these three rearrangements is the simplest but is especially important because it is the basis of the investment appraisal techniques considered in Sec. 4.3 and 4.4 below.

To rearrange the formula $P_n = (1 + i)^n P_0$ into an expression for $i$ this is what we do:

First divide by $P_0$ to obtain $\qquad\qquad\qquad\qquad (1 + i)^n = P_n/P_0$

Next take the $n$th root of each side to obtain $\quad 1 + i = (P_n/P_0)^{1/n}$

Finally subtract 1 from both sides $\qquad\qquad\qquad i = (P_n/P_0)^{1/n} - 1$

## Example 4.1.3

What annual rate of compound interest would be needed in order for £10 000 to grow to £25 000 in 8 years?

## *Solution to Example 4.1.3*

Here $P_0 = $ £10 000, $P_n = $ £25 000 and $n = 8$ so using the rearrangement of the compound interest formula seen above, we have

$$i = (25\,000/10\,000)^{1/8} - 1 = 2.5^{1/8} - 1$$

This can be found on most calculators using

$$2.5\ [x^{1/y}]\ 8\ [=]\ [-]\ 1\ [=]$$

giving an answer for $i$ of 0.12 and hence an interest rate of 12%. If your calculator will find $x^n$ but not $x^{1/n}$ you could initially find $1/8 = 0.125$ using $1\ [\div]\ 8\ [=]$ and then use

$$2.5\ [x^y]\ 0.125\ [=]\ [-]\ 1\ [=]$$

to again obtain an answer of 0.12 for $i$.

We could also answer this question by using the table in Appendix 3. Having found $P_n/P_0$ to be 2.5 we could go to the $n = 8$ row of the table and try to locate the value 2.5 in that row. The column showing a compound interest factor closest to 2.5 would then be the column for the interest rate we require. In this case we find 2.4760 in the 12% column.

To rearrange the compound interest formula into an expression for $n$ you would need logarithms, which are not covered in this foundation-level book. So for solving problems involving the finding of $n$ we'll stick to using the table in Appendix 3. The procedure is the reverse of that in Example 4.1.3. We go to the column for the given interest rate and look in that column for the figure closest to our value for $P_n/P_0$. The row showing a figure closest to our $P_n/P_0$ value is the row for the number of periods we require.

## Example 4.1.4

How many years will it take for £10 000 to grow to £30 000 if the rate of interest is 6% compounded annually?

## Solution to Example 4.1.4

Here $P_n/P_0 = 30\,000/10\,000 = 3$ so we need to look in the 6% column for the number closest to 3. We find the value 3.0256 in row 19 and hence see that it would require 19 years for the growth to £30 000 to take place.

The **reducing balance method for depreciation** is a variation on the compound interest idea. Instead of having an investment which grows by a specified percentage each period we have an asset which depreciates by a specified percentage each period. If the rate of depreciation is $r$% per period and we write $r/100$ as $i$, then using the same reasoning as applied to compound interest earlier we see that the value $P_n$ after $n$ periods of an asset initially valued at $P_0$ will be:

$$P_n = (1 - i)^n P_0$$

Thus we have the compound interest formula with '$+ i$' replaced by '$- i$'. Appendix 3 contains a table of *depreciation factors* obtained by calculating $(1 - r/100)^n$ for the selection of $n$ and $r$ values shown.

## Example 4.1.5

Find the value recorded in a company's accounts at the end of 7 years for an asset initially valued at £50 000 if reducing balance depreciation has been applied over the 7 years using an annual depreciation rate of 10%.

## Solution to Example 4.1.5

The value at the end of 7 years is

$$(1 - 0.1)^7 \times £50\,000 = 0.9^7 \times £50\,000 = 0.4783 \times £50\,000 = £23\,915$$

This could be found on a calculator using

$$[1]\,[-]\,[0.1]\,[=]\,[x^y]\,[7]\,[=]\,[\times]\,[50\,000]\,[=]$$

Note that the factor 0.4783 could have been obtained from the table of depreciation factors in Appendix 3 by referring to the 10% column and the 7 years row.

Rearrangements of the depreciation formula and reverse uses of the table of depreciation factors can be carried out using exactly the same principles as explained for compound interest above.

**Exercises 4.1**

1    You invest £40 000 in a savings account which pays simple interest monthly at a guaranteed fixed rate of 0.5% per month. Calculate the total amount of interest that would be paid to you over five years.

2    A sum of £45 000 is invested for 8 years at a compound interest rate of 5% per year paid annually. What is the final value of the investment?

3    What annual rate of compound interest would be needed in order for £24 000 to grow to £36 000 in 5 years?

4    How many years will it take for £20 000 to grow to £40 000 if the rate of interest is 8% compounded annually?

5    Find the value recorded in a company's accounts at the end of 11 years for an asset initially valued at £80 000 if reducing balance depreciation has been applied over the 11 years using an annual depreciation rate of 15%.

## 4.2 Effective Interest Rate

In all the examples and exercises we looked at in Sec. 4.1 the interest rate period was the same as the compounding period, either a monthly interest rate with monthly compounding, or an annual interest rate with annual compounding. When the compounding period and the interest rate period differ, we need to distinguish between the nominal rate and the effective rate.

The **nominal interest rate** is the rate which is named (or 'nominated'). For example, a nominal rate of 2% per month could also be described as a nominal rate of 24% per year or vice versa.

The **effective interest rate** (as a percentage) on an annual basis is the amount by which a £100 investment would grow over a year. Let's look again at the example of a nominal rate of 2% per month with monthly compounding and see what the effective annual rate is. If £100 is invested for a year at this rate, then the amount by which it will have grown by the end of the year is

$$(1 + 0.02)^{12} \times £100 - £100 = £126.82 - £100 = £26.82$$

revealing an effective annual interest rate of 26.82%.

In general we see that if a nominal rate of $r\%$ per period is compounded over $n$ periods to obtain the annual rate, then the effective annual percentage rate is

$$(1 + r/100)^n \times 100 - 100$$

The effective proportional rate, $i$, could be calculated as

$$(1 + i)^n - 1$$

For many years building societies compounded interest on savings accounts every six months so that the rate actually received was, in fact, slightly higher than the nominal rate advertised. For example, an advertised nominal annual rate of 6% actually meant 3% per six-month compounding period, so the effective annual rate was

$$i = (1 + 0.03)^2 - 1 = 1.0609 - 1 = 0.0609$$

That is to say, the effective annual rate was 6.09%.

Building societies and banks have now moved towards crediting such accounts only once a year. (It is possible to have the interest on such accounts paid as monthly income, as for the National Savings Income Bond mentioned at the beginning of Sec. 4.1. We can then invest the interest elsewhere, but the nominal rate paid when the interest is drawn monthly in this way is lower than the nominal rate on the 'normal' method.)

The main practical significance of this point, however, is not about interest paid on savings. It is about interest charged on debts. The UK parliament has considered it necessary to pass legislation to require those lending money to publish the effective annual rate (EAR) of interest they are charging. This applies to all forms of lending including credit cards and bank overdrafts. Publication of just a nominal monthly rate of 2% makes it sound like not very much. The nominal annual rate of 24% is considerable, but even this hides the further 2.82% resulting from compounding which we discovered above. So the effective annual rate of 26.82% has to be published.

## Example 4.2.1

Loans are offered at an annual rate of 20% compounded quarterly. What is the effective annual rate?

### Solution to Example 4.2.1

The nominal quarterly rate is 20%/4 = 5% so the effective annual rate is

$$i = (1 + 0.05)^4 - 1 = 0.2155$$

Thus the effective annual rate is 21.55%.

The basic point being made in this section is that the more frequently interest is compounded, for a given nominal rate, then the higher the effective annual rate will be. This is the case because more frequent compounding means that new money in the form of interest is being added to the investment earlier. Hence the money added has longer to itself go on to earn interest. To illustrate this further we consider an example of a specified nominal rate subject to a variety of different frequencies of compounding.

## Example 4.2.2

A sum of £8000 is invested at a nominal rate of interest of 12% per year. Calculate the total value of the investment after one year under each of the following frequencies of compounding:

      **a** annual    **b** quarterly    **c** monthly    **d** weekly    **e** daily

### Solution to Example 4.2.2

**a**    Value after one year = $(1 + 0.12) \times £8000 = 1.12 \times £8000 = £8960$

**b**    Nominal quarterly rate is 3% so the value of the investment after one year is

$$(1 + 0.03)^4 \times £8000 = 1.1255 \times £8000 = £9004.07$$

**c**    Nominal monthly rate is 1% so the value of the investment after one year is

$$(1 + 0.01)^{12} \times £8000 = 1.1268 \times £8000 = £9014.60$$

**d**    Nominal weekly rate as a percentage is 12/52 = 0.23077 so value after one year is

$$(1 + 0.0023077)^{52} \times £8000 = 1.12734 \times £8000 = £9018.73$$

**e**    Nominal daily rate as a percentage is 12/365 = 0.0328767 so value after one year is

$$(1 + 0.000328767)^{365} \times £8000 = 1.12747 \times £8000 = £9019.80$$

Note the increasing values.

**Exercises 4.2**

1    Loans are offered at an annual rate of 18% compounded every two months. What is the effective annual rate?

2    A sum of £60 000 is invested at a nominal rate of interest of 18% per year. Calculate the total value of the investment after one year under each of the following frequencies of compounding:

   **a** annual     **b** quarterly     **c** monthly     **d** weekly     **e** daily.

## 4.3 Net Present Value

As we saw in Sec. 4.1, the most important rearrangement of the compound interest formula is that which involves using it to express $P_0$ in terms of $P_n$, $i$ and $n$.

Starting from the formula $P_n = (1 + i)^n P_0$ the rearrangement simply involves dividing both sides by $(1 + i)^n$ to give:

$$P_0 = \frac{P_n}{(1 + i)^n}$$

or, as it is more usually written:

$$P_0 = (1 + i)^{-n} P_n$$

Because $(1 + i)^{-n}$ is an alternative way of writing $1/(1 + i)^n$

What this formula is telling us is the amount of money which, if available now (i.e. at the present time), would grow to become $P_n$ by the end of $n$ periods.

Hence, $P_0$ is called the **present value** of the amount $P_n$ which is going to be received at the end of $n$ periods. The process of reducing a future sum of money to its present value is called **discounting**, and in this context the interest rate $r$ is usually referred to as the **discount rate**. This concept of discounting is, as we shall see, of very great importance, and tables of *present value factors* $(1 + i)^{-n}$ for a selection of values of $r$ and $n$ are widely published. Appendix 3 contains such a table.

The values in this table are, of course, just the reciprocals of the compound interest factors $(1 + i)^n$.

## Example 4.3.1

What is the present value of £33 000 due to be paid in 6 years time if the discount rate over these years is taken as 5% compounded annually?

### Solution to Example 4.3.1

Present value $= (1 + 0.05)^{-6} \times £33\,000 = 0.7462 \times £33\,000 = £24\,625$
This could be found on a calculator using

$$[1]\,[+]\,[0.05]\,[=]\,[x^y]\,[6]\,[+/-]\,[=]\,[\times]\,[33\,000]\,[=]$$

Note also that the factor could have been looked up in the table of present value factors in row 6 and column 5%.

The importance of present values arises from their usefulness in evaluating investment projects. Typically, such projects involve some 'up front' investment which will be followed later by some inflows of money as the project delivers them. Because these money flows are occurring at different times, we cannot just add and subtract them as they stand. Money relating to earlier times is more valuable because it can be invested. A way in which we can make all the money flows comparable is to discount them all to present values. This takes account of their respective investment potentials.

When all the cash flows for the project—the (positive) inflows and the (negative) outflows—are reduced to present values and added together the result is called the **net present value** of the project, often abbreviated to NPV.

If this is a positive number it means that the sum of the inflows, in present value terms, is larger than the sum of the outflows, in present value terms, and the project is worth undertaking. If it is a negative number it means that the sum of the inflows, in present value terms, is smaller than the sum of the outflows, in present value terms, and the project is not worth undertaking. Furthermore, if two or more projects are to be compared, the one with the larger positive net present value would be the more suitable one to pursue.

This method (as we are using it here) assumes

1    that we can predict what all the money flows are going to be
2    that we can predict what the interest rate will be
3    that the interest rate will remain constant over the lifetime of the project.

You may think we are making a lot of assumptions here. However, the first two are unavoidable and people who have to make such decisions are to some extent being judged on, and paid for, their skill in making the necessary predictions. The third assumption can be relaxed by using more sophisticated variations on the approach allowing different (but known or predicted) rates at different times. However, we certainly won't burden you with such details in this book.

## Example 4.3.2

A company has to make a decision about which, if either, of two possible plants it should invest in. One works faster and is expected to produce higher returns in the early years of use. However, the other is expected to last longer and produce income further into the future. Each plant would require an immediate investment of £500 000 and the respective anticipated incomes (in thousands of pounds) are as follows:

| End of year | Plant 1 | Plant 2 |
|---|---|---|
| 1 | 200 | 180 |
| 2 | 180 | 130 |
| 3 | 150 | 120 |
| 4 | 100 | 80 |
| 5 | 70 | 60 |
| 6 | | 55 |
| 7 | | 50 |
| 8 | | 45 |

**a**  Calculate the Net Present Value for each of the two possible investments on the assumption of a discount rate of 8% per year.

**b**  Say whether both, one or neither of the possible investments is financially viable on the basis of your answer found in **a**.

**c**  Say which of the two possible investment projects is to be preferred on the basis of your answer found in **a**.

## Solution to Example 4.3.2

**a**  The calculations required for finding net present values are best set out in the form of a table of the kind shown below. In this table the expression 'end of year 0' is used as a way of referring to the start of year 1.

| End of year | Cash flows for plant 1 in £000s | Cash flows for plant 2 in £000s | Present value factor for 8% | Discounted cash flow for plant 1 | Discounted cash flow for plant 2 |
|---|---|---|---|---|---|
| 0 | (500) | (500) | 1.0000 | (500) | (500) |
| 1 | 200 | 180 | 0.9259 | 185.18 | 166.66 |
| 2 | 180 | 130 | 0.8573 | 154.31 | 111.45 |
| 3 | 150 | 120 | 0.7938 | 119.07 | 95.26 |
| 4 | 100 | 80 | 0.7350 | 73.50 | 58.80 |
| 5 | 70 | 60 | 0.6806 | 47.64 | 40.84 |
| 6 | | 55 | 0.6302 | | 34.66 |
| 7 | | 50 | 0.5835 | | 29.18 |
| 8 | | 45 | 0.5403 | | 24.31 |
| | | | | 79.70 | 61.16 |

b   Both projects are financially viable as they have positive net present values, indicating that the sum of the present values of the inflows exceeds that of the outflows.

c   Plant 1 is to be preferred as the net present value for this plant has a larger positive value than that for plant 2.

**Exercises 4.3**

1   What is the present value of £36 000 due to be paid in 5 years time if the discount rate over these years is taken as 7% compounded annually?

2   A company faces a choice between two investment projects A and B. Project A requires an initial investment of £50 000 and is expected to produce income of the following amounts at the times shown:

| End of year | Income in £000s |
|---|---|
| 1 | 10 |
| 2 | 11 |
| 3 | 12 |
| 4 | 13 |
| 5 | 14 |
| 6 | 14 |
| 7 | 14 |
| 8 | 14 |
| 9 | 14 |
| 10 | 14 |

Project B requires an immediate investment of £40 000 and is expected to produce income of the following amounts at the times shown:

| End of year | Income in £000s |
|---|---|
| 1 | 20 |
| 2 | 20 |
| 3 | 10 |
| 4 | 10 |

**a**  Calculate the net present value for each of the two possible investments on the assumption of a discount rate of 20% per year.

**b**  Say whether both, one or neither of the possible investments is financially viable on the basis of your answer found in **a**.

**c**  Say which of the two possible investment projects is to be preferred on the basis of your answer found in **a**.

## 4.4 Internal Rate of Return

Another method of appraising investment projects, which is very closely related to the Net Present Value method, is the Internal Rate of Return method. This method always requires the assumption of a constant discount rate throughout the lifetime of the project, but to use the method we do not need to know what the value of the discount rate will be. In the same way as the net present value method, it requires a prediction of all the money flows associated with the project. Internal rate of return is often abbreviated to IRR.

The basic calculations involved in the internal rate of return method are present value calculations, but the objective is to find the discount rate which would cause the net present value of the project to be zero. It is the discount rate which achieves zero net present value that is referred to as the **internal rate of return** of the project. The higher this value turns out to be the more desirable the project is because it means that the future inflows have got to be discounted by a larger amount to make them equal to the earlier outflows. It is possible not only to compare internal rates of return from different projects with each other but also to compare such rates with returns available from other completely different investment opportunities, since the IRR is the effective rate of interest received on the money invested in the project.

The usual method for finding an internal rate of return, called the 'method of interpolation', is to begin with an initial guess at what the rate is going to be and calculate the project's net present value for that rate. (This initial guess can be obtained by finding the total profit in simple money terms over the whole life of the project, expressing this as a percentage of the investment required and then dividing by the number of years the project runs. Because of the simple way the flows have been used, this tends to be an underestimate, and it is usually multiplied by a correction factor of 1.5 and then rounded to the nearest whole number.) If the result for the initial guess is a positive net present value, you try a larger discount rate with a view to obtaining a negative value. If the result for the initial guess is a negative net present value, then you try a smaller discount rate with a view to obtaining a positive value.

Having obtained a positive and a negative value, the internal rate of return which gives value zero can be found by interpolating between them. The interpolation can be done graphically or by means of an equivalent calculation, as illustrated by the following example.

## Example 4.4.1

A project requires an immediate investment of £500 000 and is expected to produce income (in thousands of pounds) at future times as shown below:

| End of year | Plant 2 |
|---|---|
| 1 | 180 |
| 2 | 130 |
| 3 | 120 |
| 4 | 80 |
| 5 | 60 |
| 6 | 55 |
| 7 | 50 |
| 8 | 45 |

**a**  Find the Internal Rate of Return for this investment project.
**b**  If you had a choice between this project, another having an internal rate of return of 10% and putting the money in a savings account offering a guaranteed interest rate of 7.5% per year, which investment would you most prefer and why?

## Solution to Example 4.4.1

**a**  Sum of the inflows is $180 + 130 + 120 + 80 + 60 + 55 + 50 + 45 = 720$.
The investment required is 500 so the profit is $720 - 500 = 220$.
Hence the overall percentage profit is $(220/500) \times 100 = 44\%$.
This is over 8 years so the annual percentage is $44/8 = 5.5\%$.
Multiplying this by 1.5 gives an initial guess of $1.5 \times 5.5 = 8.25\%$
which we shall round to 8%.

Carrying out the net present value calculation with 8% discount rate
we obtain the following:

| End of year | Cash flows for project in £000s | Present value factor for 8% | Discounted cash flow for project |
|---|---|---|---|
| 0 | (500) | 1.0000 | (500) |
| 1 | 180 | 0.9259 | 166.66 |
| 2 | 130 | 0.8573 | 111.45 |
| 3 | 120 | 0.7938 | 95.26 |
| 4 | 80 | 0.7350 | 58.80 |
| 5 | 60 | 0.6806 | 40.84 |
| 6 | 55 | 0.6302 | 34.66 |
| 7 | 50 | 0.5835 | 29.18 |
| 8 | 45 | 0.5403 | 24.31 |
| | | | 61.16 |

Because the net present value is positive, 8% is too small to be the internal rate of return and we need to try something larger. Suppose we try 15%. This would give us the following:

| End of year | Cash flows for project in £000s | Present value factor for 15% | Discounted cash flow for project |
|---|---|---|---|
| 0 | (500) | 1.0000 | (500) |
| 1 | 180 | 0.8696 | 156.53 |
| 2 | 130 | 0.7561 | 98.29 |
| 3 | 120 | 0.6575 | 78.90 |
| 4 | 80 | 0.5718 | 45.74 |
| 5 | 60 | 0.4972 | 29.83 |
| 6 | 55 | 0.4323 | 23.78 |
| 7 | 50 | 0.3759 | 18.80 |
| 8 | 45 | 0.3269 | 14.71 |
| | | | (33.42) |

We can now carry out a graphical interpolation by drawing a graph showing discount rate on the horizontal axis and net present value on the vertical axis, plotting the two points found above, joining them by a straight line and reading off the discount rate at the point where this line crosses the horizontal axis. This graph is shown in Fig. 4.1.

From the graph the internal rate of return can be estimated as 12.5%. This interpolation could also be done by means of an equivalent calculation as shown below. This calculation is based on taking the rate which gives the positive NPV and adding to it a proportion of the difference between this rate and the one which gives the negative value. The pro-

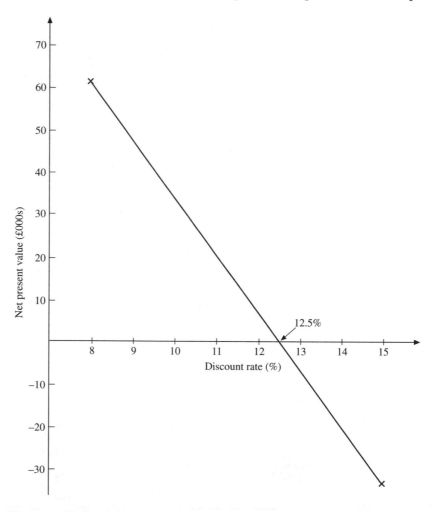

**Figure 4.1** Finding an internal rate of return by the interpolation method

portion used is the ratio of the positive NPV to the sum of the positive NPV and the absolute value of the negative NPV.

Here

$$8\% + \frac{61.16 \times (15\% - 8\%)}{61.16 + 33.42} = 8\% + 0.6436 \times 7\% = 8\% + 4.5\% = 12.5\%$$

A spreadsheet offers a good way of finding an internal rate of return. You start by putting a guess at the value of $i$ for the internal rate of return into a cell. Then enter formulae for $(1 + i)^{-n}$ in terms of that cell address for the discount factors for different years, alongside a column containing the money flow figures.

Next multiply these two columns together to give the present values of the individual flows, and the sum of this column of flows is the net present value for the project. The figure in the initial cell can then be easily varied until it makes the figure in the net present value cell become zero, so giving the internal rate of return.

Figure 4.2 shows an EXCEL spreadsheet corresponding to the solution to this example, and its construction is then explained.

In the spreadsheet in Fig. 4.2 an initial value of 0.15 was entered into cell B3, the figures 0 to 8 were entered into cells A8 to A16 for the year numbers and the cash flows were entered into cells C8 to C16. The first present value factor was then calculated in cell E8 using the formula $=(1 + \$B\$3)^\wedge(-A8)$ to give the value 1.0000 as $1 + i$ is being raised to the power zero. This formula was then copied down to cells E9 through to E16, giving the values shown.

| | A | B | C | D | E | F | G | H |
|---|---|---|---|---|---|---|---|---|
| 1 | AN EXCEL SPREADSHEET FOR CALCULATING AN INTERNAL RATE OF RETURN | | | | | | | |
| 2 | | | | | | | | |
| 3 | i = | 0.12254 | | | | | | |
| 4 | | | | | | | | |
| 5 | END OF | | CASH | | PRESENT | | DISCOUNTED | |
| 6 | YEAR | | FLOW | | VALUE | | CASH FLOW | |
| 7 | | | £ 000s | | FACTOR | | £ 000s | |
| 8 | 0 | | −500 | | 1.0000 | | −500.00 | |
| 9 | 1 | | 180 | | 0.8908 | | 160.35 | |
| 10 | 2 | | 130 | | 0.7936 | | 103.17 | |
| 11 | 3 | | 120 | | 0.7070 | | 84.84 | |
| 12 | 4 | | 80 | | 0.6298 | | 50.38 | |
| 13 | 5 | | 60 | | 0.5610 | | 33.66 | |
| 14 | 6 | | 55 | | 0.4998 | | 27.49 | |
| 15 | 7 | | 50 | | 0.4452 | | 22.26 | |
| 16 | 8 | | 45 | | 0.3966 | | 17.85 | |
| 17 | | | | | | | | |
| 18 | | | | | | | 0.00 | |

**Figure 4.2** An EXCEL spreadsheet for calculating an internal rate of return

The figure in cell G8 was then calculated using the formula =C8*E8 to give the value −500.00 and this formula was then copied down to cells G9 through to G16, giving the values shown.

Then the formula @sum(G8:G16) was used to obtain the net present value figure in cell G18.

With the value 0.15 in cell B3 the figure in G18 was −33.42 as seen in the manual solution above, showing 0.15 to be too large.

Entering 0.08 into cell B3 changed the G18 figure immediately to 61.16, also as seen in the manual solution, showing 0.08 to be too small.

Next 0.125 (the manual solution) was tried in B3 and this led to a value of −3.17 which showed this to actually be too large to be the true value for the Internal Rate of Return. Slightly smaller values were tried, with immediate feedback on each occasion, until 0.12254 was found to give a net present value equal to zero. Thus the internal rate of return was found very accurately by this method as 12.254%

**b** This project is certainly to be preferred to one offering an internal rate of return of 10% because the higher value indicates money inflows which need more discounting to bring them down to equivalence with the investment outflow.

The savings account option has the merit of offering a fixed rate of return while there are uncertainties associated with the project. However, 7.5% is so much less than 12.254% that one would expect the project to be preferred.

**Exercises 4.4**

1 A project requires an initial investment of £60 000 and is expected to yield inflows of £30 000, £30 000 and £10 000 at the ends of years 1, 2 and 3 respectively. Find the internal rate of return for this project:
   **a** by the interpolation method
   **b** by using an EXCEL spreadsheet.

## 4.5 Loan Repayments

Most people at some stage in life need to borrow money. A student loan, a mortgage to buy a house and a loan to buy a car are examples we are all familiar with. The money has to be repaid with interest through a specified number of regular equal payments.

How are the repayment amounts worked out? The method for doing this will be explained by means of an example.

## Example 4.5.1

You borrow £9000 which has to be repaid by 10 equal annual payments beginning at the end of year 1. Find the size of each repayment if the interest rate is 8% per year.

## Solution to Exercise 4.5.1

This is a particular sort of net present value problem in which there is an initial cash inflow of £8000 to be followed by 10 equal outflows of unknown size such that, with a 9% interest rate, the net present value will come to zero. If the required repayment is denoted by $x$, it would be possible to set out the calculations in the form of a table as seen in Sec. 4.4.

| End of year | Cash flows in £s | Present value factor for 8% | Present value of cash flow |
|---|---|---|---|
| 0 | 9000 | 1.0000 | 9000 |
| 1 | (x) | 0.9259 | (0.9259x) |
| 2 | (x) | 0.8573 | (0.8573x) |
| 3 | (x) | 0.7938 | (0.7938x) |
| 4 | (x) | 0.7350 | (0.7350x) |
| 5 | (x) | 0.6806 | (0.6806x) |
| 6 | (x) | 0.6302 | (0.6302x) |
| 7 | (x) | 0.5835 | (0.5835x) |
| 8 | (x) | 0.5403 | (0.5403x) |
| 9 | (x) | 0.5002 | (0.5002x) |
| 10 | (x) | 0.4632 | (0.4632x) |
| | | | 0 |

All the $x$ values and multiples of them appear in parentheses because they are outflows.

We see from this table that in order for the net present value to be zero, the sum of the outflows in the final column has to be equal to the inflow of £9000. Thus we have

$$(0.9259 + 0.8573 + 0.7938 + 0.7350 + 0.6806 + 0.6302 \\ + 0.5835 + 0.5403 + 0.5002 + 0.4632)\, x = 9000$$

Hence $x = £9000 \times \dfrac{1}{6.71} = £9000 \times 0.1490 = £1341$

So you could find the answer by a three-step process:

1   Add up the present value factors for the years when payments are to be made.
2   Find the reciprocal of this sum (i.e. 'one over' it).
3   Multiply the amount borrowed by the answer to step 2.

This is such an important application of the present value idea that tables are published which give the reciprocal of the sum of present value factors up to a specified number of years. These multipliers are called **capital recovery factors** and you will find a table of them in Appendix 3. Note that the figure in the 8% column and the 10 years row is 0.1490.

(Tables giving the direct sums of present value factors also exist, and these are called **annuity factors**. Appendix 3 also contains a table of these factors, and you will note that the value in the 10 years row and the 8% column is 6.7101, corresponding to the value of 6.71 seen above to within a rounding difference in the fourth decimal place.)

## Example 4.5.2

A loan of £15 000 is to be repaid by annual instalments over a period of 15 years with the annual rate of interest being 10%. Find the size of each instalment.

## Solution to Example 4.5.2

Looking in the 10% column and the 15 years row of the capital recovery factors table, we find the value 0.1315 so the required repayment size is £15 000 × 0.1315 = £1972.50.

(The above is all that is needed to answer this question, but you might like to confirm that if you add up the first 15 figures in the 10% column of the ordinary present value factors table in Appendix 3, the sum is 7.6060. Then 1/7.6060 = 0.1315.)

In addition to finding the size of each repayment needed to repay a loan over a specified time, it is sometimes necessary to calculate the amount which is still outstanding after some of the equal repayments have been made.

## Example 4.5.3

£9000 is borrowed and is to be repaid by 10 equal annual payments beginning at the end of year 1. The size of each of the payments if the interest rate is 8% per year was found in the answer to Example 4.5.1 to be £1341.

Find the amount that is still outstanding immediately after making

**a**   the first payment
**b**   the second payment
**c**   the third payment.

## Solution to Example 4.5.3

**a**   The interest due at the end of year 1 is £9000 × 0.08 = £720. So the first £1341 payment is actually to be set against a total debt of £9000 + £720 = £9720.

   Hence amount still owed at end of year 1 is £9720 − £1341 = £8379

**b**   So interest due at the end of year 2 is £8379 × 0.08 = £670 and the second £1341 payment is to be set against a total debt of £8379 + £670 = £9049.

   Hence amount still owed at end of year 2 is £9049 − £1341 = £7708

**c**   So interest due at the end of year 3 is £7708 × 0.08 = £617 and the third £1341 payment is to be set against a total debt of £7708 + £617 = £8325

   Hence amount still owed at end of year 3 is £8325 − £1341 = £6984

## Example 4.5.4

A loan of £15 000 is to be repaid by annual instalments over a period of 15 years with the annual rate of interest being 10%. It was found in the answer to Example 4.5.2 that the size of each repayment needed is £1972.50. Find the amount that is still outstanding immediately after making

**a**   the first instalment
**b**   the second instalment
**c**   the third instalment.

## Solution to Example 4.5.4

**a**   The interest due at the end of year 1 is £15 000 × 0.10 = £1500. So the first £1972.50 payment is actually to be set against a total debt of

   £15 000 + £1500 = £16 500

Hence amount owed at end of year 1 is £16 500 − £1972.50 = £14 527.50.

**b**   So interest due at end of year 2 is £14 527.50 × 0.10 = £1452.75 and the second £1972.50 payment is to be set against a total debt of £14 527.50 + £1452.75 = £15 980.25.

So amount owed at end of year 2 is £15 980.25 − £1972.50 = £14 007.75.

**c**   So interest due at end of year 3 is £14 007.75 × 0.10 = £1400.78 and the third £1972.50 payment is to be set against a total debt of £14 007.75 + £1400.78 = £15 408.5.

So amount owed at end of year 3 is £15 408.53 − £1972.50 = £13 436.03.

**Exercises 4.5**

1.   A debt of £80 000 is to be repaid over a period of 25 years by annual instalments. If the interest rate is 11% per year, find the size of each instalment.

2    A loan of £50 000 is to be repaid by annual instalments over a period of 15 years with the annual rate of interest being 10%.

   **a**   Show that the size of each instalment needed to achieve this repayment is £6574.

   **b**   Find the amount that is still outstanding immediately after making
   • the first instalment
   • the second instalment
   • the third instalment.

---

## Further Exercises

1    What total amount of simple interest would be earned on a sum of £20 000 invested for 5 years at an annual interest rate of 6.6%?

2    If interest at a rate of 6.6% per year is compounded annually, what is the value after 5 years of an investment initially worth £20 000?

3    If a sum of money is invested at compound interest at a nominal rate of 7.5% per year, which of the following compounding frequencies would lead to the largest total value for the investment at the end of a year?

   A. Annual compounding      B. Six-monthly compounding
   C. Quarterly compounding   D. Monthly compounding

4   An asset initially valued at £100 000 is depreciated annually by the reducing balance method using a depreciation rate of 15% per year. Which of the following represents the value (to the nearest pound) of the asset at the end of 5 years?

   A. £75 000     B. £49 718     C. £44 371     D. £25 000

5   An investment grows from an initial value of £25 000 to a value after 8 years of £50 000. If interest is at a constant rate over the 8 years and is compounded annually, which of the following is closest to the value of the interest rate?

   A. 8%          B. 9%          C. 10%          D. 11%

6   The initial valuation of an asset is £80 000. If depreciation by the reducing balance method is at a rate of 10% per year, how many years will it take for the valuation to fall to £20 000?

   A. 11 years    B. 12 years    C. 13 years     D. 14 years

7   A man staying in England for three months and needing to travel fairly extensively has to make a decision on how best to obtain use of a motor car. The best hire arrangements he can discover are as follows:

   a   A hire charge of £225 per month payable at the end of each month plus a charge of 5p per mile travelled, payable at the end of the hire period.

   b   A hire charge of £150 per month payable at the end of each month plus a charge of 10p per mile travelled, payable at the end of the hire period.

   His ability to purchase a car is limited by the outlay he is able to make. He considers the best opportunity available to him in this direction is to buy a car for £1500 which he thinks he will be able to sell at the end of the three months for £700. In addition, he expects the car to cost him £260 in maintenance charges, which he thinks he can put off paying until the end of the three months.

   Find the best course of action for the man to take if he expects to cover 8000 miles. In deciding this matter the timings of the payments and of the revenue from resale should be taken into account on the basis of an interest rate of 1% per month.

8   In order to obtain equipment of a particular kind, a manufacturer needs to make an immediate investment of £9000. His accountant recommends that the equipment should not be installed unless it yields an internal rate of return of 12%. The manufacturer expects the new equipment to produce revenue of £600 in the first year of operation, £800 in the second year and £2000 per year thereafter. The expected life of the equipment is 10 years and it has a scrap value of £500.

   a   Find the internal rate of return
   b   Say whether the equipment meets the accountant's criterion.

9   A company has a choice of two projects in which to invest. Each of these projects requires an immediate investment of £100 000 and the anticipated cash flows from the projects are as follows:

| End of year | Inflow from project 1 (£) | Inflow from project 2 (£) |
|---|---|---|
| 1 | 35 000 | 16 000 |
| 2 | 30 000 | 21 000 |
| 3 | 25 000 | 26 000 |
| 4 | 20 000 | 31 000 |
| 5 | 15 000 | 36 000 |

   a   Find the internal rate of return for project 1.
   b   Find the internal rate of return for project 2.
   c   Say which project is preferable, and how you would compare the better one with other possible ways of investing the £100 000.

10  A loan of £20 000 is to be repaid by annual instalments over a period of 5 years with the annual rate of interest being 12%.

   a   Find the size of each instalment needed to achieve this repayment.
   b   Find the amount that is still outstanding immediately after making
      • the first instalment
      • the second instalment
      • the third instalment.

## Chapter Five

# Data Collection

## 5.1 Statistical Sources

Today's companies have a thirst for information, especially numerical information. Such information is essential when making company decisions and in enhancing the competitive edge of a business, whether it is a multinational company or a one-person operation. You need to be aware of the different ways such numerical information can be collected in a clear, sensible and unbiased way.

First, an important distinction for you to understand is that between **primary** and **secondary data**. Primary data is the name given to data used for the specific purpose for which it was collected. An example would be market research that a company has commissioned. Secondary data, by contrast, is the name given to data used for purposes other than those for which it was collected. For example, the Department for Education and Employment collects data on the number of people claiming unemployment benefit, but economists might use this data as an overall indicator of the state of the economy—for them, it is secondary data. One of the advantages of primary data is that it is tailored exactly for its purpose. However, secondary data is generally much cheaper to access. For example secondary data compiled by the UK government is free to the user but gathering your own data can be very costly and time-consuming.

Today, data is collected on a massive scale, not only by the government, but also by market research firms and national organizations such as the European Union and the United Nations. By far the most important source of such statistical information in the United Kingdom is the **Office for National Statistics**, which is responsible for the publication of data that has been collected by a number of government departments. The main publications of the Office for National Statistics are:

**a**  ***Annual Abstract of Statistics***

This publication is the main source of official data and contains a large amount of useful and interesting information concerning the United Kingdom. It covers such diverse topics as population, education, weather, transport and communications, and finance.

**b**  ***Monthly Digest of Statistics***

This is a monthly version of the *Annual Abstract* and provides up-to-date information on such topics as prices, wages, population and employment.

**c**  ***Financial Statistics***

This is a monthly publication that brings together the important monetary statistics of the United Kingdom. It tabulates a wide range of financial information relating to central government, local authorities, public corporations, banks, building societies and insurance companies. In addition, there is information concerning mortgage rates, interest rates and foreign exchange rates. There is also a section dealing with overseas finance.

**d**  ***Economic Trends***

This is another monthly publication that includes graphs and numerical statistics on the main economic indicators such as prices, wages and earnings, interest rates, national income, GDP and consumers' expenditure, as well as changes in the money supply.

**e**  ***Labour Market Trends***

This is a monthly publication from the Department for Education and Employment including articles, tables and charts on manpower, employment, unemployment, hours worked, wage rates and retail prices.

**f**  ***Social Trends***

This contains information on key social and demographic issues.

As well as being published in the respective government publications the above information is also available on the Office for National Statistics' website (address http://www.ons.gov.uk/). Other publications that include important business and financial information and articles include *The Economist*, the *Financial Times* and *The Banker*. The Bank of England issues a quarterly magazine that includes data on banks in the United Kingdom, the money supply and government borrowing and financial transactions.

The European Union has a statistical office that gathers statistics from each of the member countries. The United Nations also publishes some statistics on the world economy and a *Yearbook of Labour Statistics* is published by the International Labour Organization.

The *Business Monitor* series and *Business Bulletins* contain detailed statistics on all areas of business activity including credit business, purchases by manufacturing industry, manufacturers' sales, imports and exports analysed in terms of industries. They are generally produced monthly or quarterly.

Furthermore, private companies would generally collect information for their own decision-making processes. Such data might consist of details concerning payrolls, sales records and labour turnover, and is primarily of interest to the company concerned and possibly its competitors. A summary of this information would be available from the company's annual report and accounts.

## 5.2 Sample Surveys

A great deal of statistical work is based on using a **sample** to find out something about the whole **population** from which it is drawn. For example, political pollsters typically interview a relatively small number of people about their voting intentions at a general election before concluding how the electorate at large is likely to vote. When information gathered from every member of such a population is examined we are conducting what is called a **census**.

A **census** is a survey that examines every member of the population. A **sample** is a relatively small subset of a population.

The advantage of a census is that it gives you a completely accurate view of the population. In the United Kingdom you may be aware that a census of the complete UK population takes place every 10 years (1981, 1991, 2001) and collects social and demographic information about everybody within the United Kingdom. The UK government can then use the information for its own planning and decision-making purposes, for example, the building of schools and hospitals.

There are several reasons for carrying out a sample survey rather than a census. These are listed below:

**a**    A census is time-consuming. This is important if the information is required quickly so that a conclusion can be drawn at an appropriate time. With a census the population data may be out of date before it is analysed and the results are published.

**b**    It is clearly cheaper to sample a small portion of the population than it is to view the whole population. This economy may arise out of reduced postage costs or reduced transport costs, depending on how the survey is conducted.

**c**    In a census, information is required from every member of the population. However, the entire population may not be available, possibly because not every member of the population can be contacted due to holidays, working overseas, etc., but more likely because some members would refuse to disclose the required information. This not only rules out the possibility of a census, but could also result in possible bias because the individuals who are not included may have views that are out of line with the rest of the population.

**d**    Interviewing an entire population might result in semi-skilled interviewers being used, who may not record the information correctly. A sample survey would require fewer interviewers who could be fully trained to produce more accurate information and could even be used to cover more questions.

**e**    The population might consist of a batch of electrical components (for example, a batch of light bulbs) that require testing to destruction so that the manufacturer can have clear information about the lifetime distribution. Testing the entire batch would not leave any components to sell to their customers, thus defeating the objective of the exercise. It would be better to test a sample that would give an estimate of the lifetime distribution.

**f**    Once a certain size of sample has been reached, obtaining more information does not greatly increase the accuracy of the results. A sample survey would usually yield enough information to get the required accuracy. This is true in many surveys and it is rare to carry out a survey with a size greater than 1000. Indeed in many situations it may be argued that samples yield more accurate information than a census. For example, an audit clerk who is asked to investigate a very large number of financial transactions may make mistakes due to tiredness and a lack of concentration. This may be eliminated if the clerk were to perform a more thorough investigation of a smaller sample.

You can probably see from the above why a full census happens so infrequently, and therefore for the remainder of this chapter we will concentrate on sample surveys. You also saw in Sec. 5.1 that, whenever possible, you should save yourself the trouble of gathering data by using data collected by others; that is, using secondary data. However, this may not be possible and you will then have to collect your own primary data by carrying out a sample survey.

The following situations are examples where sample surveys have been widely used.

**a**  Monitoring the quality of manufactured goods on a production line. The inspection of all products can be expensive and unnecessary so it is important to formulate a good **quality-control** scheme based on smaller samples.

**b**  Accountants need to carry out **audits** on companies that will require the inspection of accounts. If the accountant is dealing with a large company then it would be difficult to look at all the accounts.

**c**  Public **opinion polls** often provide information on political or social issues.

**d**  **Market research** is often carried out prior to the introduction of a new product.

It is quite likely that you have been a respondent in a sample survey during your life, either by filling in a questionnaire or by being stopped in the street to answer some questions. You will therefore realize that the purpose of a survey is to provide information to some organization about an issue or product. These might include:

**a**  information about your television viewing habits

**b**  your attitude to certain social issues, for example, the death penalty

**c**  your views on a newly developed product, for example, a new hair shampoo.

Before collecting data for a sample survey of this type there are certain questions that need to be considered beforehand.

First, it is important that you are clear about the **purpose of the survey**. This should clarify not only the types of questions that you should ask, but also give you an indication as to who should be questioned. For example, a holiday company may wish to gather data about the kind of people who travel on their holidays. The population of interest could be restricted to their own customers rather than the whole nation's population. We would call the travel company's own customers the **target population** in this case. The reason for gathering such information might be to find how best to market their holidays to similar potential customers. In this situation it would be sensible for the company to find out about the reading habits (newspapers and magazines) of its customers, to investigate the radio and television programmes and channels they tune into, and to evaluate any housing patterns.

Secondly, when you have clarified the purpose of the survey and hence identified the target population you need to find out if there is any list that will allow you to identify every member of the target population. The **sampling frame** is a list of the target population from which the sample is to be chosen. In the example where the holiday company has its own customers as the target population, the sampling frame would be a complete list of its customers. You could use the following sampling frames for the target populations.

| Target population | Sampling frame |
| --- | --- |
| Students at a university | University enrolment or registration list |
| UK adults | Electoral Register |
| Households in a locality | Community tax register |
| UK drivers | DVLC records |

Notice that different sampling frames will be appropriate for the collection of different information. It is also possible that no convenient sampling frame may exist for a particular population. The following are examples of this case.

**a**     The adult smokers in the UK
**b**     The customers at a supermarket

Thirdly, the next stage of a sample survey is for you to decide how the information is to be collected. If the population consists of people you need to decide whether to use **postal questionnaires**, **personal interviews** or **telephone surveys**. A comparison of these approaches is made in Sec. 5.4. If the target population consists of objects the obvious way is to inspect them. An example of this would be when a quality control inspector samples articles that are being mass-produced on a production line.

As we have already stated, when gathering primary data, either by inspection or by interviewing, it is usually impractical for you to look at the whole target population. Instead we take a sample, but how large should that sample be? The larger the sample size, the lower the likely error in any population characteristics that we might wish to estimate. Sampling is therefore a compromise between the accuracy of your findings and the amount of time or money you invest in collecting the data. The choice of sample size may be determined by:

**a**   the margin of error that you can tolerate, or the accuracy you require
**b**   the time and money you have available for data collection
**c**   the number of subpopulations into which you may wish to subdivide your data.

Given these competing influences, the final **sample size** tends to be a matter of judgement rather than a matter of calculation. As a general rule of thumb it is not advisable to have fewer than 50 respondents in any subpopulation of interest, and there would be little gain in accuracy with a total sample size above 2000. Unfortunately, for many sample surveys a 100% response rate is unlikely and so the sample size will need to be larger to ensure sufficient responses for the accuracy required.

**Exercises 5.2**

1   A large industrial company wishes to construct a 'profile' of its hourly paid workforce, with particular reference to items of information such as family structure, housing conditions and financial commitments. Assuming that all the activities of the company are concentrated in a single geographical area

   **a**   What would be the advantages and disadvantages of a sample survey of this kind as opposed to a complete census?
   **b**   How would you determine the appropriate sample size for a sample survey?

2   Write brief notes on

   **a**   Sample data and population data
   **b**   Primary data and secondary data
   **c**   Sample size and margin of error
   **d**   Sampling frame and target population

## 5.3 Sample Selection

Once you have chosen a suitable sampling frame and established the required actual sample size, you need to select an appropriate sampling technique to obtain a representative sample. There are many sampling techniques that find widespread application across a broad spectrum of subject areas. In any given situation you must select the most appropriate method for collecting the information which the survey is aiming to produce. Sampling techniques can be broadly classified into the categories of **probability sampling** and **judgement sampling**.

**Probability sampling**: every member of the population has a known chance of inclusion in the sample.

**Judgement sampling**: the sampler decides in advance on the factors that will determine whether or not a member of the population will be included in the sample.

The main methods of probability sampling are now described.

## (a) Simple Random Sampling

The simplest of all possible probability sampling techniques is **simple random sampling**. In simple random sampling every member of the population has an **equal chance** of being selected in the sample. One way in which a simple random sample can be chosen is by using **random numbers**. Each member of the population is assigned a number and a sample is selected in some predetermined fashion according to the values in a random number table or from a random number generator.

It is important to note that randomness in this context does not mean haphazardly. It is not enough for the investigator to choose members *at random* because inevitably this will incorporate an unconscious **bias**. The choice of individual observations in the sample is best achieved by the use of random number tables.

## Example 5.3.1

Each employee working in a company has been assigned an employee reference number. The codes for 60 employees working in the accounts department are shown in Table 5.1. Using the extract from a set of random number tables select a sample of size 10 from the employees in the accounts department.

| Table 5.1 Reference numbers for 60 employees | | | | | | | | | |
|------|------|------|------|------|------|------|------|------|------|
| EA01 | EA02 | EA03 | EA04 | EA05 | EA06 | EA07 | EA08 | EA09 | EA10 |
| EA11 | EA12 | EA13 | EA14 | EA15 | EA16 | EA17 | EA18 | EA19 | EA20 |
| EA21 | EA22 | EA23 | EA24 | EA25 | EA26 | EA27 | EA28 | EA29 | EA30 |
| EA31 | EA32 | EA33 | EA34 | EA35 | EA36 | EA37 | EA38 | EA39 | EA40 |
| EA41 | EA42 | EA43 | EA44 | EA45 | EA46 | EA47 | EA48 | EA49 | EA50 |
| EA51 | EA52 | EA53 | EA54 | EA55 | EA56 | EA57 | EA58 | EA59 | EA60 |

*Random numbers*

| | | | | | | | | | |
|---|---|---|---|---|---|---|---|---|---|
| 27855 | 02606 | 43347 | 65350 | 59506 | 75440 | 90827 | 03652 | 15770 | 03281 |
| 58124 | 09533 | 20322 | 82000 | 52780 | 93520 | 68773 | 67687 | 45541 | 54976 |
| 30545 | 74383 | 22814 | 36752 | 00708 | 21816 | 39615 | 03102 | 33104 | 81206 |
| 00112 | 53445 | 72459 | 66136 | 97266 | 26490 | 82429 | 90288 | 61064 | 26489 |

## Solution to Example 5.3.1

You select the first number at random (closing your eyes and pointing with a pencil usually works) as this makes sure that different random numbers are used for different sampling exercises. Starting with this number you need to select the subjects systematically until the sample size is reached. If you read off the same number a second time you should ignore it as different subjects are needed.

In this example let us assume you start at the 11th digit on the second row of the table given (starting 20322 82000 ...). As the population consists of 60 subjects, a two-digit number, you divide the table up so that the digits appear in twos; for example, 20, 32, 28, 20, 00. Mark off 10 such random numbers and select those members of the population bearing these numbers. Note that if the same number appears more than once, treat it as blank. Similarly any number greater than 60 is also ignored (for our purposes the pair 00 really represents the number 100 and is ignored as it is above 60).

Using the given random digits you should proceed in the following way.

| | |
|---|---|
| 20 | ✓ |
| 32 | ✓ |
| 28 | ✓ |
| 20 | (previously chosen) |
| 00 | (regarded as 100 and too high) |
| 52 | ✓ |
| 78 | (too high) |
| 09 | ✓ |
| 35 | ✓ |
| 20 | (previously chosen) |
| 68 | (too high) |
| 77 | (too high) |
| 36 | ✓ |
| 76 | (too high) |
| 87 | (too high) |
| 45 | ✓ |
| 54 | ✓ |
| 15 | ✓ |

Your chosen employees would therefore be, in order, EA09, EA15, EA20, EA28, EA32, EA35, EA36, EA45, EA52 and EA54.

Simple random sampling is best when you have an accurate and easily accessible sampling frame that lists the entire population, preferably stored on a computer. This is usually the case if you are dealing with employees at a company. If the population covers a large geographical region, random selection tends to result in selected subjects being widely spread. Consequently, this form of sampling is not suitable when undertaking a survey that covers a large geographical area.

## (b) Systematic Random Sampling

The practicality of the simple random sampling procedure depends on the existence of a sampling frame and also on the size and location of the population. A good approximation to simple random sampling is **systematic random sampling**, which involves selecting the sample at regular intervals from the sampling frame. For example, if you wished to select a sample of size 25 from a population of size 1000 you need to calculate

$$k = \frac{\text{Population size}}{\text{Sample size}} = \frac{1000}{25} = 40$$

then select every $k$th item from the population list. If you continue using the random number tables that were introduced in Example 5.1.1 then the following pairs of random digits might be used to generate the first number.

    49   76   30   54   57   43

The pairs of digits 49 and 76 are above 40 and can be ignored, and so 30 would be your randomly chosen number between 1 and 40. Your sample would consist of those population members numbered 30, 70, 110, 150, 190, ... until you have gone through the whole sampling frame. Systematic sampling provides a simple method for sample selection and is widely used in practice. An advantage of this method of sampling is that it can be used where no sample frame exists (but the items do exist); for example, every 20th customer to enter a shop might be chosen.

With this method of sampling you must be careful to avoid repetitive patterns in the sampling frame. For example, suppose a sampling frame consists of a list of cohabiting couples on a council house list with the male cohabitant listed first

   1  Mr Smith
   2  Miss Green
   3  Mr Brown     ✓
   4  Miss White
   5  Mr Jones
   6  Miss Bailey
   7  Mr Fletcher   ✓
   8  Miss Stone
   9  Mr Wainwright
 10  Miss Turnbull
 11  Mr Bright      ✓
 12  Miss Shaw

If the required sample size is one-quarter of the population size ($k = 4$) you would need to select every fourth customer on the list. If the first person to be selected is male, then the sample is all-male. Conversely, if you start with a female customer all those in the sample will be female. As a consequence the sample will be biased.

As with simple random sampling, systematic sampling is not really suitable if subjects are geographically spread over a wide region.

## (c) Stratified Random Sampling

Although the accuracy of sample results can be improved by increasing the sample size, this can also increase costs. One way of improving accuracy without increasing the sample size is by using **stratified random sampling**. In effect, the sampling frame is divided into a number of subgroups and then you draw a random sample, simple or systematic, from each subgroup.

Dividing the population into relevant **strata** means that the sample is more likely to be **representative**, as you can ensure that each of the strata is represented proportionally within each sample. The process of splitting into strata is likely to increase both time and costs compared with simple random or systematic sampling.

## Example 5.3.2

Suppose you wish to select a sample of 400 employees from a moderately large company to determine the attitude to a new productivity scheme of payment. You decide that the two major factors that would affect the individuals' views would be their degree of skill and their gender. The company records show that the workforce has the following breakdown.

|  | Male | Female |
| --- | --- | --- |
| Skilled | 2400 | 330 |
| Semi-skilled | 1290 | 660 |
| Unskilled | 300 | 1020 |

Indicate how you would obtain a sample that is representative of the population.

## Solution to Example 5.3.2

Your sample obtained by simple random sampling (and also systematic sampling) may look unrepresentative; for example, there is a very small possibility that the sample contains few women workers even though there is a substantial number of women among the 6000 workers. All that can be said in these circumstances is that an unlikely sample has occurred. Although a random sample ensures that the method of selection is unbiased it does not necessarily ensure that the sample itself is completely representative.

One way to make sure your sample is representative is to take a sample from each stratum. If the number of units selected from each stratum is proportional to the population size of the stratum, then the procedure is called 'proportionate stratified sampling'. Otherwise it is 'disproportionate stratified sampling'. In proportionate stratification the sampling fraction is the same for each stratum; that is

$$\frac{\text{Size of sample from a stratum}}{\text{Total size of stratum}} = k, \text{ say, for each stratum}$$

In this example you have six strata. If you require a sample of 400 employees the sampling fraction is

$$\frac{\text{Sample size}}{\text{Population size}} = \frac{400}{6000} = \frac{1}{15}$$

Hence from each stratum you require a sample of size

$$\frac{1}{15} \times \text{stratum size}$$

for example, from the skilled male stratum you take a sample of size

$$\frac{1}{15} \times 2400 = 160$$

In the same way you obtain the sample sizes from each stratum.

|              | Male | Female |
| ------------ | ---- | ------ |
| Skilled      | 160  | 22     |
| Semi-skilled | 86   | 44     |
| Unskilled    | 20   | 68     |

It should be emphasized that in stratified sampling the people from each stratum are selected randomly (using either simple random or systematic sampling as discussed earlier). This distinguishes it from quota sampling, which we describe later. The procedure of stratified random sampling is frequently used in practice. It is preferable that the stratification is based on some criterion relevant to the subject under investigation. For example, if it was required to test opinions of the government by a door-to-door enquiry it would be necessary to ensure that some views were conducted in known Conservative areas and some in known Labour regions.

## (d) Cluster Sampling

**Cluster sampling** has similarities to stratified sampling as we need to divide the population into groups, or **clusters**, prior to sampling. The groups can be based on any naturally occurring grouping such as geographical location. For cluster sampling the sampling frame is the complete list of clusters rather than the individual subjects within the population. We then select a number of clusters normally using simple random sampling. Information is then collected from every subject within the selected clusters. For example, if it is necessary to obtain a sample from a large town, it would be convenient if the sample consisted of households from the same street, or in certain areas of town. Hence the population is split into, say, 1000 areas each containing 10 dwellings and a number of those areas are chosen at random.

## Example 5.3.3

You need to select a sample of firms to undertake a survey about 'Car Parking in the Workplace' within the Midlands region. As you have limited resources with which to pay for travel explain how you might carry out your survey. Describe the advantages and disadvantages of your chosen method of sampling compared with other methods.

## *Solution to Example 5.3.3*

A list of local authority areas could form the sampling frame. Each of these areas should be numbered from 1 upwards so that a small number, five or six say, of local authority districts can be selected using simple random sampling. The sample of firms chosen for your survey would then be all the firms in the selected local authority districts. For this research you might use a local listing of companies or telephone directories to provide a suitable list of all firms within each cluster.

The great advantage of this type of sampling is the saving in time and cost incurred in visiting firms within the same district as many interviews can take place within a short space of time with a minimum of travelling. However, this sampling approach normally results in a sample which represents the total population less accurately than when individual firms are chosen randomly because it tends to be less representative of the population as a whole.

Cluster sampling is used because it requires relatively little administrative effort and it is less costly than other sampling methods. Another important reason why cluster sampling is used is that there may be no alternative. A typical example is one in which we wish to select a large sample of workers in a particular industry. It is likely that we can compile a list of employers but not a list of workers. In this situation the only way we may be able to obtain a sample is to select the firms at random and ask the employers to contact their workers on our behalf.

## *(e) Multistage Sampling*

**Multistage sampling** is a development of cluster sampling and is normally used to overcome problems associated with a geographically dispersed population when face-to-face interviews are required or where it is difficult to set up a sampling frame for a large geographical area. In market research it is often necessary to draw conclusions about the whole country. To travel over the entire country is costly and time-consuming and it would certainly be more convenient if the sample could be restricted to certain smaller areas of the country.

The procedure of multistage sampling for a national survey would involve choosing a sampling frame of relevant geographical areas (counties or districts), numbering each of the areas and selecting a small sample using simple random sampling (for example, it might be that Kent, Dorset and Staffordshire are selected). Next you subdivide each of the selected counties into smaller regions from which you select further samples randomly. Again these regions may be split into smaller units (streets, say) and a further random selection made, and so on for as many stages as required. At each stage we randomly choose three or four elements, so that you are finally left with several households which are not too isolated from other households in the sample.

As multistage sampling relies on a series of sampling frames, you need to ensure that they are all appropriate and available. We only need a sampling frame that lists all the population members for those subgroups we finally select. This provides savings in time and cost.

The five methods of sampling described in this section have all involved random selection. Consequently it is possible to determine the probability that any specific subject will be included in the sample. However, for some surveys this may not be possible. Judgement sampling provides a range of alternative techniques that do not require random selection. One such technique is **quota sampling**, which resembles stratified sampling in that the population is divided into groups. A different judgement sampling method would involve putting a questionnaire in a newspaper or magazine and asking for **volunteer respondents**.

## (f) Quota Sampling

**Quota sampling** is widely used in both opinion surveys and market research. Where it differs from stratified random sampling is in the fact that the samples are not chosen randomly from the strata. Typically, strata are defined, the sample stratum size needed for proportional allocation are calculated from overall stratum sizes in the population, and then the actual choice of elements within the strata is left to the **individual interviewers**.

Quota sampling has a number of advantages over the probability sampling methods. In particular it is less costly and can be set up quickly. Furthermore, it does not require a sample frame and therefore may be the only technique that can be used if it is not available. Quota sampling has the fundamental disadvantage that we are not able to measure the degree of accuracy given by the sample estimates.

## Example 5.3.4

The following table shows the breakdown of a college population into categories of sex, age and course.

| Course | Sex | Age | |
|---|---|---|---|
| | | Under 20 | 20 and over |
| 1 | Male | 75 | 90 |
| | Female | 60 | 63 |
| 2 | Male | 124 | 32 |
| | Female | 86 | 29 |
| 3 | Male | 73 | 44 |
| | Female | 59 | 30 |
| 4 | Male | 77 | 59 |
| | Female | 90 | 59 |

a   Construct a quota sample comprising 70 students that fully reflects the distribution of these three characteristics in the population. Calculate the numbers in each category of the quota sample.

b   Suppose that it was decided that both age and sex are no longer of importance in the survey. How would your quota sample of 70 be affected?

c   What is the major criticism of a quota sample?

## Solution to Example 5.3.4

a   You reflect the population by obtaining a sample in which the number of students in the sample is proportional to the population size. Here the population size is 1050, so the sample fraction is

$$\frac{70}{1050} = \frac{1}{15}$$

Therefore you divide each number in the above table by 15 and round to the nearest whole number to obtain the following sample sizes.

| Course | Sex | Age | |
|--------|-----|-----|-----|
| | | Under 20 | 20 and over |
| 1 | Male | 5 | 6 |
| | Female | 4 | 4 |
| 2 | Male | 8 | 2 |
| | Female | 6 | 2 |
| 3 | Male | 5 | 3 |
| | Female | 4 | 2 |
| 4 | Male | 5 | 4 |
| | Female | 6 | 4 |

You can then obtain the information by instructing the interviewers to fill the quotas for the different cells. Instead of selecting the sample at random you now select those that are easiest to find until you have the number of respondents required for each category.

b   If age and sex are no longer of importance you merely combine the classes in your quota table to give

| | |
|---|---|
| Course 1 | 19 |
| Course 2 | 18 |
| Course 3 | 14 |
| Course 4 | 19 |

c   From a theoretical viewpoint the non-randomness of quota sampling is a weakness. Samples drawn in this way are open to a risk of being biased. However, we should point out that many market researchers and administrators, who actually have to conduct surveys, defend the method on the grounds of simplicity, cheapness, speed, and the fact that there is no need for a sampling frame and therefore no real problems caused by non-response.

## Example 5.3.5

An interview survey has been carried out to establish the size of households in a large geographical area.

a   Outline the key factors influencing choice of method when sampling is required.
b   Identify (and justify) two sampling methods that are most likely to have been considered in this situation.

### Solution to Example 5.3.5

a   The key factors influencing the choice of sampling method might include
  • how geographically spread out the population is—if well spread then cluster and multistage sampling would be appropriate
  • whether or not a sampling frame is available
  • size of population and sample
  • cost and availability of time
  • whether there are several well-defined groups
  • whether the population has a repetitive pattern.
b   For the given situation it is likely that multistage or cluster sampling would be most appropriate owing to
  • the large and geographically spread population
  • the likely absence of a sampling frame that covers the whole population

**Exercises 5.3**   1   a   Define the term simple random sample and state one advantage and one disadvantage of this method of sampling.
  b   A batch of quotations is numbered from 1853 to 1952 inclusive. Use the random number table below to select a simple random sample of ten quotations, giving a brief explanation of how you select the sample.

*Extract from random number table*

46243   29764   44679   00199   79482   86193   02718   91480
87177   58142   64325   81735   45692   82390   65555   95594

  c   Explain the meaning of the term 'stratified sample' and state one advantage of this type of sampling compared with simple random sampling.

2  **a**  Sampling methods are frequently used for the collection of data. Explain the terms simple random sampling, stratified sampling and sampling frame.

   **b**  Suggest a suitable sampling frame for each of the following in which statistical data will be collected:
   - an investigation into the reactions of workers in a large factory to new proposals for shift working
   - a survey of students at a college about the relevance and quality of the teaching for their professional examinations
   - an enquiry into the use of home computers by schoolchildren in a large city.

   **c**  Explain briefly, with reasons, the type of sampling method you would recommend in each of the three situations given above.

3  A large international firm of management consultants wishes to undertake market research it offers to its clients. A small working party has been set up in the head office and you have been selected to be the technical officer advising on the terms used in sampling. You are required to write short notes on the following terms used in sampling explaining the meaning of the term and how the technique is used, setting your answer in the context of this international firm.

   **a**  Simple random sample
   **b**  Systematic sample
   **c**  Sampling frame
   **d**  Random numbers
   **e**  Quota sample

## 5.4 Questionnaires

In Sec. 5.1 we defined primary data as data collected especially for the purpose of whatever survey is being conducted. Methods of collecting primary data usually include one of the following:

**a**  Personal Interviews
**b**  Postal Questionnaires
**c**  Telephone Interviews

The two principal methods of **gathering information** for surveys are postal questionnaires and interviews. Each of these has its merits and which is best to use depends on the circumstances of the survey.

The postal questionnaire is much **less costly** to operate than the personal interview. The cheapness may in some situations be a decisive argument in favour of the former, especially if resources are limited or the population is widely scattered. Alternatively we can increase the size of the sample in order to make the results more reliable. As well as being fairly cheap, questionnaires allow information to be gathered **reasonably quickly**. We can usually expect most of the replies to arrive within a fortnight of the questionnaires being sent out. They also have the additional advantage that there is no interviewer to affect the respondent's answers. The way a question is asked could **influence** the respondent's answer.

Difficulty in obtaining a reasonable **response rate** is the most serious problem with questionnaires. In fact a response rate of 20% is quite good for a postal questionnaire. The seriousness of this is not so much the lack of information but rather the possibility that the non-response may be indicative of a certain attitude. This may lead to biased results from the questionnaires that are returned.

The major advantage of the personal interview is that it is much more likely to produce a high response rate. It seems that people are much less willing to decline an interview than they are to refuse to fill in a questionnaire. Furthermore, the interviewer is in a position to help the respondent if he or she requires additional information.

The main weakness in interviewing is that it is costly, not only due to the expense of the interviewer's wages and travel allowances, but also the cost of training the individual interviewers. A further possible weakness is interviewer bias. It is essential that the interviewer asks the questions in a neutral manner and does not load them so that the respondent feels compelled to answer them in a certain way.

Although the postal questionnaire and the personal interview are the two main methods of collecting survey information, there is an increasing use of the telephone as a medium for data collection. Telephone methods are very quick and a wide geographical area can be covered fairly cheaply. Furthermore, it may be easier to ask sensitive or embarrassing questions over the impersonal medium of the telephone. An important disadvantage of using the telephone as a medium for collecting information is that a biased sample might result from the fact that a proportion of people do not have telephones and many of those who do are ex-directory. A further disadvantage is that respondents may refuse to give information to a stranger over the phone and so response rate is lower than face-to-face interviews. Telephone surveys are primarily used in connection with the selling of a product or service.

If useful information is to be collected by means of a questionnaire care must be taken at the design stage. In fact a badly designed questionnaire can lead to administrative problems and may cause incorrect deductions to be made from the statistical analysis of the results. In order to avoid this scenario time should be spent identifying clearly what the aims of the survey are. In designing the structure of the questionnaire it is also important to have a clear idea of how the information produced from the questionnaire can be analysed later.

Before considering the design of actual questionnaire forms it is worth while to look at some important peripheral issues relating to postal questionnaires. First, there should be a **covering letter** with the questionnaire describing the reasons for the survey and assuring the respondents of **anonymity**. In addition, a **stamped addressed envelope** is essential and the inclusion of some **payment** in anticipation of response. This payment need not be in the form of money, but may be a cheap item such as a pen, or entry into a competition with more worthwhile prizes. All of these points are designed to encourage as high a response rate as possible.

As far as the postal questionnaire itself is concerned, it should be laid out as **clearly** as possible with questions in a **logical order** and with capital letters and bold type in order to emphasize key words and instructions. In addition, the questions should be as **simple to answer** as possible and it should look as if great care has been taken to reduce the number of questions to a minimum.

When wording the questions you should bear in mind the following points.

1   Your language should be clear and concise and able to be understood by all respondents; for example, we should use the word 'stop' rather than 'cease' or 'tell' rather than 'inform', and you should avoid all technical terms.

2   You should avoid leading the respondent to a particular answer; for example, questions starting 'Don't you think that . . .?' should be avoided.

3   Do not rely too much on the memory of the respondent. 'How much did you spend on food last week?' should produce a reasonably accurate answer. However, 'How much did you spend in an equivalent week last year?' will undoubtedly produce a worthless answer.

4   The use of precoded questions is a great help to the respondent; for example,

How many employees are on your payroll? Tick the appropriate box.

Less than100    ☐    100-500    ☐    More than 500    ☐

Precoded questions also make the necessary analysis easier.

5   You should address the subject courteously throughout the question-naire and none of the questions should be personal or offensive.

**Exercises 5.4**

1   **a**   Postal questionnaires and interviews are two methods of collecting data. List the advantages of each method.

      **b**   One of the main defects of surveys by interview is the problem of interviewer bias. What is interviewer bias and how can the problem be minimized?

      **c**   What are the main points to be considered in the design of a postal questionnaire?

## Further Exercises

1   Which of the following are secondary data sources?

    A. The *Annual Abstract of Statistics* as published by the Office for National Statistics

    B. Data collected for an attitude survey through personal interview

    C. Historical records of sales revenues to be used to prepare current forecasts

    D. *Labour Market Trends* as published by the Department for Education and Employment

       A. Source A and B only       B. Source B and D only

       C. Source B and C only       D. Source A and D only

2   In which of the following publications would you find information about foreign exchange rates?

       A. *Business Monitor*          B. *Financial Statistics*

       C. *Annual Abstract of Statistics*    D. *Social Trends*

3   In which of the following publications would you find up-to-date information about company share prices?

       A. *Monthly Digest of Statistics*    B. *Financial Statistics*

       C. *Social Trends*             D. *Financial Times*

4   An administrator is selecting a sample of respondents for interview-ing. The subjects are numbered sequentially. The first subject is selected randomly and is subject number 7. She then selects invoices numbered 25, 43, 61, 79 and so on. This type of sample is called

       A. Stratified     B. Systematic     C. Cluster     D. Multistage

5   In a sample survey, interviewers are provided with a set of specifications of the number of people of various types that they are required to interview:

Male, aged under 30 years     20
Male, aged 30+     30
Female, aged under 30 years     25
Female, aged 30+     40

The interviewers are free to select their own respondents, as long as they interview the correct number of each type. Which sampling method is being used?

A. Multistage     B. Stratified     C. Cluster     D. Quota

6   You work in the marketing department of a small company which only sells in its local area. You have been asked to carry out a survey of its customers.

a   Explain the different methods that are available to collect primary data giving the advantages and disadvantages of each.

b   What factors would you use to decide which method would be most suitable in this example?

c   Would your answer be different if your company were selling nationally?

7   A computer company currently employs 1500 people. To assess the reaction of the workforce to a new pay proposal the company wishes to conduct a sample survey.

a   Describe how a simple random sample of 150 employees could be selected.

b   The employees of the company are classified according to their degree of skill such that the number of employees in each class is shown in the following table:

| Class | Managerial | Clerical | Technical | Manual |
|---|---|---|---|---|
| Number of employees | 20 | 80 | 680 | 720 |

• Why might it be appropriate to choose a stratified random sample for this survey?

• Describe how a stratified random sample of 150 employees could be selected from this company.

c  The company decides to conduct a postal survey of the 150 employees. What are the advantages and disadvantages of using this method of data collection compared with a personal interview?

8  Write brief notes on the relative advantages and disadvantages of two of the following sections, as methods of collecting data:

a  the postal questionnaire and interviewing
b  a census and a survey
c  simple random sampling and quota sampling.

9  Write brief notes on two of the following:

a  simple random sampling
b  questionnaire design
c  multistage sampling
d  sampling frame.

10  A firm owning a chain of 'dry-cleaning shops' wishes to undertake a customer service survey. Interviewers will be sent to a sample of 50 branches to question customers in the shops. The number of shops in each area is as follows:

| Midlands | 120 |
| South | 170 |
| North | 130 |
| Wales | 30 |
| Scotland | 50 |

Explain how the 50 dry cleaners might be chosen if the survey is to be performed using the following sampling methods.

a  Systematic sampling
b  Stratified sampling

In each case give the relative merits of the sampling method concerned.

## Chapter Six

# Statistical Diagrams

## 6.1 Frequency Tables

In the commercial world there is great emphasis on communication; for example, you may often need to present evidence to colleagues and senior managers. To help these colleagues to understand your information you may wish to present information in the form of tables, diagrams and charts. The main purpose of using a **table**, **diagram** or **chart** is to convey information simply, clearly and quickly.

Information is data that has been processed in some way so as to make it intelligible. In short, it has been organized and summarized. Before proceeding you need to distinguish between various types of data, because the choice of diagram or chart depends on the nature of the data. The first distinction is between **numeric data** and **categorical data**. In some books this distinction is sometimes described as between **quantitative** data and **qualitative** data.

As the name suggests categorical data occurs when observations are assigned to categories. For example, a person's gender is categorized as either male or female, a hospital patient may have a specified illness or not. Other examples of categorical data include car types, holiday destinations, and supermarket preferences. Numeric data, by contrast, relate to data that can easily be recorded in meaningful numerical terms. Examples include heights, weights, the number of children in a household and company turnover.

Both numeric data and categorical data can provide useful information for a company. Numeric data is frequently used to show patterns such as how incomes in a certain industry have altered over years or how the number of car accidents have changed over recent months. Categorical data is used to find special characteristics of groups. For example, it would be useful to know the gender, age group and social class of purchasers of a magazine that might be used by a company for advertising purposes.

You can also divide numeric data into continuous data and discrete data and categorical data into nominal data and ordinal data. These divisions are shown clearly in Fig. 6.1.

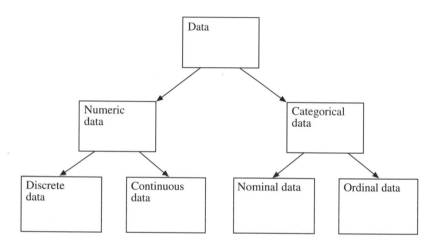

**Figure 6.1** Data divisions

You can classify numeric data as either discrete or continuous. **Discrete data** is data that can be listed without approximation. For example, the number of employees working in seven branches of a bank might be

12, 13, 14, 16, 17, 18, 15.

The data is numeric and is discrete because it can be listed exactly. In general, we call data discrete if it can be counted rather than measured. **Continuous data** is data that cannot be listed exactly. Examples of continuous data arise when measurements are involved. For example, the diameters in millimetres of ball bearings produced in a production run could be

4.11, 4.10, 4.10, 4.10, 4.15, 4.09, etc.

The accuracy of the measurement is constrained by the measuring device, and the actual diameter of the first ball bearing may be 4.1053234 millimetres. The diameters of the ball bearings are, in fact, only known to within some approximation of the true values. In general, if data can take all values in some range and it is not possible to list accurately all the possibilities which may arise, then the data is continuous.

Categorical data divides into the classes, **nominal** and **ordinal**. In the ordinal case, the categories have an ordered relationship one with another. For example, if workers are having their work judged as

> very good,   good,   fair,   poor,   or very poor

the data is ordinal. Nominal data has categories that lack any obvious order. A large company might have three retail outlets within a city: Shop A, Shop B, Shop C. When comparing these three shops in terms of their staffing or turnover there is no obvious order to them because we have assigned the categories A, B and C arbitrarily, and so the outlets would be classed as nominal data.

## Example 6.1.1

Which of the following are numeric and which are categorical? In each case divide into discrete or continuous if numeric and nominal or ordinal if categorical.

**a**   The degree of satisfaction with a management decision, recorded as 'None', 'Moderate' or 'High'.

**b**   The temperature in a factory at noon on a day in March.

**c**   The political preference of respondents to a survey, recorded as 'Conservative', 'Labour', 'Liberal Democrat' or 'Other'.

**d**   In a quality control inspection, a record of whether or not an item is satisfactory or defective.

**e**   The number of repairs in one year to a machine.

### *Solution to Example 6.1.1*

**a**   Categorical (ordinal)

**b**   Numeric (continuous)

**c**   Categorical (nominal)

**d**   Categorical (nominal)—However, it is debatable whether it should be classified as nominal or ordinal, indeed, it would clearly be ordinal if there was an intermediate category, e.g. 'capable of rework'

**e**   Numeric (discrete)

Data that has not been processed in any way is termed **raw data**. Perhaps the first thing that you should do with raw data is to make a frequency table. In general there are no problems associated with grouping ordinal and nominal data, because the data is already arranged into categories. When grouping data our main concern is with numeric data.

For discrete data a frequency table consists of a list of the possible data values and their frequencies. The frequency of a given data value is the number of times that it occurs.

## Example 6.1.2

The following values listed are the number of children in the families of 20 workers in an office.

00123  11022
41110  00001

Construct a frequency table of the data.

### Solution to Example 6.1.2

You can see clearly that eight of the workers have no children. The resulting frequency table gives us a much clearer view of the data than the original list of the 20 values.

**Table 6.1 Frequency table for the number of children in a family**

| Number of children | Number of families (frequency) |
|---|---|
| 0 | 8 |
| 1 | 7 |
| 2 | 3 |
| 3 | 1 |
| 4 | 1 |

The main aim of a frequency table is to summarize numeric data in a logical way such that an overall perspective of the data can be obtained quickly and easily. When the number of distinct data values is large, a simple frequency distribution is not appropriate because there is too much information which cannot be easily assimilated. In this situation you can use a **grouped frequency table**. A grouped frequency table organizes the data into **classes** of values and the number of items in each class, called the **class frequency**, is recorded. Note that once data has been recorded in this way information about the original individual data values is lost.

## Example 6.1.3

The following list shows the number of days in 1999 lost through illness by 60 employees in a company. Construct a grouped frequency table of the data.

| | | | |
|---|---|---|---|
| 1, 1, 3, 4, 10, | 2, 2, 5, 7, 9 | 5, 2, 1, 1, 8, | 15, 2, 4, 24, 1 |
| 11, 15, 4, 3, 1, | 1, 1, 1, 7, 8 | 1, 5, 24, 18, 1 | 12, 16, 7, 3, 5 |
| 20, 13, 16, 10, 1, | 1, 1, 2, 1, 23 | 12, 22, 4, 1, 2 | 4, 2, 3, 1, 7 |

### Solution to Example 6.1.3

You need to allocate data items to classes and so the classes have to be defined, that is, the boundaries between classes have to be determined so that you know to which class an item should be allocated.

**Table 6.2 Class boundaries for illness data**

| Number of days lost | Number of employees |
|---|---|
| 1–5 | |
| 6–10 | |
| 11–15 | |
| 16–20 | |
| 21–25 | |

Once the classes have been defined, you then need to go through the data counting the number of items that fall into each class. The usual way to do this is to have a column which you head 'tally marks'. For each item in turn in the original data you cross out and enter a mark in the tally marks column. It is a good idea to record the tally marks using a five-bar gate method so that you can add them up easily at the end.

**Table 6.3 Grouped frequency table for illness data**

| Number of days lost | Tally marks | Number of employees |
|---|---|---|
| 1–5 | ︴︴ ︴︴ ︴︴ ︴︴ ︴︴ ︴︴ ︴︴ || | 37 |
| 6–10 | ︴︴ |||| | 9 |
| 11–15 | ︴︴ | | 6 |
| 16–20 | |||| | 4 |
| 21–25 | |||| | 4 |

There is no firm rule about how many classes should be used but it is usual to have at least five and no more than 12. Less than 5 would lead to inadequate information, while more than 12 would be too many to take in easily and so would rob the frequency table of the main reason for its existence.

For any set of data the grouped frequency table is not unique. However, the following are useful guidelines for good practice when grouping data.

a   All data values should be contained in one and only one class.
b   Classes should be listed in increasing order.
c   Equal class widths should be used if possible.

The data in Tables 6.1 and 6.3 are discrete, that is, the data can only take whole numbers. With continuous data you would define the classes in a slightly different way. Suppose you have data on the annual miles travelled by a group of company sales representatives. The best approach is to define classes as '0 up to 2000 miles', '2000 up to 4000 miles', where this latter class involves all mileages from 2000 miles up to (but not including) 4000 miles. A resulting grouped frequency table might be shown in Table 6.4.

**Table 6.4 Annual miles travelled by 50 sales representatives**

| Miles travelled per year | Frequency |
|---|---|
| 0 and up to 2000 | 2 |
| 2000 and up to 4000 | 6 |
| 4000 and up to 6000 | 12 |
| 6000 and up to 8000 | 15 |
| 8000 and up to 10 000 | 8 |
| 10 000 and up to 12 000 | 4 |
| 12 000 and up to 14 000 | 2 |
| 14 000 and up to 16 000 | 1 |

For shorthand, a class such as 4000 and up to 6000 is often written 4000 < 6000. There is no ambiguity about the class into which any measurement is placed, there is no space between the various classes and all data values fall in one of them.

You obtain a **cumulative frequency table** by simply rearranging the classes of the ordinary grouped frequency table. For the Example 6.1.3 showing days of illness of 60 employees the classes are defined as 1–5, 6–10, 11–15, 16–20, 21–25 so the **class boundaries** are 5.5, 10.5, 15.5, 20.5, 25.5. To obtain a cumulative frequency table we consider as ranges of values: less than 5.5, less than 10.5, less than 15.5, etc. Thus you obtain the cumulative frequencies by accumulating those of the ordinary grouped frequency table. Table 6.5 shows the cumulative frequency table for the illness data.

**Table 6.5 Cumulative frequency table for the illness data**

| Range | Frequency |
| --- | --- |
| Less than 5.5 days | 37 |
| Less than 10.5 days | 46 |
| Less than 15.5 days | 52 |
| Less than 20.5 days | 56 |
| Less than 25.5 days | 60 |

Note that the cumulative frequency of 46 is achieved by totalling the frequencies in the first two classes (37 + 9), while the cumulative frequency of 52 is obtained by adding the frequency in the next (third) class to this value (giving 46 + 6).

**Exercises 6.1**

1   Measurement was made of the times taken by 60 employees in a factory to carry out a standard procedure. The times found, in minutes, were as follows:

| | | | | | | | | | |
|---|---|---|---|---|---|---|---|---|---|
| 16 | 18 | 21 | 31 | 25 | 15 | 10 | 16 | 14 | 17 |
| 12 | 20 | 28 | 22 | 19 | 19 | 35 | 32 | 28 | 16 |
| 21 | 26 | 19 | 30 | 19 | 27 | 20 | 30 | 25 | 20 |
| 18 | 17 | 33 | 29 | 26 | 18 | 17 | 25 | 21 | 19 |
| 15 | 26 | 10 | 20 | 16 | 19 | 14 | 20 | 17 | 22 |
| 28 | 30 | 19 | 31 | 32 | 14 | 27 | 21 | 32 | 29 |

    **a**   Group the data into six classes (6–10, 11–15, . . . , 31–35).

    **b**   Obtain a cumulative frequency table for the data.

2   Which of the following are numeric and which are categorical? In each case divide into discrete or continuous if numeric and nominal or ordinal if categorical.

    **a**   The gender of a person

    **b**   The height of a person

    **c**   The time taken from start to finish to manufacture a product

    **d**   The level of satisfaction with the performance of the present government in a survey recorded as 'very satisfied', 'satisfied', 'neutral', 'dissatisfied', or 'very dissatisfied'

    **e**   The number of products manufactured each day

3   The table below shows the salaries (in thousands of pounds) of the employees of a company.

| Salary (£000) | Number of employees |
|---|---|
| 5 and less than 10 | 35 |
| 10 and less than 15 | 75 |
| 15 and less than 20 | 96 |
| 20 and less than 25 | 42 |
| 25 and less than 35 | 52 |

Form a cumulative frequency table.

4   The following list shows the heights in metres of 20 students.

    1.21   1.65   1.23   1.45   1.31   1.54   1.65   1.33   1.69   1.67

    1.56   1.69   1.63   1.45   1.52   1.20   1.31   1.61   1.62   1.62

Classify the data as discrete or continuous and construct a grouped frequency table with five equal classes. Obtain a cumulative frequency table for this data.

## 6.2 Frequency Diagrams

Tabulating data in the form of a frequency table increases our ability to detect pattern and meaning. The use of diagrams or charts can be even more revealing and they are widely used to present data. The essential aim of any diagram or chart is to present the data clearly so that a general perspective of what the information contains can be grasped quickly. Consequently all diagrams should have the following features.

**a**  They should be clear and attractive.
**b**  They should possess a title.
**c**  If the diagram takes the form of a graph,
  • the axes should be labelled
  • the scales should be clearly marked.
**d**  If the diagram is pictorial,
  • all regions should be clearly distinguishable
  • a key/legend should be included to explain the shading used.

In short, you should be able to accurately summarize the data from the information contained on the diagram. In this section we describe a number of diagrams that improve our appreciation of what a data set is saying.

## Histograms

A **histogram** is a block diagram having one block for each class into which the data values are divided. The proper way to think about a histogram is that the width of a block is proportional to the **class** width of the class it represents and the area of the block is proportional to the class frequency. Hence the height of a block is proportional to class frequency divided by class width, which can be referred to as the **frequency density** of the class. If, however, all the classes have the same class width, then the definition above reduces to saying all blocks have the same width and the heights are proportional to the class frequencies. In summary the important features of a histogram are the following.

**a**  There is no space between the bars.
**b**  If all the class widths are equal, the vertical axis shows the frequency and the heights of the bars are proportional to the frequency.
**c**  If the class widths are not equal, the vertical axis shows

$$\textbf{frequency density} = \frac{\text{frequency}}{\text{class width}}$$

and the **area** of the bar is proportional to the frequency.

## Example 6.2.1

The following data shows the number of miles travelled by 100 sales representatives in a particular working week.

| Number of miles travelled | Number of sales representatives |
|---|---|
| 100 and up to 200 | 15 |
| 200 and up to 300 | 40 |
| 300 and up to 400 | 25 |
| 400 and up to 500 | 15 |
| 500 and up to 600 | 5 |

**a**   Draw a histogram to represent this data. Interpret the information given in this diagram.

**b**   Combine the last two classes to form a frequency table having unequal class widths. Draw the new histogram to show this modified information.

## Solution to Example 6.2.1

**a**   The histogram for the original data is shown in Fig. 6.2. The information shows clearly that sales representatives tend to travel between 100 and 400 miles per week, and that the data is centred around 280 miles. This

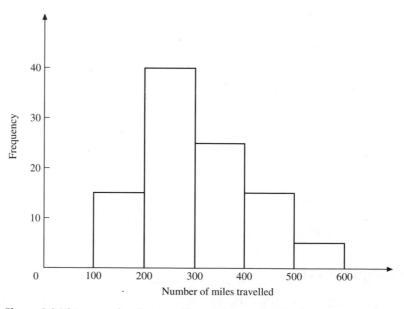

**Figure 6.2** Histogram showing travelling distances of 100 sales representatives

data set is not symmetrical. As the histogram has a tail stretching to the right, the data is described as **positively skewed**. If there had been a tail to the left, the data set would have been described as **negatively skewed**. Positively skewed data sets are fairly common in the business world. They would, for example, often be associated with distributions of incomes or of service times in an organization. Negatively skewed data sets are less common. An example of one would be the age distribution of hearing aid users.

b   You can combine the last two classes to reveal that 20 sales representatives travelled between 400 and 600 miles. As the class widths are no longer equal we calculate the frequency density for each class. This is shown in the following table.

| Number of miles travelled | Number of sales representatives | Frequency density |
| --- | --- | --- |
| 100 and up to 200 | 15 | 0.15 |
| 200 and up to 300 | 40 | 0.40 |
| 300 and up to 400 | 25 | 0.25 |
| 400 and up to 600 | 20 | 0.10 |

The resulting histogram is shown in Fig. 6.3.

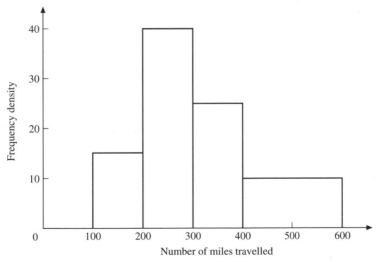

**Figure 6.3** Revised histogram from sales representatives travelling distances

If a frequency table has an open-ended class at one or both ends, the usual procedure is to assign its block a width equal to that for a class that is its immediate neighbour.

## Frequency Polygons

A frequency table can also be represented using a **frequency polygon**, which represents a frequency table by a continuous line graph. A frequency polygon is, in the most general case, drawn by plotting for each class frequency density against the midpoint of each class. The polygon is completed by joining the last point to the horizontal axis at a distance equal to the class width of the end class. Note that in all cases the points plotted to obtain a frequency polygon are the midpoints of the tops of the blocks of the corresponding histogram.

For the case where all class widths are equal the following procedure is used:

**a**    Each class is represented by the value at the midpoint of the class and the height of the point is represented by the frequency. (Use the frequency density if the class widths are not equal).

**b**    The points are joined by straight lines.

**c**    The points corresponding to the midpoints of the first and last classes are joined to the axis at the points which would correspond to the midpoints of the adjoining classes.

## Example 6.2.2

Construct a frequency polygon on the following data, met previously in Example 6.2.1.

| Number of miles travelled | Number of sales representatives |
|---|---|
| 100 and up to 200 | 15 |
| 200 and up to 300 | 40 |
| 300 and up to 400 | 25 |
| 400 and up to 500 | 15 |
| 500 and up to 600 | 5 |

## Solution to Example 6.2.2

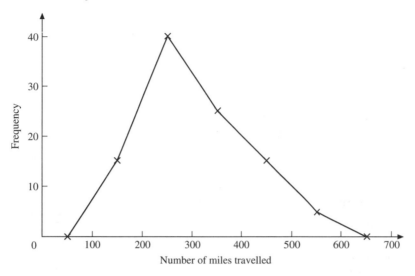

**Figure 6.4** Frequency polygon representing travelling distances of 100 sales representatives

You can draw a frequency polygon using the EXCEL package by listing the class midpoints and frequency densities in two columns of the EXCEL spreadsheet. Using the CHART icon you need to select the following:

Chart type – *xy* scatter
Chart subtype – points connected by lines
Chart title – frequency polygon
*x*-axis – miles travelled
*y*-axis – frequency

The resulting diagram is shown in Fig. 6.5.

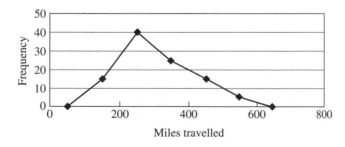

**Figure 6.5** Frequency polygon showing distances travelled by salesmen

Frequency polygons are particularly useful when comparing two frequency tables.

## Example 6.2.3

The delivery times for a certain product were obtained from two branches, Manchester and Liverpool, of a major retail outlet. Construct a frequency polygon diagram to show the distribution of delivery times and compare their performance.

| Delivery time | Number from Manchester | Number from Liverpool |
|---|---|---|
| 2-4 days | 0 | 10 |
| 4-6 days | 8 | 17 |
| 6-8 days | 12 | 13 |
| 8-10 days | 25 | 6 |
| 10-12 days | 3 | 4 |
| 12-14 days | 2 | 0 |

## *Solution to Example 6.2.3*

The frequency polygon diagram is shown in Fig. 6.6. It is clear from the frequency polygons that Liverpool tends to deliver much earlier than Manchester, as the Liverpool polygon is further to the left than that of Manchester.

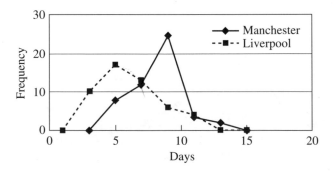

**Figure 6.6** Delivery times distribution

## Ogives

These diagrams, sometimes called 'cumulative frequency graphs', are not particularly useful in giving an immediate impression of sets of data but are valuable in the further stages of describing the data, as you will see in Chapters 7 and 8.

You construct an ogive from a cumulative frequency table by plotting the **cumulative frequencies** against the corresponding **upper class boundaries** and joining the resulting points by a smooth curve. Differing class widths have no effect on this diagram. The ogive can be used to obtain estimates for relevant values of the data.

## Example 6.2.4

A survey on a sample of 200 people led to the following table of results for weekly incomes.

| Weekly income (£) | Number of people |
|---|---|
| 100 and less than 120 | 12 |
| 120 and less than 140 | 35 |
| 140 and less than 160 | 67 |
| 160 and less than 200 | 45 |
| 200 and less than 250 | 25 |
| 250 and less than 300 | 16 |

**a**   Convert the frequency table to a cumulative frequency table.
**b**   Draw an ogive for this data.
**c**   Use the ogive to estimate
  • the number of employees earning less than £150 per week
  • the number of employees earning more than £180 per week
  • the percentage of employees earning more than £220 per week
  • the wage above which the top 20% of employees earn
  • the 90th percentile.

## Solution to Example 6.2.4

**a**   The cumulative frequency table shows the number of employees earning **less than** a given weekly wage

| Weekly income (£) | Number of people |
| --- | --- |
| Less than 100 | 0 |
| Less than 120 | 12 |
| Less than 140 | 47 |
| Less than 160 | 114 |
| Less than 200 | 159 |
| Less than 250 | 184 |
| Less than 300 | 200 |

The EXCEL package can be used to draw the ogive by putting the upper class boundaries and the cumulative frequencies in two columns of the spreadsheet, using the CHART icon and selecting the following:

Chart type – *xy* scatter
Chart subtype – points connected by curve
Chart title – ogive
*x*-axis – weekly income
*y*-axis – cumulative frequency

You can obtain the following estimates by using the cumulative frequency curve as a less than curve. Note that you would be best to draw the ogive as large as possible to get the preciseness required.

**a**    80 employees appear to earn less than £150.
**b**    140 employees appear to earn less than £180, so the remaining 60 earn more than this amount.

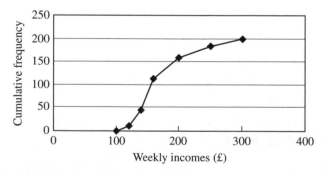

**Figure 6.7** Ogive for weekly incomes

c   170 employees earn less than £220, the remaining 30, or 15%, earn more than £220.

d   The top 20% applies to the top 40 earners, so we require the weekly income which 160 earn below, this appears to be £201.

e   A **percentile** is the value of the item located a certain percentage of the way along the ordered data set. For example, the 90th percentile is the value of the weekly income such that 90% of employees earn less than this amount. Here 90%, or 180 employees earn less than £240.

**Exercises 6.2**

1   A study was recently carried out to determine the amount of time that non-secretarial employees spend using computer terminals each week. The study involved 50 staff, and the times, in hours per week, on machines is shown in the following table.

| Hours spent | Frequency |
|---|---|
| 0 to under 5 | 4 |
| 5 to under 10 | 12 |
| 10 to under 15 | 17 |
| 15 to under 20 | 10 |
| 20 to under 25 | 7 |

a   Draw a histogram for this data.

b   Represent this information by a frequency polygon.

2   Draw a histogram for the following data on house prices.

| Class (£000) | Frequency |
|---|---|
| 0 to under 40 | 10 |
| 40 to under 80 | 22 |
| 80 to under 120 | 34 |
| 120 to under 160 | 18 |
| 160 to under 200 | 10 |
| 200 to under 300 | 6 |

3   Of 1000 people who bought new cars in 1999, the distribution of the lengths of time they had owned their previous cars is given below (in years).

| Length of time | Number |
| --- | --- |
| Less than 1 year | 180 |
| 1 year and less than 2 years | 150 |
| 2 years and less than 3 years | 240 |
| 3 years and less than 4 years | 150 |
| 4 years and less than 5 years | 110 |
| 5 years and less than 6 years | 60 |
| 6 years and less than 7 years | 60 |
| 7 years and less than 8 years | 50 |

a   Construct a cumulative frequency table for this data.
b   Draw an ogive for this data and use it to estimate:
   • the number of drivers who owned their car for less than 5.5 years
   • the percentage of drivers who owned the cars for more than 2.5 years
   • the 75th percentile.

4   The salaries of 100 male employees and 100 female employees in a certain industry are shown in the following table.

| Annual salary | Male frequency | Female frequency |
| --- | --- | --- |
| £5000 and less than £8000 | 5 | 12 |
| £8000 and less than £10 000 | 18 | 27 |
| £10 000 and less than £12 000 | 24 | 34 |
| £12 000 and less than £15 000 | 28 | 16 |
| £15 000 and less than £20 000 | 15 | 8 |
| £20 000 and less than £25 000 | 10 | 3 |

Draw a frequency polygon diagram showing both distributions and use the diagram to compare the salaries of the two genders.

## 6.3 Time-related Diagrams

A **time series** is a set of data values relating to a sequence of points in time. These points are almost always equally spaced; for example, each month, each quarter, or each year. The great majority of published statistics appear in the form of time series. For instance, the *Index of Retail Prices* is published each month. A **time series graph** is a graph with time on the horizontal axis and the value of the variable of interest on the vertical axis.

## Example 6.3.1

The following data shows the values of the retail price index in 1998 (based on January 1987 = 100).

| Month (1998) | RPI |
|---|---|
| January | 159.5 |
| February | 160.3 |
| March | 160.8 |
| April | 162.6 |
| May | 163.5 |
| June | 163.4 |
| July | 163.0 |
| August | 163.7 |
| September | 164.4 |
| October | 164.5 |
| November | 164.4 |
| December | 164.4 |

Draw a time series graph and describe the performance of the index over 1998.

## *Solution to Example 6.3.1*

The time series graph is shown in Fig. 6.8. The graph shows that the RPI increased sharply between March and May dropped slightly until July, started to rise in August and then stabilized for the rest of the year.

A **semi-log graph** is similar to a time series graph as time is plotted on the horizontal axis, but instead of plotting the values of the variable of interest on the vertical axis we plot the logs of these values. Taking logs of values is

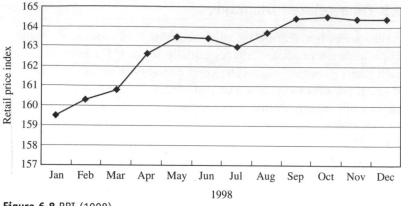

**Figure 6.8** RPI (1998)

easy when you have a calculator. For example

log 175 is obtained by entering [175] [log]

into the calculator, giving 2.243 as the answer.

In a semi-log graph equal vertical distances represent equal proportional changes. Thus sections of graphs having equal slopes represent equal proportional changes in the values of the variable of interest.

## Example 6.3.2

The values of the FTSE share index and the Dow Jones index as recorded on the first day of 10 consecutive months is shown in the following table.

Represent this information on a semi-log graph and interpret its meaning.

| Month | FTSE share index | Dow Jones Index |
|-------|------------------|-----------------|
| 1 | 4850 | 7 280 |
| 2 | 4979 | 7 562 |
| 3 | 5372 | 8 022 |
| 4 | 5480 | 8 099 |
| 5 | 5650 | 8 542 |
| 6 | 5997 | 8 964 |
| 7 | 6034 | 9 065 |
| 8 | 6080 | 9 542 |
| 9 | 6254 | 9 986 |
| 10 | 6431 | 10 065 |

## Solution to Example 6.3.2

First you need to take the log of the index values as shown in the following table.

| Month | Log(FTSE) | Log(Dow Jones) |
|---|---|---|
| 1 | 3.686 | 3.862 |
| 2 | 3.697 | 3.879 |
| 3 | 3.730 | 3.904 |
| 4 | 3.739 | 3.908 |
| 5 | 3.752 | 3.932 |
| 6 | 3.778 | 3.953 |
| 7 | 3.781 | 3.957 |
| 8 | 3.784 | 3.980 |
| 9 | 3.796 | 3.999 |
| 10 | 3.808 | 4.003 |

The resulting diagram, Fig. 6.9, shows that the two indices are growing at more or less the same percentage rate month by month. If anything, the Dow Jones index is growing at a slightly faster rate than the FTSE index. By looking at the original data you can see that the FTSE rose by 32.6% over the nine month period, while the Dow Jones rose by 38.3% over the same time.

As only proportional changes are of interest, time series measured in dif-

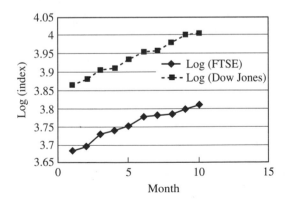

**Figure 6.9** Semi-log graph for FTSE Index and Dow Jones Index

ferent units can be compared on the same semi-log graph. Also semi-log graphs are useful in comparison situations where one of the variables being compared covers a great range of values. In such a case use of an ordinary graph would require using such a small scale on the vertical axis that significant changes in the other variable would be hidden.

## Exercises 6.3

1   The number of daily visitors to a hotel, by quarter, over the last three years is shown in the following table.

| Year | Quarter 1 | Quarter 2 | Quarter 3 | Quarter 4 |
|------|-----------|-----------|-----------|-----------|
| 1997 | 85        | 130       | 180       | 95        |
| 1998 | 110       | 150       | 210       | 125       |
| 1999 | 120       | 145       | 220       | 130       |

Draw a time series graph for this data. Identify the main features of the data.

2   The following table shows the weekly earnings (£) of males and females over the years 1988 to 1998.

| Year | Men's earnings (£) | Women's earnings (£) |
|------|--------------------|-----------------------|
| 1988 | 236.3              | 138.4                 |
| 1989 | 257.3              | 152.7                 |
| 1990 | 282.2              | 170.3                 |
| 1991 | 299.5              | 184.2                 |
| 1992 | 319.8              | 199.3                 |
| 1993 | 334.8              | 211.0                 |
| 1994 | 343.0              | 218.3                 |
| 1995 | 358.0              | 229.2                 |
| 1996 | 373.5              | 239.2                 |
| 1997 | 386.7              | 251.5                 |
| 1998 | 408.4              | 266.4                 |

Draw a semi-log graph showing both sets of data and interpret this diagram.

## 6.4 Charts

In Sec. 6.2 we examined frequency tables and diagrams for numeric data. In this section we look at tables and diagrams that describe and display categorical **characteristics** of the data. Table 6.6 is an example of a frequency table showing information about the staff employed by a factory.

| Table 6.6 Job descriptions of 100 employees | |
|---|---|
| Job description | Number of employees (Frequency) |
| Managers | 16 |
| Labourers | 21 |
| Mechanics | 38 |
| Fitters | 9 |
| Administrators | 12 |
| Draughtsmen | 4 |

We look at a number of statistical charts/diagrams which describe data of this type.

### Pie Charts

A **pie chart** divides a circle (or pie) into slices representing the sizes of the different components. A pie chart has the following features.

a    The circle is split into **sectors** (slices of the pie).
b    The area of each sector is proportional to the class frequency.
c    The classes are distinguished by shading in some way.

In order to construct a pie chart, the size of the angle at the centre of each sector (in degrees) needs to be calculated. The procedure is as follows.
- Calculate the fraction of the total number of items that each frequency represents
- Multiply each fraction by 360 to give the size of the angle, in degrees, at the centre of each of the sectors

## Example 6.4.1

Represent the data of Table 6.6 in a pie chart.

## Solution to Example 6.4.1

We first calculate the angles at the centre of each of the sectors.

| Job Description | Number of employees (frequency) | Fraction of total= frequency/total | Angle in degrees= fraction × 360 |
|---|---|---|---|
| Managers | 16 | 0.16 | 57.6 |
| Labourers | 21 | 0.21 | 75.6 |
| Mechanics | 38 | 0.38 | 136.8 |
| Fitters | 9 | 0.09 | 32.4 |
| Administrators | 12 | 0.12 | 43.2 |
| Draughtsmen | 4 | 0.04 | 14.4 |
| | Total =100 | | Total = 360 |

The method of construction of a pie chart is to divide up the circle into sectors by drawing lines radiating out from the centre at the calculated angles.

EXCEL can be used directly to produce a pie chart without the need to calculate the angles. For the above example you would only need to type the job descriptions and frequencies in adjoining columns and then to select the CHART icon (chart type – pie) to directly produce the pie chart shown in Fig. 6.10.

In general, pie charts are often used to show a total population broken down into its subcomponents and are readily understood by readers. A possible problem is that they are not always easy to construct, although modern software, including EXCEL, has overcome the problem. We should also point out that when two pie charts are used for comparison, it is essential to shade them in the same way.

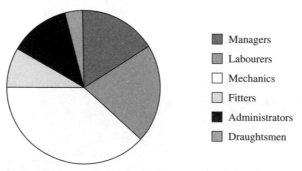

**Figure 6.10** Pie chart for job descriptions

## Bar Charts

A **bar chart** can also be used effectively to display the information describing non-numerical characteristics of a data set. As the name suggests it is a diagram which shows frequencies in the form of bars. Bar charts come in three types—simple and component and multiple.

### Simple Bar Charts

In a **simple bar chart** the height of the bar shows the size of the characteristic in question. Simple bar charts have the following features.

**a**    There is usually a space between each of the bars.
**b**    The bars are all of the same width.

Simple bar charts should not be confused with histograms that are used to display frequency tables for numeric data. Recall that for a histogram the bars are joined and they may have unequal width. Fig. 6.11 shows the bar chart for the data of Table 6.6.

Simple bar charts have the advantage that they are easy to construct and to understand. However, simple bar charts are restricted to one variable.

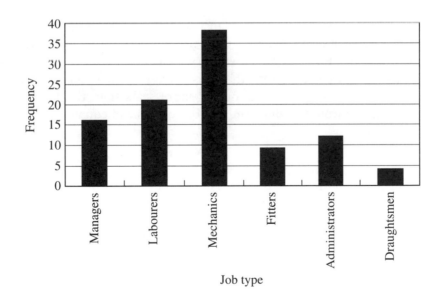

**Figure 6.11** Bar chart for job descriptions

## Example 6.4.2

Figure 6.12 was produced using the EXCEL package; shows the number of seats gained by parties in the UK general election of 9 April 1992. Interpret the information shown in the diagram.

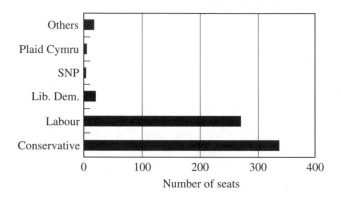

**Figure 6.12** Bar chart showing number of MPs

## Solution to Example 6.4.2

From the diagram it is difficult to read off exactly the number of seats gained by each party, but this is not usually important when interpreting such a chart. Figure 6.12 shows very clearly that the two main parties gained a high percentage of the seats (over 90%) between them with the Conservative Party having about 60 more seats than the Labour Party. You also see from this diagram that bar charts can equally well be drawn horizontally.

*Component and Multiple Bar Charts*
**Component** and **multiple bar charts** are an extension of simple bar charts that enable two or more sets of non-numeric data to be shown on the same chart.

Component bar charts have the following features.

**a**    There is one bar corresponding to each data set.
**b**    There is a space between the bars.
**c**    Components of different classes within the same data set are stacked.
**d**    The order of stacking is the same in each bar.

Multiple bar charts have the following features.

a    There is one bar corresponding to each class in each data set.
b    The same classes in the different data sets are constructed side by side.
c    There is no space between the bars of the classes of the same data set.
d    There is a space between the different data sets.

## Example 6.4.3

Table 6.7 shows holiday locations chosen by customers at a travel agent in 1994–99.

| Table 6.7 Holiday locations in the years 1994 to 1999 | | | | | | |
|---|---|---|---|---|---|---|
| Destination | 1994 | 1995 | 1996 | 1997 | 1998 | 1999 |
| Europe | 254 | 238 | 226 | 241 | 227 | 263 |
| America | 174 | 198 | 211 | 234 | 215 | 242 |
| Middle East/Africa | 104 | 116 | 132 | 146 | 140 | 142 |
| Other | 143 | 165 | 156 | 172 | 186 | 180 |
| Total | 675 | 717 | 725 | 793 | 768 | 827 |

A component bar chart and a multiple bar chart showing the data are shown in Figs 6.13 and 6.14. Interpret the information and compare the two charts.

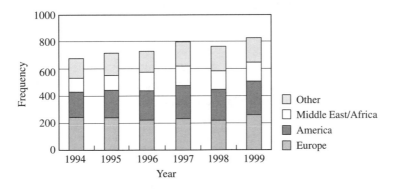

**Figure 6.13** Component bar chart for holiday locations

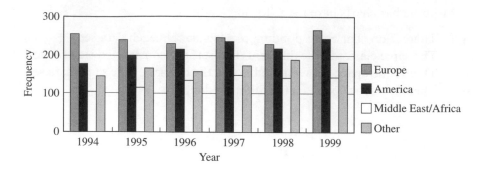

**Figure 6.14** Multiple bar chart for holiday locations

## Solution to Example 6.4.3

The charts show that the number of holiday makers going to America, Middle East/Africa and Other have generally increased over the time period of interest, whereas the numbers going to Europe have remained fairly constant. Consequently, total numbers have generally increased over the six-year period.

Both component bar charts and multiple bar charts are able to represent items belonging to two variables simultaneously. This advantage is balanced by the increased difficulty in interpreting the charts. For both charts it is important that the bars are shaded (or coloured) in a consistent way, otherwise it becomes very difficult to interpret the data. In general, a component bar chart is preferable to a multiple bar chart if the overall totals are the main items for comparison, while the multiple bar chart is preferable if there is a greater need to compare the total frequencies of the individual components.

### Pictograms

A **pictogram** is a chart that represents the frequencies of the non-numeric values by using only simple descriptive pictures. Pictograms are most useful in cases where the number of classes is small.

## Example 6.4.4

The pictogram shown in Fig. 6.15 displays the information first shown in Table 6.6. Use the pictogram to try to reproduce the frequencies.

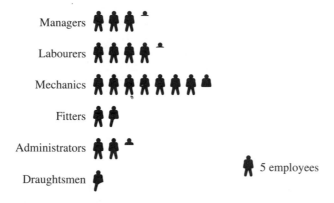

**Figure 6.15** Pictogram showing job locations

## Solution to Example 6.4.4

The main advantage of pictograms is that they are visually pleasing, allowing the creator some artistic licence, but accuracy is inevitably lost in the attempt to represent data using pictures.

Do you get similar frequencies to those given in Table 6.6?

**Exercises 6.4**

1   Sales in four regions are given in the following table. Draw a pie chart to represent this data.

| Region | Sales |
|--------|-------|
| North  | 25    |
| South  | 10    |
| East   | 45    |
| West   | 25    |

2   There are five hospitals in a Health District, and they classify the number of beds in each hospital as:

|  | Hospital | | | | |
|---|---|---|---|---|---|
|  | Amazon | Bluetown | Congo | Deeside | Emburey |
| Maternity | 35 | 52 | 24 | 0 | 0 |
| Surgical | 64 | 75 | 42 | 36 | 40 |
| Medical | 82 | 96 | 60 | 62 | 70 |
| Psychiatric | 41 | 20 | 12 | 7 | 42 |

Represent this information in a component bar chart.

3    The following table shows the marital status of the adult population by sex.

| Percentages | Never-married | Married | Divorced | Widowed |
|---|---|---|---|---|
| Males | 41 | 46 | 10 | 3 |
| Females | 33 | 45 | 12 | 10 |

Draw a multiple bar chart to illustrate this data. What are the main differences in marital status between the two sexes?

## Further Exercises

1   The following table represents the total production costs for a factory in one year.

| Cost | Amount |
|------|--------|
| Direct labour | £35 200 |
| Direct materials | £12 600 |
| Production overhead | £8 200 |

A pie chart is drawn to show the division in these three costs. How large is the angle in the pie chart representing direct materials?

    A. 81°        B. 99°        C. 108°        D. 120°

2   A component bar chart showed the number of employees in each of three grades. The data are shown in the following table.

| Grade | 1999 | 2000 |
|-------|------|------|
| Managers | 45 | 70 |
| Administrators | 125 | 130 |
| Clerks | 30 | 40 |

The bar for 1999 was 15 cm long. How high is the administrators' segment on the 2000 bar?

    A. 8.25 cm    B. 9.25 cm    C. 9.75 cm    D. 11.5 cm

3   The following frequency table shows the weekly wages in a company.

| Wage | Frequency |
|------|-----------|
| Below £100 | 24 |
| £100 up to but not including £125 | 36 |
| £125 up to but not including £150 | 54 |
| £150 and above | 11 |

What percentage of these employees earn £125 or more?

A. 40%          B. 48%          C. 50%          D. 52%

4   A Company records the number of hours lost through lateness each
    week over a 12-month period.

| Hours lost | Frequency |
|---|---|
| 0 and up to 4 | 16 |
| 4 and up to 6 | 20 |
| 6 and up to 8 | 10 |
| 8 and up to 10 | 6 |

When a histogram is drawn to represent this data the height of the
'4–6 hours' column is 10 centimetres, what is the height of the '0–4
hours' column?

A. 2 cm          B. 4 cm          C. 8 cm          D. 16 cm

5   The number of employees in a certain industry is given in the table
    below.

| Year | Number of employees ('000s) |
|---|---|
| 1975 | 84 |
| 1985 | 66 |
| 1995 | 45 |

In a pictogram representing this data, a symbol of a man represents
5000 employees. How many of these symbols are needed to represent
the number of employees in 1995?

A. 8          B. 9          C. 19          D. 38

6.  You have been asked to investigate the price of a particular holiday
    offered by 40 different travel agents nationwide. After spending some
    time telephoning the travel agents the following prices (in £) were
    identified.

| | | | | | | | | | |
|---|---|---|---|---|---|---|---|---|---|
| 435 | 475 | 541 | 539 | 476 | 479 | 499 | 452 | 412 | 521 |
| 431 | 479 | 452 | 431 | 409 | 477 | 421 | 405 | 497 | 489 |
| 455 | 469 | 431 | 427 | 489 | 485 | 445 | 433 | 476 | 518 |
| 466 | 421 | 465 | 438 | 505 | 479 | 441 | 489 | 499 | 450 |

Group the data using the group £400 up to but not including £420, £420 up to but not including £440, and so on. Draw a frequency polygon for the grouped data.

7 The table below shows the number of disputes taking place in a particular industry during the period 1995–99 in each three-month period.

| Year | Quarter | Number | Year | Quarter | Number |
|---|---|---|---|---|---|
| 1995 | 1 | 8 | 1998 | 1 | 6 |
| | 2 | 11 | | 2 | 9 |
| | 3 | 13 | | 3 | 14 |
| | 4 | 10 | | 4 | 9 |
| 1996 | 1 | 6 | 1999 | 1 | 9 |
| | 2 | 9 | | 2 | 12 |
| | 3 | 14 | | 3 | 15 |
| | 4 | 9 | | 4 | 12 |
| 1997 | 1 | 5 | | | |
| | 2 | 8 | | | |
| | 3 | 11 | | | |
| | 4 | 7 | | | |

Draw a time series graph to show the pattern of disputes over the five-year period. Describe this pattern.

8 The price relatives for 400 commodities, all with respect to base prices 10 years ago, were grouped to give the following distribution.

| Price relative | Frequency |
|---|---|
| 29 and under 65 | 3 |
| 65 and under 101 | 19 |
| 101 and under 137 | 90 |
| 137 and under 173 | 114 |
| 173 and under 209 | 87 |
| 209 and under 245 | 66 |
| 245 and under 281 | 15 |
| 281 and under 317 | 3 |
| 317 and under 353 | 3 |

Construct an ogive for the above data. Hence estimate

**a**   the number of price relatives less than 200
**b**   the percentage of price relatives greater than 250
**c**   the 90th percentile.

9   The table below shows the results of a random sample of 100 daily expense claims made by a firm's executives.

| Amount of claim | Number of claims |
|---|---|
| Under £10 | 9 |
| £10 and under £15 | 22 |
| £15 and under £20 | 25 |
| £20 and under £25 | 17 |
| £25 and under £30 | 11 |
| £30 and under £35 | 8 |
| £35 and under £40 | 5 |
| £40 and under £45 | 3 |

Draw a histogram of this grouped data.

10  The number of offences recorded as homicide within a certain region, by age of victim, is given in the following table.

| Age group | Number of offences |
|---|---|
| Under 1 | 52 |
| 1-4 | 8 |
| 5-15 | 5 |
| 16-29 | 21 |
| 30-49 | 17 |
| 50-69 | 8 |
| 70+ | 9 |

It would be usual to represent this type of continuous information in a histogram. However, the first column (representing the under 1 age group) would be far taller than the other columns. Hence draw a simple bar chart showing this information, but explain the drawback of using this type of chart here.

## Chapter Seven

# Averages

## 7.1 Mean

In business life it is not unusual to meet phrases similar to '*the average sales revenue per month is £35 000*' or '*the average company wage is £12 500*'. However, is it clear what is meant by this term **average**? Broadly speaking, the term is used to replace a collection of measurements by just one value. Indeed, the average of a set of numbers may be thought of as a number somewhere at the centre of the set and typical of the set as a whole. However, the word 'average' can be used to deliberately mislead or confuse as the word does have more than one meaning. In this chapter three measures of average are described; they are called the **mean**, the **median** and the **mode**.

First, the **mean**, or the **arithmetic mean** as it is sometimes called, is found by adding the set of numbers together and dividing by the number of items involved. For example, the mean of the numbers 12, 8, 6, 4, 9 and 3 is

$$\frac{12 + 8 + 6 + 4 + 9 + 3}{6} = \frac{42}{6} = 7$$

Suppose the numbers are 20, 110, 80, 50, and 60. These have a mean equal to

$$\frac{20 + 110 + 80 + 50 + 60}{5} = \frac{320}{5} = 64$$

To get a feel for this, you can interpret the mean in the following way:

Annabel has 20p, Brian has 110p, Claire has 80p, David has 50p and Eyal has 60p. How much would each receive if they put their money into a pool and then took out an equal share of this pool? The amount of the pool would be 20 + 110 + 80 + 50 + 60 = 320p. There are five of them to share it and so the share each would have is 320/5 = 64p.

You obtain the mean of a set of numbers by adding all the values and then dividing the total by the number of items.

You usually represent the mean and its calculation by a mathematical shorthand. In the above example there are five numbers 20, 110, 80, 50, 60. Suppose, more generally, there are $n$ numbers, represented by

$$x_1, x_2, x_3, \ldots, x_n,$$

The shorthand notation for 'add all the $x$-values together' is $\Sigma x$ (read 'sigma $x$'or 'sum of $x$'—$\Sigma$ is a capital S in Greek). For example

$$x_1 = 6, x_2 = 9, x_3 = 4, x_4 = 15, x_5 = 8, x_6 = 2, x_7 = 12$$
$$\Sigma x = 56$$

is obtained by adding the seven individual values on a calculator.

The sum, 56 here, is then divided by the number of items, 7, in order to find the mean of $x$. This is often written $\bar{x}$ (read '$x$-bar'). In this example the mean is $^{56}/_7 = 8$. So

$$\bar{x} = \frac{\Sigma x}{n}$$

is a shorthand way of representing the method of calculation of the mean when individual values are available. If the word 'average' is used in any technical publication or announcement it will probably be the mean that is being referred to.

## Example 7.1.1

A survey took place to investigate hotel prices in London. The investigator went into 15 hotels one Saturday and requested the prices of an overnight stay (bed and breakfast) in £ and the standard price of an evening meal (to the nearest £). These prices are recorded in Table 7.1.

| Table 7.1 Hotel prices | | | | | | | | | | | | | | | |
|---|---|---|---|---|---|---|---|---|---|---|---|---|---|---|---|
| Hotel | A | B | C | D | E | F | G | H | I | J | K | L | M | N | O |
| Bed & breakfast (£) | 75 | 80 | 86 | 90 | 74 | 78 | 69 | 82 | 79 | 94 | 79 | 85 | 94 | 70 | 80 |
| Evening meal (£) | 17 | 15 | 18 | 20 | 15 | 15 | 11 | 15 | 19 | 18 | 15 | 17 | 12 | 13 | 12 |

Determine

**a**   the mean cost of an overnight stay
**b**   the mean price of a standard evening meal

in these 15 hotels.

## Solution to Example 7.1.1

**a**   Using the formula $\bar{x} = \dfrac{\Sigma x}{n}$ for the prices of an overnight stay

$\Sigma x = 75 + 80 + 86 + \ldots + 80 = 1215$

and so $\bar{x} = \dfrac{1215}{15} = 81$

The mean price of an overnight stay at a London hotel is £81
**b**   For prices of evening meals,

$\Sigma x = 17 + 15 + 18 + \ldots + 12 = 232$

and so $\bar{x} = \dfrac{232}{15} = 15.47$

The mean price of an evening meal is £15.47, or £15.50 to a more appropriate degree of accuracy.

The EXCEL software package can be used to find the basic statistical measures, such as the mean of individual values. A number of statistical functions are available from the function list. To use these you need to type the relevant data into cells B2 to C16 as shown in Fig. 7.1, then type [= **average (B2:B16)**] and [= **average (C2:C16)**] in cells B17 and C17. Alternatively you might use the average function via the function wizard and follow the instructions given by this function.

| | A | B | C |
|---|---|---|---|
| 1 | Hotel | B&B price (£) | Meal price (£) |
| 2 | A | 75 | 17 |
| 3 | B | 80 | 15 |
| 4 | C | 86 | 18 |
| 5 | D | 90 | 20 |
| 6 | E | 74 | 15 |
| 7 | F | 78 | 15 |
| 8 | G | 69 | 11 |
| 9 | H | 82 | 15 |
| 10 | I | 79 | 19 |
| 11 | J | 94 | 18 |
| 12 | K | 79 | 15 |
| 13 | L | 85 | 17 |
| 14 | M | 94 | 12 |
| 15 | N | 70 | 13 |
| 16 | O | 80 | 12 |
| 17 | MEAN | = AVERAGE (B2:B16) | = AVERAGE (C2:C16) |

**Figure 7.1** EXCEL formulae for finding the mean of raw data

Cells B17 and C17 should contain the values £81 and £15.47 respectively.

In the above example the prices of the evening meals might have been recorded in a **frequency table**, as in Table 7.2. This table shows, for example, that 5 out of the 15 hotels estimated the price of a standard evening meal at £15. From the definition of the mean

$$\bar{x} = \frac{\text{Total of meal prices}}{\text{Number of hotels}}$$

**Table 7.2 Frequency table of hotel meal prices**

| Price per evening meal | Number of hotels |
|---|---|
| 11 | 1 |
| 12 | 2 |
| 13 | 1 |
| 15 | 5 |
| 17 | 2 |
| 18 | 2 |
| 19 | 1 |
| 20 | 1 |
| **Total** | **15** |

From the table, the number of hotels is 15. The total of the prices for these meals is

$$1 \times 11 + 2 \times 12 + 1 \times 13 + 5 \times 15 + 2$$
$$\times 17 + 2 \times 18 + 1 \times 19 + 1 \times 20 = 232$$

The mean $= \dfrac{232}{15} = £15.47$, as before.

When you have a **frequency table** showing a list of possible discrete observed values and their frequencies then the formula for calculating the mean is

$$\bar{x} = \frac{\Sigma xf}{\Sigma f}$$

where $\Sigma xf$ is the sum of the observed value $\times$ frequency and $\Sigma f$ is the sum of the frequencies.

You will see later that this formula is also used for a grouped frequency table where the data is organized into classes of values and the number of items that fall in each class. In this case the observed value, $x$, is replaced by the class midpoint.

## Example 7.1.2

Table 7.3 shows the daily demand for hire cars belonging to White Cars Ltd. Find the mean daily car demand.

**Table 7.3 Demand for cars**

| Daily demand | Frequency |
| --- | --- |
| 1 | 3 |
| 2 | 4 |
| 4 | 7 |
| 5 | 12 |
| 6 | 12 |
| 8 | 7 |
| 9 | 4 |
| 10 | 1 |

## Solution to Example 7.1.2

The relevant calculations are shown in the following table:

| $x$ | $f$ | $xf$ |
|-----|-----|------|
| 1 | 3 | 3 |
| 2 | 4 | 8 |
| 4 | 7 | 28 |
| 5 | 12 | 60 |
| 6 | 12 | 72 |
| 8 | 7 | 56 |
| 9 | 4 | 36 |
| 10 | 1 | 10 |
|  | 50 | 273 |

$$\bar{x} = \frac{\Sigma xf}{\Sigma f} = \frac{273}{50} = 5.46$$

The mean demand is 5.46 cars per day.

The use of a frequency table is of particular value when there is a large volume of data. It reduces the amount of calculation in finding the mean.

Although EXCEL does not have a function for finding the mean from a frequency table directly, you can carry out the calculations by putting mathematical formulae in appropriate cells. First the data from Table 7.3 should be entered then the respective formulae should be entered to perform the appropriate calculations (noting that many of these formulae can be entered using the 'copy down' routines). Figure 7.2 shows the formulae that should be entered to find the mean of the demand for cars described in Table 7.3.

|  | A | B | C |
|----|----|----|----|
| 1 | Demand | Frequency | xf |
| 2 | 1 | 3 | = A2*B2 |
| 3 | 2 | 4 | = A3*B3 |
| 4 | 4 | 7 | = A4*B4 |
| 5 | 5 | 12 | = A5*B5 |
| 6 | 6 | 12 | = A6*B6 |
| 7 | 8 | 7 | = A7*B7 |
| 8 | 9 | 4 | = A8*B8 |
| 9 | 10 | 1 | = A9*B9 |
| 10 |  | = SUM (B2:B9) | = SUM (C2:C9) |
| 11 |  |  |  |
| 12 | MEAN = | = C10/B10 |  |

**Figure 7.2** EXCEL formulae for finding the mean from a frequency table

A similar process takes place when the data is not available in raw form but already compiled in a grouped frequency table. Table 7.4 shows the times taken by maintenance staff to repair a particular type of equipment fault.

**Table 7.4 Times to repair equipment**

| Time taken (mins) | Frequency |
| --- | --- |
| 0 and under 10 | 28 |
| 10 and under 20 | 42 |
| 20 and under 30 | 56 |
| 30 and under 40 | 74 |
| 40 and under 50 | 32 |
| 50 and under 60 | 8 |

You have seen earlier that to calculate a mean, two pieces of information are needed (here, the number of repairs and the total time taken to carry out these repairs). The first of these is straightforward as you can total the frequency column to obtain 240. But how do you find out the total time taken to carry out these repairs?

The first class consists of the 28 repairs that take up to 10 minutes. Without any extra information you have to assume that all the times in the class fall at the centre of the class; that is, the midpoint of 0 and 10, which is 5 minutes. This value would also be appropriate when the values are spread evenly through the class. You repeat this for all the classes. For example in the second class you assume that all 42 times take the value of 15 minutes. Now you proceed as before by multiplying the midpoint by the frequency to give an estimate for the total time taken by the repairs falling in that class. When totalled for all classes you have a good estimate for the total time taken to carry out all the repairs. The mean is then obtained by dividing by the overall frequency. The procedure is normally set out using a table in the way shown by Table 7.5.

$$\text{Mean repair time} = \frac{6640}{240} = 27.67 \text{ minutes}$$

It is important to realize that the mean from grouped data here may not give exactly the same answer as that given by finding the actual mean of the original 240 repair times. The mean from the grouped data provides an estimate only of the mean of the actual values as the grouping process inevitably loses some accuracy.

**Table 7.5 Calculations for mean repair time**

| Times (mins) | Midpoint, $x$ | Frequency, $f$ | Midpoint × frequency |
|---|---|---|---|
| 0–10 | 5 | 28 | 140 |
| 10–20 | 15 | 42 | 630 |
| 20–30 | 25 | 56 | 1400 |
| 30–40 | 35 | 74 | 2590 |
| 40–50 | 45 | 32 | 1440 |
| 50–60 | 55 | 8 | 440 |
| | Total | 240 | 6640 |

## Example 7.1.3

The value of 100 invoices issued by a firm on one day is shown in Table 7.6.

**Table 7.6 Value of 100 invoices**

| Value (£) | Frequency |
|---|---|
| 0 and under 5 | 2 |
| 5 and under 10 | 12 |
| 10 and under 15 | 29 |
| 15 and under 20 | 22 |
| 20 and under 25 | 18 |
| 25 and under 30 | 10 |
| 30 and under 40 | 5 |
| 40 and under 50 | 2 |

Find the mean value per invoice.

## Solution to Example 7.1.3

The calculations are shown in Table 7.7.

**Table 7.7 Calculations for mean invoice table**

| Class | Midpoint, $x$ | Frequency, $f$ | $xf$ |
|-------|---------------|----------------|------|
| 0–5 | 2.5 | 2 | 5 |
| 5–10 | 7.5 | 12 | 90 |
| 10–15 | 12.5 | 29 | 362.5 |
| 15–20 | 17.5 | 22 | 385 |
| 20–25 | 22.5 | 18 | 405 |
| 25–30 | 27.5 | 10 | 275 |
| 30–40 | 35 | 5 | 175 |
| 40–50 | 45 | 2 | 90 |
| | Total | 100 | 1787.5 |

$$\overline{x} = \frac{1787.5}{100} = £17.88$$

The mean invoice value is £17.88.

To perform the calculation in an EXCEL worksheet, it is necessary to enter the lower class boundary and the upper class boundary in separate columns. Figure 7.3 shows the data and required formulae to find the mean of the data in Table 7.6. Remember that many of the formulae can be entered using the 'copy down' routine.

| | A | B | C | D | E |
|---|---|---|---|---|---|
| 1 | Lower | Upper | Frequency | Midpoint | xf |
| 2 | 0 | 5 | 2 | = (A2+B2)/2 | = C2*D2 |
| 3 | 5 | 10 | 12 | = (A3+B3)/2 | = C3*D3 |
| 4 | 10 | 15 | 29 | = (A4+B4)/2 | = C4*D4 |
| 5 | 15 | 20 | 22 | = (A5+B5)/2 | = C5*D5 |
| 6 | 20 | 25 | 18 | = (A6+B6)/2 | = C6*D6 |
| 7 | 25 | 30 | 10 | = (A7+B7)/2 | = C7*D7 |
| 8 | 30 | 40 | 5 | = (A8+B8)/2 | = C8*D8 |
| 9 | 40 | 50 | 2 | = (A9+B9)/2 | = C9*D9 |
| 10 | | | = SUM (C2:C9) | | = SUM (E2:E9) |
| 11 | | | | | |
| 12 | MEAN = | = E10/C10 | | | |

**Figure 7.3** Data and formulae to find the mean of the data in Table 7.6

| | A | B | C | D | E |
|---|---|---|---|---|---|
| 1 | Lower | Upper | Frequency | Midpoint | xf |
| 2 | 0 | 5 | 2 | 2.5 | 5 |
| 3 | 5 | 10 | 12 | 7.5 | 90 |
| 4 | 10 | 15 | 29 | 12.5 | 362.5 |
| 5 | 15 | 20 | 22 | 17.5 | 385 |
| 6 | 20 | 25 | 18 | 22.5 | 405 |
| 7 | 25 | 30 | 10 | 27.5 | 275 |
| 8 | 30 | 40 | 5 | 35 | 175 |
| 9 | 40 | 50 | 2 | 45 | 90 |
| 10 | | | 100 | | 1787.5 |
| 11 | | | | | |
| 12 | Mean = | 17.875 | | | |

**Figure 7.4** Results from an EXCEL spreadsheet

Figure 7.4 shows the results of the EXCEL calculations.

The chief merit of the mean is that it has a body of mathematical theory behind it which makes it useful in further statistical work. Also the mean makes arithmetical use of every item in the data set.

## Exercises 7.1

1  Five workers earn £180, £195, £195, £200 and £220 a week. What is their average wage? What must a sixth worker earn if the average of the six is to be £1 more?

2  A car travels for 2 hours at 25 miles per hour and 90 minutes at 30 miles per hour. Find the total time, total distance and average speed.

3  Find the mean wage for the following group of people described in Table 7.8.

**Table 7.8 Wage Distribution**

| Wage(£) | Frequency |
|---|---|
| 172 | 15 |
| 175 | 20 |
| 180 | 40 |
| 185 | 35 |
| 190 | 17 |
| 192 | 13 |
| 195 | 10 |

4    The average monthly earnings of 200 employees working for Tritown Ltd are shown in Table 7.9.

**Table 7.9 Monthly earnings**

| Monthly earnings(£) | Number of employees |
|---|---|
| 400 and under 600 | 24 |
| 600 and under 800 | 50 |
| 800 and under 1000 | 64 |
| 1000 and under 1200 | 42 |
| 1200 and under 1400 | 20 |

Find the mean monthly earnings for these 200 employees.

## 7.2 Median

The second type of average is the **median**, or middle value, where half of the numbers are less than or equal to the median and half are more than or equal to the median.

To find the median of a set of numbers, arrange them in ascending order of size and pick out the one in the middle. For example

2, 4, 9, 7, 5     has median 5

for arranged in order they are 2, 4, 5, 7, 9 and 5 is in the middle.

Another example is

1, 2, 4, 5, 6, 6, 8, 9, 10     which has median 6.

These are already in ascending order and the value of the one in the middle is 6. It does not matter that there is another 6 as well.

In both of these examples there have been an odd number of items. If the number of items is even, the definition given at the beginning has to be modified slightly. Then you arrange the values in ascending order and pick out the two in the middle. You then find the median by computing the mean of these two numbers. For example

11, 8, 6, 2, 3, 12, 10, 14     has median 9

for arranged in order they are 2, 3, 6, 8, 10, 11, 12, 14; the two in the middle are 8 and 10, and these two numbers have mean 9.

## Example 7.2.1

Table 7.10 shows the number of children in 30 households.

| Table 7.10 Number of children in 30 households | | | | | | | | | |
|---|---|---|---|---|---|---|---|---|---|
| 2 | 1 | 0 | 7 | 4 | 1 | 2 | 0 | 2 | 3 |
| 3 | 4 | 2 | 1 | 2 | 5 | 1 | 3 | 2 | 4 |
| 2 | 1 | 0 | 2 | 3 | 3 | 1 | 2 | 3 | 2 |

Determine the median number of children per household.

## *Solution to Example 7.2.1*

In ascending order the data is

0, 0, 0, 1, 1, 1, 1, 1, 1, 2, 2, 2, 2, 2, 2, 2, 2, 2, 2, 3, 3, 3, 3, 3, 3, 4, 4, 4, 5, 7

There are 30 numbers, so the median is given by the mean of the 15th and 16th numbers. Counting from the left the 15th number is 2, as is the 16th number.

Median = 2

thus indicating that an average or typical family has 2 children.

If there are a large number of items, it may be easier to find the median by alternatively striking out the largest and smallest numbers. Using this last example

| 2 | 1 | 0 | 7 | 4 | 1 | 2 | 0 | 2 | 3 |
|---|---|---|---|---|---|---|---|---|---|
| 3 | 4 | 2 | 1 | 2 | 5 | 1 | 3 | 2 | 4 |
| 2 | 1 | 0 | 2 | 3 | 3 | 1 | 2 | 3 | 2 |

first strike out the largest in the set (7), then strike out the smallest (0), next strike out the second largest (5), then strike out the second smallest (0). Continue in this way, alternatively striking out the largest remaining value and the smallest remaining value until one number (or two numbers if the number of items is even) is left.

| | A | B | C | D | E | F | G | H | I | J |
|---|---|---|---|---|---|---|---|---|---|---|
| **1** | 2 | 1 | 0 | 7 | 4 | 1 | 2 | 0 | 2 | 3 |
| **2** | 3 | 4 | 2 | 1 | 2 | 5 | 1 | 3 | 2 | 4 |
| **3** | 2 | 1 | 0 | 2 | 3 | 3 | 1 | 2 | 3 | 2 |
| **4** | | | | | | | | | | |
| **5** | Median = | 2 | | | | | | | | |

**Figure 7.5** EXCEL output from using the MEDIAN command

An alternative way of determining the median would be to enter the original values into an EXCEL worksheet and using the MEDIAN function in the same way as the AVERAGE function was used in Sec. 7.1. Figure 7.5 shows the use of this function for the data of Example 7.2.1, where cell B5 contains [=**MEDIAN (A1:C10)**].

## Example 7.2.2

The daily demand for a product is given in the Table 7.11.
State the median.

**Table 7.11 Product demand**

| Demand | Frequency |
|---|---|
| 2 | 4 |
| 3 | 6 |
| 4 | 4 |
| 5 | 7 |
| 6 | 2 |
| 7 | 4 |

## Solution to Example 7.2.2

Writing the 27 values out in order gives

2, 2, 2, 2, 3, 3, 3, 3, 3, 3, 3, 4, 4, 4, 4, 5, 5, 5, 5, 5, 5, 5, 6, 6, 7, 7, 7, 7

The middle (14th) value is 4.

## Example 7.2.3

The incomes of six bank employees are

$$£15\,000 \quad £17\,000 \quad £12\,500 \quad £14\,500 \quad £19\,000 \quad £18\,000$$

Find **a** the mean and
     **b** the median.

### Solution to Example 7.2.3

**a**   Mean $= \dfrac{\text{total}}{6} = \dfrac{96\,000}{6} = £16\,000$

**b**   Median $= (15\,000 + 17\,000)/2 = £16\,000$

Referring to the last example imagine now that the bank employee earning £19\,000 earns not £19\,000 but £39\,000. What happens to the mean and median?

The median does not change, but the mean increases to £19\,333. It is true that the mean is now unrepresentative because it is significantly influenced by the extreme value. This is a major advantage that the median has over the mean. Extreme values are not uncommon in economic data, and so the median is often a more suitable measure for such data than is the mean. The great disadvantage of the median is that it cannot be as readily used in further statistical work as can the mean.

When data is not available in its raw form and has already been compiled into a grouped frequency table, the median is still the value in the middle, and we have to find the number such that half the items are below it and half above.

Thus when finding the median of a grouped data set you need to use a cumulative frequency table or the corresponding ogive. We consider first finding the median from an ogive and then see how this method extends to the calculation of the median from a cumulative frequency table.

## Example 7.2.4

As part of an investigation into the market for fast personal computer systems the information technology director has found the following data on the price of machines.

**Table 7.12 Prices of personal computers**

| Price class (£) | Frequency |
|---|---|
| 500 and up to 700 | 8 |
| 700 and up to 900 | 12 |
| 900 and up to 1100 | 27 |
| 1100 and up to 1300 | 33 |
| 1300 and up to 1500 | 32 |
| 1500 and up to 1700 | 18 |
| 1700 and up to 1900 | 12 |
| 1900 and up to 2100 | 8 |

a  Draw a cumulative frequency curve and hence estimate the median.
b  Use the cumulative frequency table to estimate the median directly.

## Solution to Example 7.2.4

a  The first step is to form a cumulative frequency table

**Table 7.13 Cumulative frequencies for computer prices**

| Price range (£) | Number of prices (cumulative frequency) |
|---|---|
| Under 700 | 8 |
| Under 900 | 20 |
| Under 1100 | 47 |
| Under 1300 | 80 |
| Under 1500 | 112 |
| Under 1700 | 130 |
| Under 1900 | 142 |
| Under 2100 | 150 |

From this table you can draw an ogive as shown in Fig. 7.6.

The total frequency is 150 and to obtain the median you divide this by 2, giving 75. You then draw a line at the 75 level on the cumulative frequency axis as far as the ogive. By dropping from the ogive to the horizontal axis you obtain the median. Figure 7.6 illustrates the method for obtaining the median. From this figure we can estimate the median as £1250.

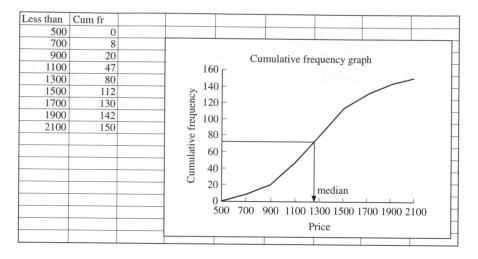

| Less than | Cum fr |
|---|---|
| 500 | 0 |
| 700 | 8 |
| 900 | 20 |
| 1100 | 47 |
| 1300 | 80 |
| 1500 | 112 |
| 1700 | 130 |
| 1900 | 142 |
| 2100 | 150 |

**Figure 7.6** Cumulative frequency graph showing computer prices

To see how a median for grouped data can be calculated, consider again Table 7.13. Because the half-way frequency of 75 is between the frequencies 47 and 80 in the cumulative table, the median must lie between the class boundaries 1100 and 1300 which correspond to those two cumulative frequencies. The class '1100 and under 1300' is called the **median class**. How far into this class you need to go to reach the median is found as that proportion of the class width equal to the proportion of the class frequency that 75 is above 47. Thus you calculate

$$\text{Median} = £1100 + \frac{75-47}{80-47} \times £200 = £1270$$

The median price is £1270.

**Exercises 7.2**

1   The incomes of seven employees are

£14 000    £16 000    £18 000    £11 000    £19 000    £21 000    £18 000

Find the median income. Imagine an eighth employee joins the team and earns an income of £15 000. What is the new value of the median?

2   The frequency table below indicates the ages of 24 lorries possessed by a haulage company.

| Age | Frequency |
|-----|-----------|
| 4 | 2 |
| 5 | 8 |
| 6 | 9 |
| 7 | 4 |
| 8 | 1 |

What is the median age?

3  The sales, each day, of carpets at a warehouse is given below.

8 12 6 7 9 11 12 10 14 9 6 3 4 3 7 9 11 11 12 13 10 9 7 6 8 9 6 5 7 9

Find the median for this data.

4  Table 7.14 shows the values of 40 invoices issued by a firm on a particular day.

**Table 7.14 Values of 40 invoices**

| Invoice value (£) | Frequency |
|-------------------|-----------|
| 20 and under 60 | 1 |
| 60 and under 100 | 6 |
| 100 and under 140 | 6 |
| 140 and under 180 | 10 |
| 180 and under 220 | 8 |
| 220 and under 300 | 9 |

Estimate the median.

## 7.3 Mode

The third type of average is the **mode** which is used to indicate the value (or type) that occurs most often. The mode is an 'average' in the sense that it is the most common.

You find the mode by counting the number of times each value occurs and then selecting the value with the highest frequency. For example, the numbers

4, 8, 12, 10, 7, 5, 8, 14, 20

have a mode equal to 8 because it occurs twice and no other number occurs that often. You can only use the MODE function in EXCEL if the spread-sheet contains the discrete raw data. It will not work if the data has already been grouped into classes. It is therefore probably unwise to use the MODE function in EXCEL.

## Example 7.3.1

A worker at a post office keeps a record of the postage stamps sold at his branch. In one day 160 postage stamps were sold to its customers. The cost and frequency of each is shown in Table 7.15. Determine the mode.

**Table 7.15 Type and frequency of postage stamps**

| Type of postage stamp | Frequency |
|---|---|
| 20p | 45 |
| 26p | 64 |
| 31p | 10 |
| 37p | 4 |
| 44p | 2 |
| 50p | 7 |
| 100p | 18 |

## Solution to Example 7.3.1

The postage stamp most frequently bought is that which costs 26p. This is the mode.

The mode of a set of grouped data is usually found graphically from a histogram. Having drawn the histogram your first step is to find the **modal class**. For data where all classes have the same class width this is the class with the largest frequency, while if class widths differ you need the class for which the frequency density is highest, where

$$\text{Frequency density} = \frac{\text{Frequency}}{\text{Class width}}$$

Consider again the data on computer prices as shown originally in Table 7.12.

| Price class (£) | Frequency |
|---|---|
| 500–700 | 8 |
| 700–900 | 12 |
| 900–1100 | 27 |
| 1100–1300 | 33 |
| 1300–1500 | 32 |
| 1500–1700 | 18 |
| 1700–1900 | 12 |
| 1900–2100 | 8 |

Figure 7.7 shows the histogram for this data, together with the construction on the block corresponding to the modal class. From the definition of the modal class you should see that it always corresponds to the tallest block of the histogram.

The construction involves joining the corners of the top of the modal class with the tops of the neighbouring classes, and dropping a vertical line from the point of intersection of the two diagonal lines to meet the horizontal axis. Here, our estimate of the mode is £1270.

In the case where the neighbouring column on the left of the modal class is taller than the one on the right the mode is smaller than the midpoint of the modal class, while in cases such as this example, where the neighbouring column on the right is taller, the mode will be larger than the modal class midpoint.

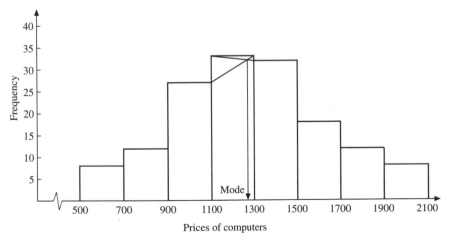

**Figure 7.7** Determination of the mode using a histogram

The mode has intuitive appeal as a measure of average in that it is the most typical value in a set. The value it takes will, for ungrouped data, be one which actually occurs in the set and will be plausible as the centre of the data. Also the mode for ungrouped data requires no calculation. A further merit of the mode is that it can be used for data which is not even numerical. For example, you might wish to find the mode for the colour of a car. You could say that the modal car colour is blue, but it would make no sense to talk about a mean colour or a median colour. In some situations where numbers are used they are little more than descriptions and therefore the mode would again be the most appropriate summary measure. An example of such a situation would be in respect of shoe sizes.

To see the greatest problem involved with the mode, consider the situation where we had to find the mode of the numbers

6, 3, 9, 15, 3, 7, 9, 10

Both 3 and 9 have a claim to be the mode because they both occur twice and no other number occurs more than once. This data is **bimodal**. More generally, there could be several modes, and the data would then be described as **multimodal**.

You have seen how the mean, median and mode can be obtained from a set of numbers. All three of these measures can be used to indicate the 'average' of the numbers in their different meanings. Consequently the word 'average' might lead to confusion if the type of average is not indicated. Consider the following example.

## Example 7.3.2

The annual income of 20 households in one street is shown in Table 7.16. In each case the annual income is recorded to the nearest £100.

**Table 7.16 Annual incomes (£)**

| | | | | |
|---|---|---|---|---|
| 5 400 | 6 000 | 6 000 | 6 300 | 6 600 |
| 7 200 | 7 500 | 9 000 | 9 000 | 9 000 |
| 9 600 | 10 200 | 10 800 | 12 000 | 12 000 |
| 13 500 | 14 400 | 15 000 | 18 000 | 22 500 |

Determine **a** the mean;   **b** the median;   **c** the mode.
Explain why the mean gives the highest of the three values.

### Solution to Example 7.3.2

**a**    The total of all annual incomes is

$$\Sigma x = 5400 + 6000 + 6000 + \ldots + 22\,500 = 210\,000$$

The mean income $= \dfrac{210\,000}{20} = £10\,500$

**b**    The incomes are already in ascending order.

The median income $= \dfrac{9000 + 9600}{2} = £9300$

**c**    The income that occurs most frequently, and hence the mode, is £9000.

These three values are all different, emphasizing the need for clarity when using the term 'average'. You notice that the mean gives the highest of the three values. This is because it is strongly influenced by the two highest values in the data set whereas the median and mode are not influenced in this way. As pointed out in Chapter 6, income distributions are often positively skewed leading to a higher arithmetic mean.

**Exercises 7.3**

1    Find the mode of the following set of data:

5 4 2 7 3 4 6 2 9 8 2 4 1 3 5 7 4 9 8 6 4 2 9 8 7 6 6 4 3 4

2    The table below indicates the colour of car passing a particular point in a one-hour interval.
     Which colour was most common?

| Colour | Frequency |
|--------|-----------|
| Blue   | 32        |
| Red    | 51        |
| Black  | 8         |
| White  | 15        |
| Green  | 20        |

3    A shop sells 2 pairs of shoes size 6, 7 pairs of size 8, 8 pairs of size 9, 4 pairs of size 10 and 1 pair of size 11. State the modal size of shoe sold.

4   The following table, originally Table 7.14, shows the values of 40 invoices issued by a firm on a particular day.

| Invoice value (£) | Frequency |
|---|---|
| 20 and under 60 | 1 |
| 60 and under 100 | 6 |
| 100 and under 140 | 6 |
| 140 and under 180 | 10 |
| 180 and under 220 | 8 |
| 220 and under 300 | 9 |

Construct a histogram from this data and hence estimate the mode.

## Further Exercises

1   Eight different tour operations organize a seven-day holiday to a certain hotel in a Spanish holiday resort. The quoted price of each of these holidays in £s is

384,    396,    354,    387,    389,    399,    355,    360

Determine the mean price of a tour to this hotel.

    A. 378        B. 382        C. 387        D. 388

2   At eight performances of a play in a week the numbers present were

873    681    752    942    621    826    1036    1092

Determine the median attendance per performance.

    A. 749.5        B. 826        C. 849.5        D. 873

3   A footwear shop sells sports shoes in whole sizes only. One summer, 260 pairs of sports shoes were sold at this shop. A breakdown of the shoe sizes sold can be seen in Table 7.17. What is the modal size of shoe?

**Table 7.17 Frequency table of shoe sizes**

| Shoe size | Frequency |
|---|---|
| 3 | 8 |
| 4 | 12 |
| 5 | 25 |
| 6 | 43 |
| 7 | 65 |
| 8 | 57 |
| 9 | 32 |
| 10 | 18 |

A. 6            B. 6.5            C. 7            D. 8

4   Brian travelled to work by car. His journey times, in minutes, over a three-week period are shown in Table 7.18.

**Table 7.18 Journey times (minutes)**

|  | Mon | Tues | Wed | Thurs | Fri |
|---|---|---|---|---|---|
| Week 1 | 42 | 38 | 39 | 36 | 47 |
| Week 2 | 43 | 41 | 35 | 38 | 44 |
| Week 3 | 41 | 36 | 37 | 39 | 42 |

Determine the median

A. 38            B. 39            C. 41            D. 42

5   Sales of product X in May and June were 70 units and 50 units respectively. The mean of monthly sales for the period January to April was 48 units per month. What is the mean of monthly sales for the period January to June?

A. 48            B. 52            C. 54            D. 56

6   The arithmetic mean of nine numbers is 20. When a tenth number is added the overall mean becomes 21. What is the value of this new number?

A. 21            B. 25            C. 29            D. 30

7   The transport manager has recorded the following daily distances travelled by vehicles in the department.

| Distances travelled per day (miles) | | |
| --- | --- | --- |
| At least | Less than | Frequency |
| 0 | 10 | 5 |
| 10 | 20 | 12 |
| 20 | 30 | 16 |
| 30 | 40 | 11 |
| 40 | 50 | 6 |

What is the mean distance travelled per day?

A. 24.6 miles     B. 25.2 miles     C. 27.8 miles     D. 28.2 miles

8   The number of breakdowns last month of seven different machines was as follows:

3,    7,    8,    5,    9,    12,    6

What is the median?

A. 6                B. 7                C. 8                D. 9

*Information for Questions 9 and 10*
The number of jobs held by a group of young people since leaving school is as follows:

| Number of jobs | Frequency |
| --- | --- |
| 0 | 3 |
| 1 | 7 |
| 2 | 14 |
| 3 | 12 |
| 4 | 9 |
| 5 | 3 |
| 6 | 2 |

9   What is the median number of jobs held since leaving school?

A. 1                B. 2                C. 3                D. 4

10 What is the mode of the number of jobs held since leaving school?

  A. 1                B. 2                C. 3                D. 4

11 Petrol prices (per litre) at twelve different garages in a given town centre were

  67.9p,   65.5p,   64.9p,   69.9p,   68.2p,   67.9p
  68.9p,   66.3p,   67.5p,   67.9p,   66.6p,   68.7p

Determine **a** the mean, **b** the median, **c** the mode.
Which of these averages do you think is the most appropriate?

12 An analysis of sales invoices outstanding at the end of December is as follows:

| Invoice value | | |
| --- | --- | --- |
| At least (£) | Less than (£) | Number of invoices |
| 10 | 30 | 6 |
| 30 | 50 | 17 |
| 50 | 70 | 26 |
| 70 | 90 | 23 |
| 90 | 110 | 15 |
| 110 | 130 | 11 |
| 130 | 150 | 2 |

Estimate **a** the mean, **b** the median, **c** the mode, and compare their values.

13 The following frequency distribution shows the number of times 120 machines have broken down in the last year:

| Number of breakdowns | Number of machines |
| --- | --- |
| 5 | 8 |
| 6 | 17 |
| 7 | 40 |
| 8 | 32 |
| 9 | 16 |
| 10 | 7 |

Find **a** the mean, **b** the median, **c** the mode.

14  The average monthly earnings of 200 employees working for Tritown Ltd were shown in Table 7.9

| Monthly earnings (£) | Number of employees |
|---|---|
| 400 and under 600 | 24 |
| 600 and under 800 | 50 |
| 800 and under 1000 | 64 |
| 1000 and under 1200 | 42 |
| 1200 and under 1400 | 20 |

Estimate the median monthly earnings for these 200 employees and compare with the mean, as found in Exercise 7.1.4.

## Chapter Eight

# Spread

## 8.1 Range

In the last chapter we used three measures of centrality or average, the mean, median and mode, to describe and summarize a set of data. You often need to provide additional information to indicate how closely the data is concentrated about the average.

Suppose you want to compare the average weekly earnings (£) of sales representatives in two companies, Acme and Benley. Table 8.1 shows the earnings for 10 sales representatives in each company.

**Table 8.1 Earnings of sales representatives**

| Acme   | 230 | 240 | 240 | 260 | 220 | 250 | 280 | 250 | 260 | 270 |
|--------|-----|-----|-----|-----|-----|-----|-----|-----|-----|-----|
| Benley | 230 | 220 | 280 | 150 | 200 | 300 | 240 | 270 | 260 | 350 |

You can calculate the mean to be £250 in each case. However, the weekly incomes for Acme are much more concentrated about the mean. Therefore the mean of £250 is more typical of the weekly earnings for Acme. In other words, the mean of Benley earnings is less reliable than that of Acme as an indication of a typical value. Figure 8.1 illustrates the differences in variability graphically between the two companies.

One of the simplest measures of spread is the **range**, which is the difference between the largest value and the smallest.

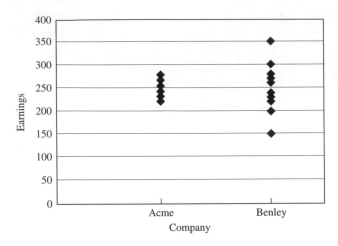

**Figure 8.1** Company earnings of two companies

For the Acme company you can see that the largest observed value is £280 and the smallest is £220. The 10 weekly wages range between £220 and £280. In statistical terms

Range = 280 − 220 = £60

In the Benley company

Range = 350 − 150 = £200

This illustrates that the weekly earnings of the Benley employees seem to be more spread out compared with the other company.

The spreadsheet EXCEL does not directly have a RANGE command, but it does have commands that find the minimum and maximum values of a data set, and so the range can be found by subtracting these two values, as shown in Fig. 8.2.

## Example 8.1.1

A major oil company is considering the inclusion of an additive in its petrol in order to increase the number of miles per litre obtainable by a certain make of car. Under test at the moment are two additives, Xtra and Yper, which are available from different suppliers. To test the performance of the two additives an independent agency tests five cars with each additive, all

| | Acme | Benley |
|---|---|---|
| | 230 | 230 |
| | 240 | 220 |
| | 240 | 280 |
| | 260 | 150 |
| | 220 | 200 |
| | 250 | 300 |
| | 280 | 240 |
| | 250 | 270 |
| | 260 | 260 |
| | 270 | 350 |
| MIN | **220** | **150** |
| MAX | **280** | **350** |
| RANGE | **60** | **200** |

**Figure 8.2** EXCEL spreadsheet calculating range of earnings

cars being of the same make, type and size. The results are presented in the table below.

| Table 8.2 Mileage per litre | |
|---|---|
| Xtra | Yper |
| 10.4 | 10.7 |
| 10.7 | 11.3 |
| 10.7 | 9.9 |
| 10.6 | 10.5 |
| 10.6 | 10.1 |

For each additive find

**a**    the mean mileage per litre and
**b**    the range

and interpret your answers.

## Solution to Example 8.1.1

For Xtra, the mean is 10.6 miles per litre and the range is $10.7 - 10.4 = 0.3$
For Yper, the mean is 10.5 miles per litre and the range is $11.3 - 9.9 = 1.4$

It appears that, on average, Xtra gives an increased mileage per litre and that this additive yields more consistent results. Clearly samples of size 5 are far too small to make conclusive statements.

You see that the calculation of the range is easy but this measure uses only the extreme values within the data set. Small changes to other values will not affect the range. For this reason, the range tends not to be used in practical statistical analysis. An important exception to this last point is in small sample quality control, where use is made of small random samples of constant size (typically four to five items) to identify if some measured dimension is under control.

**Exercises 8.1**   1   Find the range of each of the following small data sets:

a 3,   7,   2,   9,   12,   4,   13
b 0,   1,   2,   4,   2
c 8,   18,   15,   27,   32,   16

2   The following data were obtained from a manufacturing process each day for a week.

| Monday    | 40, | 41, | 42, | 44 |
|-----------|-----|-----|-----|----|
| Tuesday   | 44, | 38, | 41, | 40 |
| Wednesday | 39, | 41, | 43, | 40 |
| Thursday  | 38, | 40, | 45, | 41 |
| Friday    | 40, | 43, | 37, | 36 |

For each day calculate the mean and range of the process and comment on its stability.

## 8.2 Standard Deviation

The previous section illustrated the need for a measure of **spread** for data, but indicated that the range is not always a suitable measure. The most common measure of spread in statistics is the **standard deviation**. The standard deviation uses all the available data to measure the variation within a set of data and is based on the differences of the data values from the mean. The more spread out the data, the greater the differences are and the higher is the measure of spread. Thus a low standard deviation indicates that the data is concentrated tightly around the mean.

The standard deviation for a set of data is defined as

$$s = \sqrt{\{\Sigma(x - \bar{x})^2/n\}}$$

To use the formula, you must first calculate the mean and then for each data value:

a    subtract the mean, $\bar{x}$, to give $x - \bar{x}$
b    square $(x - \bar{x})$ to give $(x - \bar{x})^2$.

You then add together the values of $(x - \bar{x})^2$ for each data value and divide by $n$, the number of data values. Finally, you take the square root to give the standard deviation. A table is often used to help to perform the calculation. We use an example to illustrate the calculation.

## Example 8.2.1

The mileages recorded for a sample of company vehicles during a given week yielded the following data:

164    132    125    157    158    147    148    144    126    179

a    Determine the mean and standard deviation.
b    The data below now becomes available on the mileages of the six other cars belonging to the company.

234    267    179    260    198    230

Recalculate the mean and standard deviation and comment on the changes to these values.

## Solution to Example 8.2.1

a    The mean of 10 mileages are

$$(164 + 132 + 125 + 157 + 158 + 147 + 148 + 144 + 126 + 179)/10$$

$$= 1480/10$$

$$= 148$$

The first data item is 164. Therefore we have

$$(x - \bar{x}) = 164 - 148 = 16$$

which gives us

$$(x - \bar{x})^2 = (16)^2 = (16) \times (16) = 256$$

This process is repeated for each data item. The table below shows the calculations involved.

| $x$ | $(\bar{x})$ | $(x - \bar{x})$ | $(x - \bar{x})^2$ |
|---|---|---|---|
| 164 | 148 | 16 | 256 |
| 132 | 148 | −16 | 256 |
| 125 | 148 | −23 | 529 |
| 157 | 148 | 9 | 81 |
| 158 | 148 | 10 | 100 |
| 147 | 148 | −1 | 1 |
| 148 | 148 | 0 | 0 |
| 144 | 148 | −4 | 16 |
| 126 | 148 | −22 | 484 |
| 179 | 148 | 31 | 961 |
| | | | Total = 2684 |

The standard deviation for the mileages is

$$s = \sqrt{(2684/10)}$$
$$= \sqrt{268.4}$$
$$= 16.38 \text{ miles}$$

**b**   When the other six cars are added the mean of the 16 cars is

$$2848/16 = 178 \text{ miles}$$

The standard deviation is

$$s = \sqrt{(32570/16)}$$
$$= \sqrt{2035.625}$$
$$= 45.12 \text{ miles}$$

You can see from the means that the additional six cars have increased the mean mileage by 30 miles per car. Also the additional six cars have substantially increased the spread of the mileages; that is, they are more widely spread around the mean.

The standard deviation is in practice a very important measure of spread because of its mathematical properties, which allow valuable results to be readily deduced. The mean and standard deviation together provide a powerful summary of a set of data. Note that the standard deviation is never a negative number. This is because $\Sigma(x - \bar{x})^2$ is a sum of terms which is always greater than or equal to zero, and the standard deviation is defined as the positive square root of this sum.

EXCEL has a function that calculates directly the standard deviation of a set of values. The required command that calculates the standard deviation, in the form described in this chapter, of 10 numbers in the cells A1 ... A10 is

$$= \text{Stdevp (A1:A10)}$$

## Example 8.2.2

The temperature of an industrial process is measured at ten different times during the day. The results are as follows (in °C)

    38.0   37.7   38.6   37.0   36.8   37.4   38.8   37.5   37.8   38.4

Find the mean and standard deviation.

## Solution to Example 8.2.2

The mean temperature is $\bar{x} = (38.0 + 37.7 + \ldots + 38.4)/10$
$$= 37.8$$

| $x$ | $(\bar{x})$ | $(x - \bar{x})$ | $(x - \bar{x})^2$ |
|------|------|------|------|
| 38.0 | 37.8 | 0.2 | 0.04 |
| 37.7 | 37.8 | − 0.1 | 0.01 |
| 38.6 | 37.8 | 0.8 | 0.64 |
| 37.0 | 37.8 | − 0.8 | 0.64 |
| 36.8 | 37.8 | − 1.0 | 1.00 |
| 37.4 | 37.8 | − 0.4 | 0.16 |
| 38.8 | 37.8 | 1.0 | 1.00 |
| 37.5 | 37.8 | − 0.3 | 0.09 |
| 37.8 | 37.8 | 0.0 | 0.00 |
| 38.4 | 37.8 | 0.6 | 0.36 |
| | | Total = | 3.94 |

$$s = \sqrt{(3.94/10)}$$
$$= \sqrt{0.394}$$
$$= 0.63$$

| | A | B | C | D | E |
|---|---|---|---|---|---|
| 1 | 38 | 37.4 | 38.6 | 37 | 36.8 |
| 2 | 37.4 | 38.8 | 37.5 | 37.8 | 38.4 |
| 3 | FORMULAE | | | RESULTS | |
| 4 | mean = | = AVERAGE (A1:E2) | | 37.77 | |
| 5 | st dev = | = ST DEVP (A1:E2) | | 0.64 | |

**Figure 8.3** EXCEL spreadsheet showing standard deviation formula for raw data

Figure 8.3 gives the printout from an EXCEL spreadsheet showing the mean and standard deviation.

It is useful to know that there are different formulae for finding the standard deviation of a set of data. A well-used formula, which gives the same answer as that given by the current approach is

$$s = \sqrt{\{\Sigma x^2/n - \bar{x}^2\}}$$

where $\Sigma x^2$ is the sum of squares of all the numbers in the data set. This formula is generally easier and quicker to use, particularly when the mean is not an easy-to-use whole number.

For the data of Example 8.2.2 the mean $\bar{x} = 37.8$, and

$$\Sigma x^2 = 38.0^2 + 37.7^2 + 38.6^2 + 37.0^2 + 36.8^2 + 37.4^2$$
$$+ 38.8^2 + 37.5^2 + 37.8^2 + 38.4^2$$
$$= 14292.34$$

Consequently, the standard deviation is

$$\sqrt{\{14292.34/10 - 37.8^2\}}$$
$$= \sqrt{\{1429.234 - 1428.84\}}$$
$$= \sqrt{0.394}$$
$$= 0.63$$

which agrees with the answer given by the alternative approach. It is particularly important to keep as much accuracy as possible when using this latter approach for calculating the standard deviation.

Looking at Example 8.2.1 again, this latter approach also gives the same answers as that given earlier.

Here the data set for the first 10 cars was 164, 132, 125, 157, 158, 147, 148, 144, 126, and 179 with a mean of 148. The standard deviation could have been calculated using

$$\Sigma x^2 = 164^2 + 132^2 + \ldots + 179^2 = 221\,724$$
$$s = \sqrt{\{221724/10 - 148^2\}}$$
$$= \sqrt{\{22172.4 - 21904\}}$$
$$= \sqrt{268.4} = 16.38$$

A major advantage of using this formula is that when data for the additional six cars is available, we don't have to start the whole calculation again from the beginning. It is only necessary to add the extra $x^2$ values into $\Sigma x^2$ and the extra $x$ values into $\Sigma x$.

The standard deviation for grouped data is defined by an extension of the ungrouped definition in the same way as we have seen the group mean defined by extension of the ungrouped mean. That is to say, we behave as if every member of a class were equal to the midpoint of that class and then proceed as for the ungrouped case. Consider the data in Table 8.3, which shows, for one machine, the number of rejects in each successive period of five minutes.

**Table 8.3 The number of rejects in successive 5-minute periods**

| Number of rejects | Number of periods |
| --- | --- |
| 0–4 | 2 |
| 5–9 | 5 |
| 10–14 | 8 |
| 15–19 | 9 |
| 20–24 | 13 |
| 25–29 | 8 |
| 30–34 | 5 |
| | 50 |

The calculation of both the mean and standard deviation is based on assuming that 2 periods have 2 rejects, 5 periods have 7 rejects, 8 periods have 12 rejects, etc. Thus we emerge with the formula

$$s = \sqrt{\{\Sigma(x - \overline{x})^2 f / \Sigma f\}}$$

It is again usual to set out the calculation in tabular form. Firstly the mean has to be found:

| Number of rejects | Midpoint, $x$ | Frequency, $f$ | $xf$ |
|---|---|---|---|
| 0–4 | 2 | 2 | 4 |
| 5–9 | 7 | 5 | 35 |
| 10–14 | 12 | 8 | 96 |
| 15–19 | 17 | 9 | 153 |
| 20–24 | 22 | 13 | 286 |
| 25–29 | 27 | 8 | 216 |
| 30–34 | 32 | 5 | 160 |
| | | 50 | 950 |

The mean is $\bar{x} = 950/50 = 19$ rejects.
Then we can find the standard deviation.

| $x$ | $x - \bar{x}$ | $(x - \bar{x})^2$ | $f$ | $(x - \bar{x})^2 f$ |
|---|---|---|---|---|
| 2 | −17 | 289 | 2 | 578 |
| 7 | −12 | 144 | 5 | 720 |
| 12 | −7 | 49 | 8 | 392 |
| 17 | −2 | 4 | 9 | 36 |
| 22 | 3 | 9 | 13 | 117 |
| 27 | 8 | 64 | 8 | 512 |
| 32 | 13 | 169 | 5 | 845 |
| | | | 50 | 3200 |

$$s = \sqrt{3200/50}$$
$$= \sqrt{64}$$
$$= 8.0$$

As with individual values there is an alternative formula for finding the standard deviation of grouped data. This formula is often called the computational formula because it is generally easier to use. This computational formula is

$$s = \sqrt{\{(\Sigma x^2 f / \Sigma f) - (\bar{x})^2\}}$$

This formula is used in the next example.

## Example 8.2.3

The time when a computer is out of action due to breakdown or failure is called 'downtime'. Table 8.4 shows the downtimes (in minutes) of a computer for the last 100 working days.

**Table 8.4 Downtimes for the last 100 days**

| Downtimes | Number of days |
|---|---|
| 0–10 | 5 |
| 10–20 | 12 |
| 20–30 | 25 |
| 30–40 | 30 |
| 40–60 | 20 |
| 60–120 | 8 |

Estimate the mean and standard deviation.

## *Solution to Example 8.2.3*

| Downtime | Midpoint, $x$ | Frequency, $f$ | $xf$ . | $x^2 f$ |
|---|---|---|---|---|
| 0–10 | 5 | 5 | 25 | 125 |
| 10–20 | 15 | 12 | 180 | 2700 |
| 20–30 | 25 | 25 | 625 | 15 625 |
| 30–40 | 35 | 30 | 1050 | 36 750 |
| 40–60 | 50 | 20 | 1000 | 50 000 |
| 60–120 | 90 | 8 | 720 | 64 800 |
|  |  | 100 | 3600 | 170 000 |

$$\text{Mean downtime} = \frac{3600}{100} = 36 \text{ minutes}$$

$$\text{Standard deviation} = \sqrt{\left\{ \frac{170\,000}{100} - (36)^2 \right\}}$$

$$= \sqrt{\{1700 - 1296\}}$$

$$= \sqrt{404} = 20.1$$

| | A | B | C | D | E | E |
|---|---|---|---|---|---|---|
| 1 | Lo class | Up class | Frequency | Midpoint | xf | x2f |
| 2 | 0 | 4 | 2 | = (A2+B2)/2 | = C2*D2 | = D2*E2 |
| 3 | 5 | 9 | 5 | = (A3+B3)/2 | = C3*D3 | = D3*E3 |
| 4 | 10 | 14 | 8 | = (A4+B4)/2 | = C4*D4 | = D4*E4 |
| 5 | 15 | 19 | 9 | = (A5+B5)/2 | = C5*D5 | = D5*E5 |
| 6 | 20 | 24 | 13 | = (A6+B6)/2 | = C6*D6 | = D6*E6 |
| 7 | 25 | 29 | 8 | = (A7+B7)/2 | = C7*D7 | = D7*E7 |
| 8 | 30 | 34 | 5 | = (A8+B8)/2 | = C8*D8 | = D8*E8 |
| 9 | | | = SUM (C2:C8) | | = SUM(E2:E8) | = SUM(F2:F8) |
| 10 | | | | | | |
| 11 | | mean = | = E9/C9 | | | |
| 12 | | st dev = | = SQRT(F9/C9-(C11*C11)) | | | |

**Figure 8.4** EXCEL spreadsheet showing standard deviation formula for grouped data

There is no direct way to compute the standard deviation of grouped data using EXCEL, but the calculations can be carried out using appropriate formulae. Figure 8.4 shows this latter formula to find the mean and standard deviation for the data given in Table 8.3.

You often need to consider the variation in two sets of data whose items are measured in different units, or are of different sizes. Suppose that you are asked to compare the variability of sets of salaries; for example, the weekly earnings of a group of workers in the United Kingdom and a group of workers in the same profession in the United States. The values of the standard deviation may not be meaningful, even if the data is measured on a common scale (e.g. pounds or dollars). If the two data sets have mean values of £120 and £250 respectively, and they both have a standard deviation of £25, then in relative terms the spread of the second data set is less than that of the first.

We are able to compare the spread (or variability) of the data set by considering the spread in the data relative to the mean. The coefficient of variation, $CV$, is defined as the standard deviation divided by the mean, and is often expressed as a percentage; that is, it is calculated as

$$CV = \frac{\text{Standard deviation}}{\text{Mean}} \times 100\%$$

## Example 8.2.4

You wish to compare the day-to-day variabilities in mileage and petrol consumption for a travelling sales representative. The mileages per day have a mean of 200 miles with a standard deviation of 30 miles, while the petrol consumption has a daily mean consumption of 25 litres and a standard deviation of 6 litres. Calculate the coefficient of variation for both mileage and petrol consumption.

### Solution to Example 8.2.4

With the given information it is difficult to compare the variability in mileage and petrol consumption. You can calculate the coefficients of variation to aid the comparison.

For mileage:

$$\text{Coefficient of variation} = \frac{30}{200} \times 100\% = 15\%$$

that is, the standard deviation is 15% of the mean.

For petrol consumption:

$$\text{Coefficient of variation} = \frac{6}{25} \times 100\% = 24\%$$

This indicates a greater variability in petrol consumption than in mileage.

## Example 8.2.5

A small engineering firm has recorded the bonuses paid to its nine work-shop staff:

£17   £12   £24   £8   £10   £20   £25   £16   £30

Determine the mean, standard deviation and coefficient of variation.

### Solution to Example 8.2.5

$n = 9$ and the mean is $162/9 = £18$. If $x$ represents bonus payments,

$$\Sigma x^2 = 17^2 + 12^2 + 24^2 + 8^2 + 10^2 + 20^2 + 25^2 + 16^2 + 30^2 = 3354$$

The standard deviation is

$$\sqrt{\{3354/9 - 18^2\}}$$
$$= \sqrt{\{372.6667 - 324\}}$$
$$= \sqrt{48.6667}$$
$$= £6.98$$

The coefficient of variation is $\dfrac{6.98}{18} \times 100\% = 39\%$

**Exercises 8.2**   1   The earnings (£ per week) of ten employees of department A are

237   245   283   296   253   249   236   254   305   242

Given that the employees of department B have a mean weekly wage of £366 and a standard deviation of £29, compare the earnings of the two departments.

2   A company has two factories situated in two different parts of the country. Managerial turnover in Factory Y is much higher than in Factory X, and a possible cause of this is the greater inequality of income in Factory Y. The following data are collected:

| Factory | Mean income | Standard deviation |
|---------|-------------|--------------------|
| X       | £15 000     | £5 000             |
| Y       | £20 000     | £15 000            |

Calculate the coefficient of variation for each factory. What would you conclude?

3   In April 1999 a survey of customer transaction values was carried out by a retail business. The following data was collected:

| Transaction value | Number of customers |
|-------------------|---------------------|
| Below £1.00       | 137                 |
| £1.00–£1.99       | 259                 |
| £2.00–£2.99       | 297                 |
| £3.00–£3.99       | 378                 |
| £4.00–£4.99       | 193                 |
| £5.00–£5.99       | 84                  |
| £6.00–£8.00       | 52                  |

a   For the above data calculate:
   • the mean transaction value
   • the standard deviation.

b   A similar survey had been carried out two years previously. The resulting data gave a mean transaction value of £2.79 and a standard deviation of £1.43. Comment on how the spending pattern has changed between the two years.

4    A quality control inspector found the following number of defective parts on eight different days on an assembly line production

    3   10   8   9   6   10   12   6

Calculate the mean and standard deviation.

## 8.3 Quartiles

Just as the mean can be unduly influenced by values that are not really typical of the data, so can the standard deviation. In this section we look at measures that help to indicate the spread of the data in situations where the median might be used as a measure of average. Examples of these situations include the comparison of groups of salaries (where the mean and standard deviation may be influenced by a few people with particularly high incomes). **Quartiles**, and in particular the **quartile deviation**, would normally be used to compare the spread of such data sets.

From the previous chapter we know that the median is the figure which has half the data values below it and half above. In a similar way the quartiles are the quarter points of the data. The **first quartile**, denoted $Q1$, has 25% of the data below it and 75% above, and the **third quartile**, denoted $Q3$, has 75% below it and 25% above. Figure 8.5 illustrates the position of the quartiles.

**Figure 8.5** Quartiles

Having found $Q1$ and $Q3$ an established measure of spread is the quartile deviation, which is defined as

$$\text{Quartile deviation} = \frac{Q3 - Q1}{2}$$

Essentially $Q3 - Q1$ measures the range of the middle half of the data, that is, the range of the data where the smallest quarter and the largest quarter of the data values are removed. Unlike the standard deviation, the quartile deviation is not influenced by any **extreme values** in the data.

For ungrouped data values, it is necessary to calculate the median first. The first quartile, $Q1$, is defined to be the median of the data below the median and the third quartile, $Q3$, is defined to be the median of the data above the median. For example, consider the data set with 15 items arranged in order:

$$5, \ 7, \ 8, \ 9, \ 9, \ 10, \ 12, \ 14, \ 15, \ 17, \ 20, \ 21, \ 25, \ 32, \ 50$$
$$\uparrow$$
$$\text{Median} = 14$$

The median is the 8th value, 14. Now we find the median of the two data sets either side of the median:

$$5, \ 7, \ 8, \ 9, \ 9, \ 10, \ 12 \qquad\qquad 15, \ 17, \ 20, \ 21, \ 25, \ 32, \ 50$$
$$\uparrow \qquad\qquad\qquad\qquad\qquad \uparrow$$
$$Q1 = 9 \qquad\qquad\qquad\qquad\qquad Q3 = 21$$

The quartile deviation is, therefore, $\text{QD} = \dfrac{21 - 9}{2} = 6$

However, the quartiles and the quartile deviation are more usually employed for grouped data, where the quartiles are found in a similar way to the median, that is, by drawing lines at the 25% and 75% cumulative frequency levels on the ogive and dropping to the horizontal axis (or by calculating the appropriate distance across the classes containing the quartiles).

## Example 8.3.1

Consider again the data of Example 8.2.3 describing the downtime of a computer for 100 consecutive days.

| Downtime (mins) | Number of days | Cumulative frequency |
|---|---|---|
| 0–10 | 5 | 5 |
| 10–20 | 12 | 17 |
| 20–30 | 25 | 42 |
| 30–40 | 30 | 72 |
| 40–60 | 20 | 92 |
| 60–120 | 8 | 100 |

Use an ogive to estimate the values for the first quartile, $Q1$, and the third quartile, $Q3$. Hence estimate the quartile deviation.

## Solution to Example 8.3.1

Figure 8.6 shows an ogive for this data; for example, on 42 days the downtime is less than 30 minutes. As described in Chapter 6 the ogive is a plot of the cumulative frequencies against the upper class boundaries. The points are joined to allow estimation between the points.

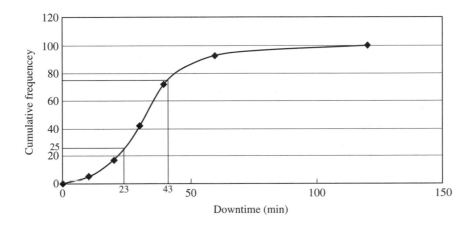

**Figure 8.6** Ogive for computer downtime

To obtain the quartiles, $Q1$ and $Q3$, the lines relative to the 25th and 75th data values can be read off the ogive.

The estimates of $Q1$ and $Q3$ are 23 minutes and 43 minutes respectively.

$$\text{The quartile deviation is } QD = \frac{43 - 23}{2} = 10.$$

The quartile deviation has similar properties to the median. It does not use all the available data and does not therefore represent the full set of values. This can be advantageous if some extreme observations are thought to be untypical of the data set. For this reason the quartile deviation is usually used when the data does contain extreme values (such as income data). In addition, the quartile deviation can be used when we do not know all the values; for example, when there are open-ended classes. The standard deviation is generally easier to calculate arithmetically and is used in more advanced statistical applications.

**Exercises 8.3**

1   You have been asked to investigate the price of a particular printer and recommend the choice of supplier. By looking in computer magazines you have found the following range of prices, in £s. Find the quartile deviation for this data set.

| | | | | | | | | | |
|---|---|---|---|---|---|---|---|---|---|
| 299 | 269 | 259 | 275 | 276 | 299 | 249 | 280 | 285 | 295 |
| 260 | 271 | 279 | 275 | 255 | 289 | 275 | 251 | 269 | 249 |
| 289 | 299 | 279 | 275 | 270 | | | | | |

2   The senior partner in your firm has been looking at the market for training courses and has obtained the following data on the cost of one-day courses.

| Cost of course, (£) | Number of courses |
|---|---|
| 25 and up to 75 | 2 |
| 75 and up to 125 | 2 |
| 125 and up to 175 | 28 |
| 175 and up to 225 | 19 |
| 225 and up to 275 | 17 |
| 275 and up to 325 | 18 |
| 325 and up to 425 | 7 |
| 425 and above | 7 |

Draw an ogive for this data. Estimate the median, quartiles and quartile deviation.

3   Determine the quartile deviation from the data given in the table.

| Distance to work (miles) | Frequency |
|---|---|
| Under 1 | 12 |
| 1 and under 3 | 15 |
| 3 and under 5 | 28 |
| 5 and under 10 | 48 |
| 10 and under 20 | 44 |
| 20 and under 30 | 32 |
| 30 and above | 21 |

## Further Exercises

1   The number of breakdowns each day on a section of road were
    recorded for a sample of 8 days.

        7    12    19    14    9    8    15    16

    Determine the standard deviation for this data

        A. 1.2          B. 2.2          C. 4.0          D. 5.7

2   The number of new orders received by a company over the last 25
    working days were recorded as follows:

        8      15     24     20     25     12     16     18
        21     10     12     10     24     20     9      12
        26     21     10     7      12     15     16     14     12

    Determine the quartile deviation.

        A. 3.25         B. 4.75         C. 5.75         D. 7.5

3   The number of faults recorded on a sample of 10 cars is given
    below:

        6    8    2    4    3    5    4    2    8    7

    Determine the coefficient of variation.

        A. 44%          B. 88%          C. 133%         D. 199%

4   The quarterly electricity bills of 20 consumers is recorded in the
    following table.

    | Quarterly electricity bill (£) | Frequency |
    |---|---|
    | 20 and under 40 | 4 |
    | 40 and under 60 | 8 |
    | 60 and under 80 | 5 |
    | 80 and under 100 | 3 |

    Calculate the standard deviation.

        A. 7.5          B. 12.1         C. 14.7         D. 19.3

5    The following table shows the monthly tax payments of 40 employees.

| Monthly tax payment (£) | Frequency |
| --- | --- |
| Under 50 | 4 |
| 50 and under 80 | 6 |
| 80 and under 100 | 15 |
| 100 and under 140 | 10 |
| 140 and under 200 | 5 |

Use an ogive to estimate the quartile deviation.

A. 10            B. 20            C. 30            D. 40

6    The times (in minutes) taken to repair machines of two types are recorded below:

| | | | | | |
| --- | --- | --- | --- | --- | --- |
| Machine type A | 82 | 90 | 100 | 85 | 95 |
| Machine type B | 24 | 30 | 15 | 32 | 40 |

Calculate the mean, standard deviation, and coefficient of variation to compare the repair times of the machine types.

7    A sample of the transfer times of data from an intelligent terminal, in microseconds, are as follows.

| Time (microseconds) | Frequency |
| --- | --- |
| 10 and less than 20 | 6 |
| 20 and less than 30 | 10 |
| 30 and less than 35 | 15 |
| 35 and less than 40 | 12 |
| 40 and less than 45 | 8 |
| 45 and less than 55 | 6 |
| 55 and less than 65 | 3 |

a    Find the mean and standard deviation of the transfer times,
b    Draw an ogive of the data,
c    Using your ogive find the median and quartile deviation.

8 As part of the investigation into the market for fast personal computer systems, the information technology director has found the following data on the price of machines. The data collectors had already processed the data into groups.

| Price | | |
|---|---|---|
| Greater than or equal to (£) | Less than (£) | Frequency |
| 500 | 1000 | 3 |
| 1000 | 1500 | 8 |
| 1500 | 2000 | 12 |
| 2000 | 2500 | 14 |
| 2500 | 3000 | 20 |
| 3000 | 3500 | 11 |
| 3500 | 4500 | 8 |
| 4500 | 5500 | 4 |

a  Calculate the mean and standard deviation of the data.
b  Draw an ogive and hence determine the median and quartile deviation.

9 The data below shows the number of orders which individual sales representatives have secured over the previous month.

| 12 | 15 | 21 | 17 | 22 | 13 | 25 | 21 | 20 | 16 | 12 |
| 15 | 18 | 23 | 21 | 18 | 22 | 10 | 14 |

a  Calculate the mean and standard deviation.
b  Find the median and the quartile deviation.

10 The amount, in £s, spent on food per week by 100 households is given in the following table

| Amount spent (£) | Number of households |
|---|---|
| 20 but under 30 | 5 |
| 30 but under 40 | 12 |
| 40 but under 50 | 15 |
| 50 but under 60 | 24 |
| 60 but under 80 | 20 |
| 80 but under 100 | 15 |
| 100 but under 120 | 9 |

a   Calculate the mean and standard deviation.
b   Determine the coefficient of variation.

## Chapter Nine

# Index Numbers

## 9.1 Price Relatives

Index number calculations are basically percentage calculations, rather like the ones you met in Chapter 2. Index numbers are most commonly associated with measuring changes in prices.

Suppose the price of an item was recorded on 1 January for each of 10 years and resulted in the following set of data:

| Year | 1 | 2 | 3 | 4 | 5 | 6 | 7 | 8 | 9 | 10 |
|------|----|----|----|----|----|----|----|----|----|----|
| Price (£) on 1 Jan | 30 | 35 | 38 | 40 | 42 | 45 | 47 | 50 | 52 | 55 |

A way in which we could look at how prices are changing over the 10 years is to express each of the prices as a proportion of the price at one particular time. Suppose, for the sake of illustration, that year 4 were used for this purpose. The resulting proportions would be as calculated below.

Year 1      30/40 = 0.750
Year 2      35/40 = 0.875
Year 3      38/40 = 0.950
Year 4      40/40 = 1.000
Year 5      42/40 = 1.050
Year 6      45/40 = 1.125
Year 7      47/40 = 1.175
Year 8      50/40 = 1.250
Year 9      52/40 = 1.300
Year 10     55/40 = 1.375

These proportions are called **price relatives**. They tell us the price at the time concerned relative to the price in year 4.

An index number expresses a price change as a percentage rather than as a proportion, so price relatives can be changed into index numbers simply by multiplying by 100:

| Year | 1 | 2 | 3 | 4 | 5 | 6 | 7 | 8 | 9 | 10 |
|------|---|---|---|---|---|---|---|---|---|----|
| Index | 75.0 | 87.5 | 95.0 | 100.0 | 105.0 | 112.5 | 117.5 | 125.0 | 130.0 | 137.5 |

These figures are telling us that the price of the item in year 1 was 75% of the price in year 4, the price in year 2 was 87.5% of the price in year 4, and so on through to year 10 where the price was 137.5% of the price in year 4.

This **index number series** has year 4 as its **base time** because all the prices are expressed as percentages of the year 4 price. The time for which an index value is calculated is called the **given time**. Note that the index value for year 4 is 100 because it is calculated by dividing the year 4 price by itself before multiplying by 100. This would be true of any time that was used as the base time. So we declare the base date for an index number series by using a statement like:

Year 4 = 100

This is the way the base date is declared in published index series.

To **re-base** an index series to a new base year, all we need to do is divide each index value by the index for the new base year and multiply by 100. If in our example we wanted to make year 8 the base year, we would divide each of the index values by 125.0 and multiply by 100.

For year 1 this would give $(75.0 / 125.0) \times 100 = 0.6 \times 100 = 60$
For year 2 it would give $(87.5 / 125.0) \times 100 = 0.7 \times 100 = 70$

The full index series rebased to year 8 is

| Year | 1 | 2 | 3 | 4 | 5 | 6 | 7 | 8 | 9 | 10 |
|------|---|---|---|---|---|---|---|---|---|----|
| Index | 60.0 | 70.0 | 76.0 | 80.0 | 84.0 | 90.0 | 94.0 | 100.0 | 104.0 | 110.0 |

This set of figures gives the price in each of the years as a percentage of the price in year 8. Using the original prices and expressing each of them as a percentage of the year 8 price would have led to the same values.

What we are most often interested in is the year on year percentage changes in prices. We can find these by taking the original prices or the index series with any base year, and expressing each value in the series as a percentage of the preceding one. The earliest time for which this can be done in our example is year 2 as year 1 has no predecessor.

For year 2, using the latest version of the index series above, we have

$$(70.0/60.0) \times 100 = 1.167 \times 100 = 116.7$$

This is saying that the price in year 2 was 116.7% of what it was in year 1, an increase of 16.7%. This is the most important thing to know, as the change in **points** is dependent on when the base time is. Using year 4 as the base time, the change from year 1 to year 2 was

$$87.5 - 75.0 = 12.5 \text{ points}$$

while using year 8 as base it was

$$70.0 - 60.0 = 10 \text{ points}$$

The very simple index numbers considered so far have a useful property called **time reversal**. This means that if we interchange the base time and the given time, then the index value which is calculated still tells the same 'story'.

In the example we have been using a base time of year 4 led to an index value of 125.0 for year 8 as given time. That is to say, the price in year 8 was one and a quarter times the price in year 4. When year 8 was taken as base we found an index value of 80 for year 4 as given time. That is to say, the price in year 4 was four-fifths of the price in year 8.

These two statements are equivalent, showing that we do indeed have time reversal. When dealing with index numbers that are more complicated than just one number divided by another, time reversal is not always achieved. It is desirable if it can be, and if it cannot be achieved exactly, it is important that the calculations the two different ways round do not make substantially different statements.

Index numbers have many uses and they form a large part of the material published by the Office for National Statistics. The **retail prices index (RPI)** is given particular attention as a 'cost of living index' and as a measure of inflation in the economy. Its accuracy and integrity are broadly trusted. (This index is looked at in more detail in Sec. 9.3.) The RPI is used for updating certain Social Security benefits from year to year and for revaluing one form of National Savings certificate. It is also used in determining the size of annual pay awards, particularly in the public sector. The existing value of the item concerned in each case is scaled up by the percentage increase in the index from a year earlier. Similar procedures are used with insurance policies to adjust the amount of cover needed, and hence to increase premiums year by year. For this purpose, however, especially in the case of buildings policies, it is more usual to employ specialised indices, say relating to building costs, rather then the RPI.

Another use of the RPI is to **deflate** a series of figures relating to a sequence of points in time by dividing the figures by the RPI value at a specified time and multiplying by 100. This has the effect of adjusting all the values concerned to prices at the specified time and so allowing a more realistic comparison than is possible with the raw figures.

Suppose we have a set of gross domestic product (GDP) figures for 9 years as shown below in billions of pounds and have also the RPI figures for those years based on year 6:

| Year | 1 | 2 | 3 | 4 | 5 | 6 | 7 | 8 | 9 |
|------|-----|-----|-----|-----|-----|-----|-----|-----|-----|
| GDP | 231 | 255 | 278 | 303 | 323 | 354 | 379 | 414 | 430 |
| RPI | 71 | 79 | 86 | 90 | 94 | 100 | 103 | 108 | 113 |

The GDP series can be deflated to year 6 prices by dividing each of the figures by the RPI for the year concerned, and then multiplying by 100. We obtain the results shown below.

| | |
|--------|------------------------------|
| Year 1 | $231/71 \times 100 = 325.4$ |
| Year 2 | $255/79 \times 100 = 322.8$ |
| Year 3 | $278/86 \times 100 = 323.3$ |
| Year 4 | $303/90 \times 100 = 336.7$ |
| Year 5 | $323/94 \times 100 = 343.6$ |
| Year 6 | $354/100 \times 100 = 354.0$ |
| Year 7 | $379/103 \times 100 = 368.0$ |
| Year 8 | $414/108 \times 100 = 383.3$ |
| Year 9 | $430/113 \times 100 = 380.5$ |

**Exercises 9.1**

1   The price of an item on 1 January in each of seven years was as follows:

| Year | 1 | 2 | 3 | 4 | 5 | 6 | 7 |
|------|-----|-----|-----|-----|-----|-----|-----|
| Price (£) on 1 Jan | 71 | 94 | 114 | 130 | 144 | 172 | 204 |

    **a**  Derive an index number series, for this item using year 2 as the base year.

    **b**  Rebase your index number series found in **a** to year 5 as the base year.

2   The sales revenue for Toytown plc in five consecutive years, together with the RPI is given below:

| Year | 1 | 2 | 3 | 4 | 5 |
|------|------|-------|-------|-------|-------|
| Sales revenue(£million) | 32.5 | 36.9 | 42.7 | 43.4 | 44.2 |
| RPI | 100 | 103.5 | 107.4 | 111.6 | 114.7 |

Deflate the sales revenues to year 1 prices. Comment on the general trend of the company's revenues.

## 9.2 Aggregative Indices

The index number calculations in Sec. 9.1 were very simple because only one item was being considered. In this section we consider the much more usual situation where we need to combine together the changes in prices of several items to arrive at a **composite index**. Consider the following example data relating to daily sales by a small grocer:

|  | January 1997 | | January 1998 | |
|---|---|---|---|---|
|  | Price | Quantity | Price | Quantity |
| Milk | 25p per pt | 6000 pt | 30p per pt | 6250 pt |
| Sugar | 44p per kg | 2300 kg | 59p per kg | 2600 kg |
| Tea | 150p per lb | 1600 lb | 165p per lb | 1800 lb |
| Bread | 35p per loaf | 4200 loaves | 40p per loaf | 4300 loaves |

The principle involved in calculating an aggregative index is to compare in aggregate the prices at the given time with those at the base time. It is not good enough, however, simply to add the prices alone for each of these periods because the differences in the quantities consumed of the different items mean that some must be given more weight than others.

This brings us to the idea of a **weighted aggregative index**.

In order to calculate a weighted aggregative index we need to weight the prices in both the numerator and denominator of the aggregative index calculations with a set of figures for quantities sold. It is essential that the *same* set of quantity weights is used in both the numerator and the denominator so that the resulting value reflects only a price change and is not mixed up with a change in quantities sold as well.

We shall be concentrating on the two main types of weighted aggregative index which are the **Laspeyres** index and the **Paasche** index.

In the Laspeyres index the prices in both the numerator and denominator of the index calculation are weighted by the base time quantities. What this amounts to is calculating:

$$\frac{\text{What the base time quantities would have cost at given time prices}}{\text{What the base time quantities actually cost at base time prices}} \times 100$$

For this example we have

$$\frac{30 \times 6000 + 59 \times 2300 + 165 \times 1600 + 40 \times 4200}{25 \times 6000 + 44 \times 2300 + 150 \times 1600 + 35 \times 4200} \times 100$$

$$= \frac{180\,000 + 135\,700 + 264\,000 + 168\,000}{150\,000 + 101\,200 + 240\,000 + 147\,000} \times 100$$

$$= \frac{747\,700}{638\,200} \times 100 = 117.16$$

In the Paasche index the prices in both the numerator and denominator of the index calculation are weighted by the given time quantities. What this amounts to is calculating

$$\frac{\text{What the given time quantities actually cost at given time prices}}{\text{What the given time quantities would have cost at base time prices}} \times 100$$

For this example we have

$$\frac{30 \times 6250 + 59 \times 2600 + 165 \times 1800 + 40 \times 4300}{25 \times 6250 + 44 \times 2600 + 150 \times 1800 + 35 \times 4300} \times 100$$

$$= \frac{187\,500 + 153\,400 + 297\,000 + 172\,000}{156\,250 + 114\,400 + 270\,000 + 150\,500} \times 100$$

$$= \frac{809\,900}{691\,150} \times 100 = 117.18$$

The layout above is intended to make clear how the Laspeyres and Paasche indices are operating, but from the point of view of actually carrying out calculations it is more efficient to set out the figures in a series of columns. These are shown below for the example data.

| Items | A<br>Base time price | B<br>Base time quant | C<br>Given time price | D<br>Given time quant | C × B | A × B | C × D | A × D |
|-------|------|------|------|------|---------|---------|---------|---------|
| Milk  | 25  | 6000 | 30  | 6250 | 180 000 | 150 000 | 187 500 | 156 250 |
| Sugar | 44  | 2300 | 59  | 2600 | 135 700 | 101 200 | 153 400 | 114 400 |
| Tea   | 150 | 1600 | 165 | 1800 | 264 000 | 240 000 | 297 000 | 270 000 |
| Bread | 35  | 4200 | 40  | 4300 | 168 000 | 147 000 | 172 000 | 150 500 |
|       |     |      |     |      | 747 700 | 638 200 | 809 900 | 691 150 |

Then Laspeyres index $= \dfrac{C \times B}{A \times B} \times 100 = \dfrac{747\,700}{638\,200} \times 100 = 117.16$

and Paasche index $= \dfrac{C \times D}{A \times D} \times 100 = \dfrac{809\,900}{691\,150} \times 100 = 117.18$

This way of laying out the index number calculation also lends itself readily to the use of a spreadsheet. Figure 9.1 shows output from EXCEL obtained by entering the prices and quantities as given above into the first four cells of columns A, B, C and D respectively.

| | A | B | C | D | E | F | G | H |
|---|---|---|---|---|---|---|---|---|
| 1 | 25 | 6000 | 30 | 6250 | 180000 | 150000 | 187500 | 156250 |
| 2 | 44 | 2300 | 59 | 2600 | 135700 | 101200 | 153400 | 114400 |
| 3 | 150 | 1600 | 165 | 1800 | 264000 | 240000 | 297000 | 270000 |
| 4 | 35 | 4200 | 40 | 4300 | 168000 | 147000 | 172000 | 150500 |
| 5 | | | | | 747700 | 638200 | 809900 | 691150 |
| 6 | | | | | | | | |
| 7 | | | | | Laspeyres = 117.1576 | | Paasche = 117.1815 | |

**Figure 9.1** EXCEL spreadsheet output showing the calculation of Laspeyres and Paasche price indices

The figure of 180 000 in cell E1 is then obtained by means of the formula

=**C1\*B1**.

The figures in cells E2, E3 and E4 are then obtained by copying this formula down. Similarly

F1 is obtained as **=A1\*B1** and copied down as far as F4
G1 is obtained as **=C1\*D1** and copied down as far as G4
and H1 is obtained as **=A1\*D1** and copied down as far as H4.

The total in cell E5 is then obtained using **=sum(E1:E4)** and this is copied across to cells F5, G5 and H5.

Then the Laspeyres index calculation, shown in F7, is **=E5/F5\*100** and the Paasche index calculation, shown in H7, is **=G5/H5\*100**

The Laspeyres and Paasche formulae do not have the time reversal property, but the values calculated using January 1998 as base time and January 1997 as given time will actually be found to differ by not very much from the reciprocals of the values calculated above.

## Quantity Indices

So far we have considered index numbers only for looking at changes in prices. Another type of change which they are commonly used to measure is change in quantity. This could be quantity produced in the case of an **index of production** or quantity sold in the case of a **sales index**. The principles involved are exactly the same as for price index numbers and all the same types of index number are available. We shall illustrate these by reference to the example data on grocery sales which we have been using throughout Sec. 9.2. This set of data is reproduced below.

|  | January 1997 | | January 1998 | |
|---|---|---|---|---|
|  | Price | Quantity | Price | Quantity |
| Milk | 25p per pt | 6000 pt | 30p per pt | 6250 pt |
| Sugar | 44p per kg | 2300 kg | 59p per kg | 2600 kg |
| Tea | 150p per lb | 1600 lb | 165p per lb | 1800 lb |
| Bread | 35p per loaf | 4200 loaves | 40p per loaf | 4300 loaves |

In calculating a quantity index more expensive items need to be regarded as more important in our assessment of overall production or sales than cheaper items. Hence we need to weight the quantities by the prices of the respective items, and this leads us to the use of Laspeyres and Paasche quantity index numbers.

In the **Laspeyres quantity index** the quantities in both the numerator and denominator of the index calculation are weighted by the base time prices. What this amounts to is calculating

$$\frac{\text{What the given time quantities would have cost at base time prices}}{\text{What the base time quantities actually cost at base time prices}} \times 100$$

For this example we have

$$\frac{25 \times 6250 + 44 \times 2600 + 150 \times 1800 + 35 \times 4300}{25 \times 6000 + 44 \times 2300 + 150 \times 1600 + 35 \times 4200} \times 100$$

$$= \frac{156\,250 + 114\,400 + 270\,000 + 150\,000}{150\,000 + 101\,200 + 240\,000 + 147\,000} \times 100$$

$$= \frac{691\,150}{638\,200} \times 100 = 108.30$$

In the Paasche quantity index the quantities in both the numerator and denominator of the index calculation are weighted by the given time quantities. What this amounts to is calculating

$$\frac{\text{What the given time quantities actually cost at the given time prices}}{\text{What the base time quantities would have cost at given time prices}} \times 100$$

For this example we have

$$\frac{30 \times 6250 + 59 \times 2600 + 165 \times 1800 + 40 \times 4300}{30 \times 6000 + 59 \times 2300 + 165 \times 1600 + 40 \times 4200} \times 100$$

$$= \frac{187\,500 + 153\,400 + 297\,000 + 172\,000}{180\,000 + 135\,700 + 264\,000 + 168\,000} \times 100$$

$$= \frac{809\,900}{747\,700} \times 100 = 108.32$$

As in the case of price index numbers, these calculations can be more effectively set out in the form of a table. In fact the table required is the same one as was used earlier for the price index calculations. The only difference is in the combinations of column totals which we have to use in the calculations at the final stage. Thus, we see a further advantage in the table method if both price index calculations and quantity index calculations are required. The earlier table is reproduced below and the Laspeyres and Paasche quantity indices are calculated using it.

| Items | A Base time price | B Base time quant | C Given time price | D Given time quant | C × B | A × B | C × D | A × D |
|-------|------|------|------|------|------|------|------|------|
| Milk | 25 | 6000 | 30 | 6250 | 180 000 | 150 000 | 187 500 | 156 250 |
| Sugar | 44 | 2300 | 59 | 2600 | 135 700 | 101 200 | 153 400 | 114 400 |
| Tea | 150 | 1600 | 165 | 1800 | 264 000 | 240 000 | 297 000 | 270 000 |
| Bread | 35 | 4200 | 40 | 4300 | 168 000 | 147 000 | 172 000 | 150 500 |
| | | | | | 747 700 | 638 200 | 809 900 | 691 150 |

Then Laspeyres quantity index $= \dfrac{A \times D}{A \times B} \times 100 = \dfrac{691\,150}{638\,200} \times 100 = 108.30$

and Paasche quantity index $= \dfrac{C \times D}{C \times B} \times 100 = \dfrac{809\,900}{747\,700} \times 100 = 108.32$

## The Value Index

The final index number calculation we consider in this section is that of a weighted aggregative index which is neither a price index nor a quantity index. The **value index** is a measure of change in the total *value* of sales, production or whatever. It works by expressing the total value of the sales at the given time as a percentage of the total value of sales at the base time. In doing this it combines together changes in both the price and the quantity between the base time and the given time.

The value index calculation is:

$$\frac{\text{What the given time quantities cost at given time prices}}{\text{What the base time quantities cost at base time prices}} \times 100$$

So for the example data on the groceries we have

$$\frac{30 \times 6250 + 59 \times 2600 + 165 \times 1800 + 40 \times 4300}{25 \times 6000 + 44 \times 2300 + 150 \times 1600 + 35 \times 4200} \times 100$$

$$= \frac{187\,500 + 153\,400 + 297\,000 + 172\,000}{150\,000 + 101\,200 + 240\,000 + 147\,000} \times 100$$

$$= \frac{809\,900}{638\,200} \times 100 = 126.9$$

This is saying that the total value of the grocery sales in January 1998 was 26.9% up on the total value in January 1997.

As price change and quantity change are being combined, we would expect to see the value index being equal, to within a factor of 100, to the product of the price index and the quantity index. If, for example, a price index indicated that price had doubled between base time and given time while output had tripled, we should hope this would correspond to the value index telling us that the overall value of production had increased by a factor of $2 \times 3 = 6$.

An index formula for which this is exactly true is said to have the property of **factor reversal**. This property is not possessed by either the Laspeyres index or the Paasche index, though calculation of price index $\times$ quantity index for either of these would in practice lead, when divided by 100, to a result not very far from the value index.

However, it is the case that the value index is exactly equal to

$$\frac{\text{Laspeyres price index} \times \text{Paasche quantity index}}{100}$$

and also to

$$\frac{\text{Laspeyres quantity index} \times \text{Paasche price index}}{100}$$

For the groceries example we have for the first of these

$$(117.16 \times 108.32)/100 = 126.9$$

and for the second we have

$$(117.18 \times 108.30)/100 = 126.9$$

The corresponding products for Laspeyres alone and for Paasche alone come to 126.88 and 126.93 respectively, which are not so far from the value index.

## Relative Utility of Laspeyres and Paasche Indices

The Laspeyres index, which is the most commonly used of the weighted aggregative indices, has the following points in its favour.

1   It is good from an administrative point of view because once the weights have been found they are fixed until it is decided to move to a new base date.
2   Every value in a published Laspeyres series is referring to the same basket of goods so it is completely valid to compare the index values in the series with each other.

Disadvantages of the Laspeyres index are as follows:

1   If the pattern of demand, production or whatever is subject to serious change, then continued use of the base time weights could result in a weighting system significantly different to the current pattern.
2   In times of inflation the Laspeyres price index will tend to overstate the inflation rate since no account is taken of the effect on the cost of living of reduction in demand for items whose prices have risen particularly rapidly.

The Paasche index, on the other hand, is less commonly used. It has one chief merit: it uses an up-to-date basket of goods and so is talking about the change in price of what is *now* actually being bought, produced or whatever. This is especially useful if the pattern is subject to marked changes.

Disadvantages to be noted in the case of the Paasche index are:

1   There may be some understatement of inflation because of reduction in demand for some items whose prices have risen rapidly.
2   Obtaining up-to-date weights can present a major practical problem; the amount of data collection may be very expensive or difficult, perhaps impossibly so.
3   Each time a Paasche index is calculated the reference is to a different basket of goods, so successive values in a Paasche series are not strictly comparable with each other. (However, the incremental nature of the changes in the weights from one time point to another are such that we can for practical purposes treat the values as if they were comparable.)

**Exercises 9.2**    1   A firm producing three products X, Y and Z, sold the following numbers in 1997 and 1998 at the prices shown.

|  | 1997 | | 1998 | |
| Item | Price (£) | Number | Price (£) | Number |
| --- | --- | --- | --- | --- |
| X | 3.00 | 32 | 3.40 | 48 |
| Y | 4.50 | 68 | 5.00 | 60 |
| Z | 4.00 | 54 | 4.60 | 56 |

Using 1997 as base year and 1998 as given year in each case, calculate:

a   the Laspeyres price index
b   the Laspeyres quantity index
c   the Paasche price index
d   the Paasche quantity index
e   the value index.

2   An organization employs four grades of staff. The numbers employed and the hourly wage rates, in pounds, for each of the grades in 1997 and 1998 were as follows:

| Grade | 1997 | | 1998 | |
|---|---|---|---|---|
| | Hourly wage (£) | Number | Hourly wage (£) | Number |
| 1 | 9.85 | 44 | 10.27 | 45 |
| 2 | 9.60 | 37 | 9.95 | 29 |
| 3 | 9.25 | 23 | 9.60 | 31 |
| 4 | 8.57 | 18 | 8.85 | 15 |

**a** Calculate the Laspeyres wage index using 1997 as base year and 1998 as given year.

**b** Calculate the Paasche index for number of employees using 1997 as base year and 1998 as given year.

**c** Calculate the index for the total wage bill using 1997 as base year and 1998 as given year.

**d** Explain the relationship between your answers to parts **a**, **b** and **c**.

3   A company wishes to measure the change in its performance using an index calculated from the data given below on numbers of items sold and their prices in 1997 and 1998.

| Item | 1997 | | 1998 | |
|---|---|---|---|---|
| | Price (£) | Number | Price (£) | Number |
| A | 2.50 | 90 | 2.70 | 200 |
| B | 3.80 | 150 | 4.00 | 160 |
| C | 4.10 | 180 | 4.50 | 120 |

Calculate

**a** the value index

**b** the Laspeyres quantity index

**c** the Paasche quantity index

(In all these calculations 1997 should be used as base year and 1998 as given year.)

**d** state with reasons which of the indices calculated in your answers to parts **a**, **b** and **c** you consider to be the best measure of the company's change in performance.

## 9.3 Retail Price Index

This is probably the best known of all UK official statistics and is generally accepted by both sides of industry and by people of most political persuasions as an indicator of domestic price inflation. It is sometimes criticized as being not properly representative of the inflation experienced by some sections of the community and for omitting certain items which some people feel should be included, such as the capital element of mortgage repayments, insurance and pension contributions, and income tax. However, the retail price index is widely respected as a fair attempt to give an overall measure of price inflation. The index is referred to by both sides in wage negotiations, it has been used for certain government-backed savings schemes including currently index linked National Savings Certificates, many pensions, particularly in the public sector, are linked to it, and certain subindices are used for annual updating of insurance cover. In essence the retail prices index is a weighted mean of price relatives with its base date at 13 January 1987.

It is not possible to include every imaginable product and service in the index and it would not materially improve the index if this could be done. What is needed is a representative selection of products and services, and 350 are used. These 350 items can be classified into 95 sections which can in turn be classed into 11 groups. The first step is to obtain a price relative for each of the 350 items using the Tuesday nearest the middle of the month for which the index is to be quoted as the given time and the Tuesday nearest the middle of the immediately preceding January as base time. This requires obtaining on the Tuesday nearest the middle of each month 150 000 separate price quotations. Some of these can be obtained centrally but discovering most of the shop prices involves Department for Education and Employment staff from unemployment benefit offices visiting a set sample of shops all over the country to record prices actually being charged.

Having obtained the 350 price relatives a weighted mean is calculated within each of the 95 section indices. The weights used for this purpose are the proportions, expressed as parts in 1000 of expenditure on each of the 350 items as found by the Family Expenditure Survey for the year ended the previous June. Hence during each year a different set of weights is being used, and this helps keep the index up to date in its weighting pattern. Having found the 95 section indices, a weighted average of these is calculated using their total section weights to give the 11 group indices.

Combining the 11 group indices together using their weights, then gives the overall index for the month of interest as given time and the preceding January as base time. We have a **link-based** series of index numbers. For publication purposes reference must be made back to January 1987 as base date. This involves multiplying the index as calculated above by all January-to-January indices back to January 1987. For example, the published index for July 1989 was obtained as follows:

(Calculated index with July 1989 given and January 1989 as base)
× (index for January 1989 given and January 1988 as base)
× (index for January 1988 as given and January 1987 as base)

Note that the product of the last two terms in the above is what would be published as the index for January 1989. The advantage of this procedure over relating the original relatives directly to January 1987 before calculating the weighted mean is that it allows the proportional change in price in any particular period to be weighted by an up-to-date basket of goods. Separate quarterly indices are published for one-person and two-person pensioner households, but although the weighting pattern differs considerably from that of the general index (in whose calculation such households are omitted if at least three-quarters of the income is from National Insurance sources) the actual index differs very little from the general index. This is an encouragement to believe in the general index as a reasonable average inflation measure.

The retail price index is published each month under its eleven main group headings: food, alcoholic drink, tobacco, housing, fuel and light, durable household goods, clothing and footwear, transport and vehicles, services, meals bought and consumed outside the home. Some of these groups are broken down for publication purposes into subgroups. For example, the transport and vehicles group is broken down into two subgroups: motoring and cycling, fares. For each group and subgroup included there is shown both its own index and its weighting in the overall index as parts in one thousand.

As an example of how a subgroup index is made up from sections and their representative items, consider the motoring and cycling subgroup of the transport and vehicles group.

| Subgroup | Section | Items |
|---|---|---|
| Motoring and cycling | Purchase of vehicles | Specified models of second-hand cars<br>Motor scooters |
| | Maintenance of vehicles | Charges for specified jobs<br>Car and motor cycle tyres<br>Petrol<br>Engine oil |
| | Motor licences | Annual car road tax<br>Annual motor cycle road tax |
| | Motor insurance | Third-party insurance rates for specified cars and motor cycles |

First news of the retail price index comes in a press release from the Department for Education and Employment usually on the Friday four and a half weeks after the Tuesday on which the prices were collected. Initial publication of the index broken down into groups, subgroups and sections is in the monthly *Labour Market Trends*. It is subsequently repeated in various summary statistical publications including the *Monthly Digest of Statistics*, *Economic Trends* and the *Annual Abstract of Statistics*.

**Exercises 9.3**

1   Discuss the extent to which the Retail Price Index is valid and useful as a measure of inflation to:

a   the Chancellor of the Exchequer
b   you as an individual.

2   Explain how the retail price index is used to obtain the final value of an index linked National Savings Certificate purchased for £10 000 and held for 5 years. (A National Savings leaflet obtainable from your local Post Office could be useful for answering this question.)

## Further Exercises

1   A price index was calculated using 1980 as base year and 1998 as given year, and the value found was 200. If the same data were used to calculate the price index for 1998 as base year and 1980 as given year, which one of the following would you expect to be closest to the result obtained?

A. 20          B. 50          C. 100          D. 200

2   In 1990 there were 1000 of item X sold at £4 each and 2000 of item Y sold at £6 each. In 1998 there were 1500 of item X sold at £5 each and 2500 of item Y sold at £7 each. Which of the following figures is closest to the Laspeyres quantity index for these two items using 1990 as base year and 1998 as given year ?

A. 118.75          B. 119.05          C. 131.25          D. 156.25

3   For a particular set of data the value index is 135 and the Laspeyres price index is 108. Which of the following numbers is closest to the value of the Paasche quantity index ?

A. 145.8          B. 120.7          C. 80.0          D. 125.0

4   Which of the following can be regarded as an advantage of the Paasche price index over the Laspeyres price index?

    A. The Paasche index requires less data collection than the Laspeyres.

    B. The Laspeyres price index is inclined to understate the rate of price increase.

    C. The Paasche index uses a more up-to-date basket of goods than the Laspeyres index.

    D. Figures in a Paasche price index series are strictly comparable with each other while those in a Laspeyres series are not.

5   A company sells two products, A and B. The total number of units sold of A and B combined in 1998 was the same as in 1997. However, equal numbers of A and B were sold in 1997, while in 1998 twice as many A were sold as B. If each unit of A cost £3 in both 1997 and 1998, while each unit of B cost £2 in both 1997 and 1998, which of the following is closest to the value index using 1997 as base year and 1998 as given year?

    A. 200        B. 159        C. 107        D. 100

6   If a Paasche price index is multiplied by a Paasche quantity index, and the result is divided by 100, which of the following will result?

    A. Value index               B. Laspeyres price index
    C. Laspeyres quantity index    D. None of A, B or C

7   If a Paasche price index is multiplied by a Laspeyres quantity index, and the result is divided by 100, which of the following will result?

    A. Value index               B. Laspeyres price index
    C. Paasche quantity index      D. None of A, B or C

8   A Paasche price index was calculated as 200 for 1988 as base year and 1998 as given year. The value index was calculated for the same base year and given year and came out as 300. Which of the following, calculated for 1988 as base year and 1998 as given year, must come out as 150?

    A. Laspeyres quantity index    B. Laspeyres price index
    C. Paasche quantity index     D. Simple mean of quantity relatives

9  **a**  In 1996 a company produced product A and sold it throughout the year at a price of £5 per unit. On 1 January 1997 the price of product A was increased to £5.20 and it was sold at this price throughout 1997.
   - Calculate the price index for product A using 1996 as base year and 1997 as given year.
   - Calculate the price index for product A using 1997 as base year and 1996 as given year, and explain how the answer relates to your answer to part **a**.

   **b**  On 1 January 1997 the company added product B to its range and sold this throughout 1997 at £4 per unit. On 1 January 1998 the price of A was increased to £5.40 per unit and that of B was increased to £4.25 per unit. At these prices, which prevailed throughout 1998, the company sold 20 000 units of A and 15 000 units of B.
   - Calculate a weighted aggregative price index for 1997 as base year and 1998 as given year using the quantities indicated as weights.
   - Say what kind of index you have calculated in answer to part **a** and explain the information conveyed by it.

10  The prices and numbers of units sold for three items in 1987 and 1997 were as follows:

| Item | 1987 Price (£) | 1987 Units (in '000s) | 1997 Price (£) | 1997 Units (in '000s) |
|------|------|------|------|------|
| A | 120 | 35 | 150 | 15 |
| B | 80 | 40 | 80 | 40 |
| C | 100 | 25 | 90 | 45 |

   **a**  Calculate the Laspeyres price index if 1987 is taken as the base year and 1997 as the given year.
   **b**  Calculate the Paasche price index if 1987 is taken as the base year and 1997 as the given year.
   **c**  Explain why the Laspeyres and Paasche price indices differ by a substantial amount for this set of data.

## Chapter Ten

# Correlation

## 10.1 Scatter Diagrams

Correlation is about closeness of association between variables. In its most basic form, it is about how closely *two* variables are associated in one of two specific ways:

Either **The two variables increase together.**

Or **One variable decreases as the other increases.**

As a first step towards seeing whether any such association exists, we can plot what is known as a **scatter diagram**. To do this we take a sample of pairs of readings for the two variables and plot one against the other on a graph. Look at Example 10.1.1.

If the two variables increase together, the plotted points will lie close to a straight line sloping *upwards* as in Fig. 10.1(a). If one variable decreases as the other increases, the plotted points will lie close to a straight line sloping *downwards* as in Fig. 10.1(b).

## Example 10.1.1

An insurance company recorded the number, $x$, of policies issued during each of six months and the total hours, $y$, of overtime worked each month in the issuing department:

| Policies, $x$ | 150 | 300 | 100 | 400 | 350 | 500 |
|---|---|---|---|---|---|---|
| Overtime hrs, $y$ | 10 | 20 | 10 | 40 | 30 | 35 |

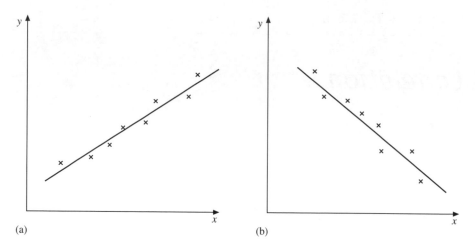

**Figure 10.1** A scatter diagram where (a) the variables increase together, and (b) one variable decreases as the other increases

Draw a scatter diagram showing the numbers of overtime hours plotted against the numbers of policies issued, and explain what it shows.

## Solution to Example 10.1.1

Figure 10.2 shows the scatter diagram.

Another way we can plot this scatter diagram is by using EXCEL. Here,

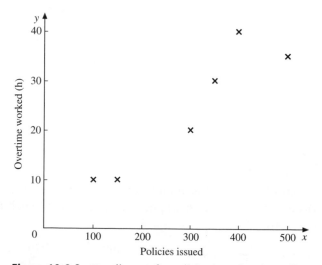

**Figure 10.2** Scatter diagram for policies issued and overtime worked

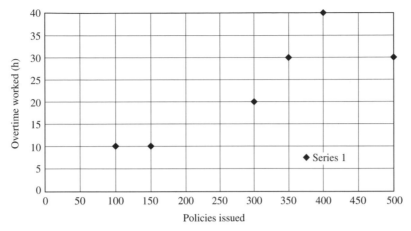

**Figure 10.3** Scatter diagram for policies issued and overtime worked

we enter the values in cells A1 to B6 and use the Chart Wizard with the *xy*-scatter plot option. Figure 10.3 shows the result.

We see from Figs 10.2 and 10.3 that the points lie reasonably close to an upward-sloping line, indicating that these two variables increase together.

## Example 10.1.2

You have collected figures over a 10-week period on levels of output and cost per unit of output of radio/cassette players:

| Output, $x$: (in 000s of units) | 10 | 18 | 25 | 20 | 16 | 30 | 32 | 34 | 5 | 24 |
|---|---|---|---|---|---|---|---|---|---|---|
| Cost per unit, $y$ (£) | 20 | 14 | 12 | 14 | 15 | 9 | 9 | 8 | 25 | 11 |

Draw a scatter diagram showing cost per unit plotted against output, and comment on what the diagram shows.

## *Solution to Example 10.1.2*

Figure 10.4 shows the scatter diagram.

We can plot this scatter diagram in EXCEL by entering the values in cells A1 to B10 and using the Chart Wizard with the *xy*-scatter plot option. The result is shown in Fig. 10.5.

We see from Figs 10.4 and 10.5 that the points lie reasonably close to a downward-sloping line, indicating that cost per unit decreases as total output increases.

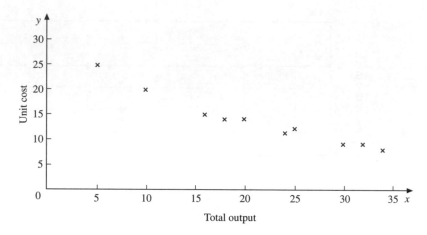

**Figure 10.4** Scatter diagram for total output and unit cost

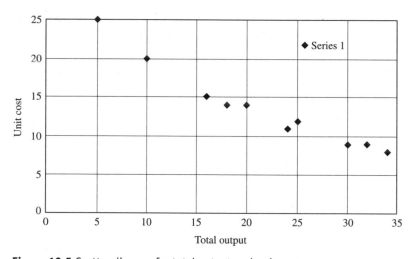

**Figure 10.5** Scatter diagram for total output and unit cost

**Exercises 10.1**   1   The figures in the table below show the time it takes to do different clerical tasks (A–H) and the cost of doing each of them.

| Task | A | B | C | D | E | F | G | H |
|------|---|---|---|---|---|---|---|---|
| Time needed, $x$ (in mins) | 7 | 8 | 10 | 12 | 14 | 16 | 20 | 24 |
| Cost, $y$ (£) | 4 | 7 | 8 | 9 | 10 | 14 | 17 | 18 |

   **a**   Draw a scatter diagram showing the cost of doing a particular task plotted against the time needed to do that task.

**b**  Using EXCEL draw a scatter diagram showing the cost of doing a particular task plotted against the time needed to do that task.

**c**  Comment on your results for parts (a) and (b).

2  The following table shows, for a group of 12 production workers, the number of months' experience each of them had and the numbers of defective items they produced during a particular week.

| Worker | 1 | 2 | 3 | 4 | 5 | 6 | 7 | 8 | 9 | 10 | 11 | 12 |
|---|---|---|---|---|---|---|---|---|---|---|---|---|
| Rejects, $y$ | 26 | 20 | 28 | 16 | 23 | 18 | 24 | 26 | 38 | 22 | 32 | 25 |
| Exp'nce, $x$ (months) | 7 | 9 | 6 | 14 | 8 | 12 | 10 | 4 | 2 | 11 | 1 | 8 |

**a**  Draw a scatter diagram showing rejects plotted against number of months of experience.

**b**  Draw using EXCEL a scatter diagram showing rejects plotted against number of months of experience.

**c**  Comment on what is shown by your results for parts (a) and (b).

## 10.2 Product–Moment Correlation

We can go beyond scatter diagrams and *measure* the extent of association between two variables. The most basic calculation we can use for this purpose is the **correlation coefficient**. This is always represented by the letter $r$. (It is sometimes given the fuller name of **product–moment correlation coefficient** to distinguish it from other measures which we shall come to later.)

We shall see in a moment how to calculate $r$ for a specific set of data pairs, but our main concern is not with how to calculate $r$, or with why $r$ is a measure of association. What is important at this stage is understanding what a particular value of $r$ is telling us about the association between two variables. The key points are these:

> **If $r$ comes out close to $+1$ we have two variables which increase together, such as in Example 10.1.1 above.**
>
> **If $r$ comes out close to $-1$, one variable decreases as the other increases, such as in Example 10.1.2 above.**
>
> **If $r$ comes out close to $0$, neither of these types of association exists between the variables.**

We can also say that:

1  The fact of $r$ being close to $+1$ or to $-1$ does not necessarily mean that

increases in one variable are responsible for increases or reductions in the other. A strong correlation does not of itself imply that there is a **causal relationship** between the variables.

When a value of $r$ is close to $+1$ or to $-1$ and there is no causal relationship we call it a **spurious correlation.**

2    The fact that $r$ is close to 0 does not necessarily mean that there is no relationship of any kind between the two variables. It is possible that there is an association of a type other than the two types we have been considering. The points might, for example, lie close to the graph for a non-linear function. It is also possible that different relationships might apply over different parts of the ranges of values of the variables.

In summary, a low value for the correlation coefficient does not of itself imply that the two variables are **independent** of each other. Look at Fig. 10.6. Here, for small values of $x$ we have $y$ decreasing as $x$ increases, while for larger values of $x$ the two variables increase together. Yet $r$ would come out close to zero.

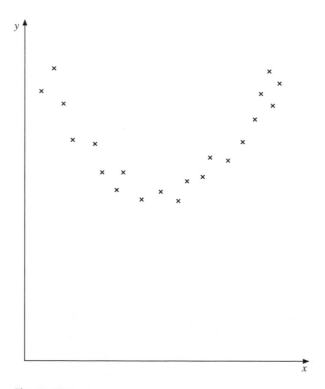

**Figure 10.6**

To obtain the value of $r$ for a set of data pairs, let's go back to the data presented in Examples 10.1.1 and 10.1.2 and first see how to do it using an EXCEL spreadsheet. We shall then show the manual calculations.

## Example 10.2.1

An insurance company recorded the number, $x$, of policies issued during each of six months and the total hours, $y$, of overtime worked each month in the issuing department:

| Policies, $x$ | 150 | 300 | 100 | 400 | 350 | 500 |
| Overtime hrs, $y$ | 10 | 20 | 10 | 40 | 30 | 35 |

a   Use EXCEL to find the correlation coefficient $r$ between number of policies issued and number of hours of overtime worked.
b   Calculate $r$ manually for this set of data.
c   Interpret the value found for $r$.

## *Solution to Example 10.2.1*

a   Enter the $x$ values into cells A1 to A6.
Enter the $y$ values into cells B1 to B6.
Click on the Function Wizard icon.
Choose Statistical as the Function Category in the left-hand column of the dialogue box.
Choose CORREL as the Function Name in the right-hand column of the dialogue box.
Click on Next in the bottom line of the dialogue box.
Enter A1:A6 as the array 1 cells.
Enter B1:B6 as the array 2 cells.

The value 0.926330784 will appear in the top right of the dialogue box as the value of the correlation coefficient, $r$.

Click on Finish in the bottom line of the dialogue box.

The value 0.926331 will appear in the cell of the worksheet where the cursor was left.
b   The formula needed for the calculation of $r$ is as follows:

$$r = \frac{n\sum xy - (\sum x)(\sum y)}{\sqrt{\{(n\sum x^2 - (\sum x)^2)(n\sum y^2 - (\sum y)^2)\}}}$$

where $n$ is the number of pairs of values you have.

When entering numbers into this formula it is crucially important to know the precise meanings of the summation expressions.

$\Sigma xy$ with no brackets in sight means **work out each individual product and then add these products together**. So for this example it means:

$$150 \times 10 + 300 \times 20 + 100 \times 10 + 400 \times 40 + 350 \times 30 + 500 \times 35$$
$$= 1500 \quad + \quad 6000 \quad + \quad 1000 \quad + \quad 16\,000 \quad + \quad 10\,500 \quad + \quad 17\,500$$
$$= 52\,500$$

$(\Sigma x)(\Sigma y)$ means **find the sum of the $x$ values, then find the sum of the $y$ values, and finally multiply the two sums together**. Here, we have:

$$(150 + 300 + 100 + 400 + 350 + 500) \times (10 + 20 + 10 + 40 + 30 + 35)$$
$$= \qquad\qquad\qquad 1800 \qquad\qquad \times \qquad\qquad 145$$
$$= 261\,000$$

$\Sigma x^2$ with no bracketing means **first square each of the individual $x$ values and then add the squares together**. So for the example, we have:

$$150^2 \quad + \quad 300^2 \quad + \quad 100^2 \quad + \quad 400^2 \quad + \quad 350^2 \quad + \quad 500^2$$
$$= 22\,500 + 90\,000 + 10\,000 + 160\,000 + 122\,500 + 250\,000$$
$$= 655\,000$$

$(\Sigma x)^2$ means **add up the $x$ values and then square the sum**. Here, we have:

$$(150 + 300 + 100 + 400 + 350 + 500)^2 = 1800^2 = 3\,240\,000$$

In the same way, for the $y$ values, the two notations mean:

$$\Sigma y^2 = 10^2 + 20^2 + 10^2 + 40^2 + 30^2 + 35^2$$
$$= 100 + 400 + 100 + 1600 + 900 + 1225 = 4325$$
$$(\Sigma y)^2 = (10 + 20 + 10 + 40 + 30 + 35)^2 = 145^2 = 21\,025$$

The value of $n$ in this case is 6 because there are six pairs of values. So the formula given above for $r$ leads to the following calculation:

$$r = \frac{6 \times 52\,500 - 261\,000}{\sqrt{\{(6 \times 655\,000 - 3\,240\,000)(6 \times 4325 - 21\,025)\}}}$$

$$= \frac{315\,000 - 261\,000}{\sqrt{\{(3\,930\,000 - 3\,240\,000)(25\,950 - 21\,025)\}}} = \frac{54\,000}{\sqrt{\{690\,000 \times 4925\}}}$$

$$= \frac{54\,000}{58\,294.51} = 0.926331$$

c   The $r$ value of 0.926331 is close to $+1$ so the two variables increase together. That is to say, the number of hours of overtime worked increases as the number of policies issued increases, as we should expect.

## Example 10.2.2

You have collected figures over a ten week period on levels of output and cost per unit of output of radio/cassette players:

| Output, $x$ (in 000s of units) | 10 | 18 | 25 | 20 | 16 | 30 | 32 | 34 | 5 | 24 |
|---|---|---|---|---|---|---|---|---|---|---|
| Cost per unit, $y$ (£) | 20 | 14 | 12 | 14 | 15 | 9 | 9 | 8 | 25 | 11 |

a  Use EXCEL to find the correlation coefficient $r$ between number of units output and the cost per unit of output.
b  Calculate $r$ manually for this set of data.
c  Interpret the value found for $r$.

## *Solution to Example 10.2.2*

a  The procedure here is the same as in part (a) of Example 10.2.1 to set up the $x$ values in cells A1 to A10 as array 1 and the $y$ values in cells B1 to B10 as array 2.

  The value $-0.969977225$ will appear in the top right of the dialogue box as the value of the correlation coefficient, $r$. The value $-0.96998$ will appear in the cell of the worksheet where the cursor was left.

b  Having used the answer to part (b) of Example 10.2.1 to emphasize the meaning of the summation notations, we shall set out the calculations for this answer in a tabular form. You will find this is the most effective layout if you ever need to calculate a correlation coefficient manually yourself.

| $x$ | $y$ | $xy$ | $x^2$ | $y^2$ |
|---|---|---|---|---|
| 10 | 20 | 200 | 100 | 400 |
| 18 | 14 | 252 | 324 | 196 |
| 25 | 12 | 300 | 625 | 144 |
| 20 | 14 | 280 | 400 | 196 |
| 16 | 15 | 240 | 256 | 225 |
| 30 | 9 | 270 | 900 | 81 |
| 32 | 9 | 288 | 1024 | 81 |
| 34 | 8 | 272 | 1156 | 64 |
| 5 | 25 | 125 | 25 | 625 |
| 24 | 11 | 264 | 576 | 121 |
| 214 | 137 | 2491 | 5386 | 2133 |

The value of $n$ in this case is 10 because there are 10 pairs of values. So the formula given for $r$ leads to the following calculation:

$$r = \frac{10 \times 2491 - 214 \times 137}{\sqrt{\{(10 \times 5386 - 214 \times 214)(10 \times 2133 - 137 \times 137)\}}}$$

$$= \frac{24\,910 - 29\,318 \quad -4408}{\sqrt{\{(53\,860 - 45\,796)(21\,330 - 18\,769)\}} \; \sqrt{\{8064 \times 2561\}}}$$

$$= \frac{-4408}{4544.4366} = -0.96998$$

On most calculators the calculations needed for the first row in each of the last three columns of the above table are as follows:

[10] [×] [20] [=]
[10] [$x^2$]
[20] [$x^2$]

We could find the first column summation as:

[10][+][18][+][25][+][20][+][16][+][30][+][32][+][34][+][5][+]
[24][=]

We could find the summations in the third, fourth and fifth columns without writing out the table if we use the calculator memory appropriately. Always ensure that the memory is *cleared* before starting on any operations involving the memory.

To find the sum of the third column, obtain each $xy$ value on the calculator display and follow it by [M+] to add it into the memory. After pressing the last [M+], use [MR] to read the memory. We have set out the full set of keystrokes for this calculation but we shan't do it every time!

[10] [(] [20] [=] [M+] [18] [(] [14] [=] [M+] [25] [(] [12] [=] [M+] [20]
[(] [14] [=] [M+] [16] [(] [15] [=] [M+] [30] [(] [9] [=] [M+] [32] [(] [9]
[=] [M+] [34] [(] [8] [=] [M+] [5] [(] [25] [=] [M+] [24] [(] [11] [=]
[M+] [MR]

We can find the summation for the fourth column, after clearing the memory, by entering each $x$ value in turn followed by the [$x^2$] key and then the [M+] key to add its square into the memory. After pressing the last [M+], use [MR] to read the memory.

Having found the summations, the numerator of $r$ is calculated as:

[10] [×] [2941] [=] [M+] [214] [×] [137] [=] [M–] [MR]

We can then, similarly, evaluate each of the two brackets in the denominator. Finally, we can calculate the correlation coefficient itself by using:

$$[8064]\,[\times]\,[2561]\,[=]\,[\sqrt{}]\,[M+]\,[4408]\,[+/-]\,[\div]\,[MR]\,[=]$$

The **coefficient of determination** is another way of measuring strength of association between variables. It is very closely related to the correlation coefficient. In fact it is just the correlation coefficient squared. We usually denote it by the symbol $r^2$. As $r$ has to be in the range $-1$ to $+1$, it follows that $r^2$ must be a value in the range 0 to $+1$.

If we have a strong association, with both variables increasing together, the coefficient of determination will be close to $1^2$ which is 1. If we have a strong association with one variable decreasing as the other increases, then the coefficient of determination will be close to $(-1)^2$ which is also 1. If there is no strong association of either type, the coefficient of determination will be the square of something close to zero which means that it will itself be close to zero.

We can also regard the coefficient of determination as the proportion of the variation in one variable which can be explained by its association with the other variable. This is often multiplied by 100 to give $100r^2$ as the percentage of variation explained by the association.

## Example 10.2.3

An insurance company recorded the number, $x$, of policies issued during each of six months and the total hours, $y$, of overtime worked each month in the issuing department:

| Policies, $x$ | 150 | 300 | 100 | 400 | 350 | 500 |
|---|---|---|---|---|---|---|
| Overtime hrs, $y$ | 10 | 20 | 10 | 40 | 30 | 35 |

Calculate the coefficient of determination for this set of data.

## Solution to Example 10.2.3

We found in answer to Example 10.2.1 that $r = 0.926331$. Hence the coefficient of determination is

$$r^2 = 0.926331^2 = 0.858$$

This means that 85.8% of the variation in the number of overtime hours worked can be explained by the association of this variable with the number of policies issued.

We can calculate the coefficient of determination from the correlation coefficient here by keying in:

[0.926331] [$x^2$]

We then convert it to a percentage by using:

[0.858] [×] [100] [=]

## Example 10.2.4

You have collected figures over a 10 week period on levels of output and cost per unit of output of radio/cassette players:

| Output, $x$ (in 000s of units) | 10 | 18 | 25 | 20 | 16 | 30 | 32 | 34 | 5 | 24 |
|---|---|---|---|---|---|---|---|---|---|---|
| Cost per unit, $y$ (£) | 20 | 14 | 12 | 14 | 15 | 9 | 9 | 8 | 25 | 11 |

Calculate the coefficient of determination for this set of data.

## Solution to Example 10.2.4

We found in answer to Example 10.2.2 that $r = 0.96998$. Hence, the coefficient of determination is

$$r^2 = 0.96998^2 = 0.941.$$

So we can say that 94.1% of the variation in the cost per unit is explained by its association with the number of units of output.

**Exercises 10.2**

1   The figures in the table below show the time it takes to do different clerical tasks (A–H) and the cost of doing each of them.

| Task | A | B | C | D | E | F | G | H |
|---|---|---|---|---|---|---|---|---|
| Time needed, $x$ (in mins) | 7 | 8 | 10 | 12 | 14 | 16 | 20 | 24 |
| Cost, $y$ (£) | 4 | 7 | 8 | 9 | 10 | 14 | 17 | 18 |

a   Use EXCEL to find the correlation coefficient $r$ between time required to complete the task and the cost involved.

b   Calculate $r$ manually for this set of data.

c   Interpret the value found for $r$.

d   Find the coefficient of determination and interpret it in terms of percentage of variation explained.

2    The following table shows, for a group of 12 production workers, the number of months' experience each of them had and the numbers of defective items they produced during a particular week.

| Worker | 1 | 2 | 3 | 4 | 5 | 6 | 7 | 8 | 9 | 10 | 11 | 12 |
|---|---|---|---|---|---|---|---|---|---|---|---|---|
| Rejects, $y$ | 26 | 20 | 28 | 16 | 23 | 18 | 24 | 26 | 38 | 22 | 32 | 25 |
| Exp'nce, $x$ (months) | 7 | 9 | 6 | 14 | 8 | 12 | 10 | 4 | 2 | 11 | 1 | 8 |

a    Use EXCEL to find the correlation coefficient $r$ between number of rejects produced and the number of months' experience the worker has.

b    Calculate $r$ manually for this set of data.

c    Interpret the value found for $r$.

d    Find the coefficient of determination and interpret it in terms of percentage of variation explained.

## 10.3 Rank Correlation

In Chapter 6 we looked at the way data is divided into numeric and categorical, and how these can be further subdivided into nominal and ordinal (for categorical) or discrete and continuous (if numeric). In this section we remind you of this division for the case of categorical data.

**Nominal** data, where the word 'nominal' means *name*, describes numbers that are being used merely as names or labels. An example would be to code blue cars 1, red cars 2, green cars 3 and cars of any other colour 4. There is no numerical relationship between these labels and it would be meaningless to calculate, for example, the mean of the scores for a sample of cars.

**Ordinal** data, where the word 'ordinal' relates to the idea of *order*, describes data values in which there is a definite order to the numbers used. Suppose you were asked to give a 'tastiness score' in the range 1 to 10 to each of several food items. If you gave one item a score of 8 and another a score of 4, it would be safe to say that the first was tastier than the second. However, it would be dangerous to interpret it as being 'twice as tasty' or even to believe that the 'tastiness difference' between them was the same as that between two items scoring 6 and 2. We can believe in data values of this kind to the extent of their rank ordering.

Correlation coefficient calculations of the type we saw in Sec. 10.2 are not reliable if the values being used are only ordinal data. In this case what should in principle be done is to replace the stated values by their positions in the rank ordering of the data set, and then calculate the correlation coefficient using the ranks instead. The resulting value can be interpreted as a measure of association as for an ordinary correlation coefficient.

In practice, a **rank correlation coefficient**, $r'$, (sometimes referred to as **Spearman's rank correlation coefficient**) is actually much easier to calculate than a product–moment correlation coefficient. After the ranking process has been carried out the $x$ values are replaced by the numbers 1 to $n$ in some order and the $y$ values also are replaced by the numbers 1 to $n$ in some (usually different) order. When the sums and sums of squares needed for the correlation coefficient calculation take this simple form, the formula for the coefficient itself reduces to:

$$r' = 1 - \frac{6 \sum d^2}{n(n^2 - 1)}$$

where the $d$'s are the differences in the data pairs after ranking has been carried out.

## Example 10.3.1

Twelve students were tested and then ranked on their written and verbal abilities. The two sets of ranks were as follows:

| Student | Ann | Ben | Chris | Don | Eric | Faye | Gill | Harry | Ian | Joy | Ken | Liz |
|---|---|---|---|---|---|---|---|---|---|---|---|---|
| Written rank | 2 | 3 | 1 | 6 | 7 | 4 | 8 | 5 | 12 | 11 | 9 | 10 |
| Verbal rank | 1 | 2 | 3 | 5 | 4 | 6 | 7 | 8 | 10 | 9 | 11 | 12 |

Calculate the rank correlation coefficient and interpret your result.

## Solution to Example 10.3.1

This is the simplest kind of rank correlation problem. Both sets of values are presented from the start in ranked form. So, we can proceed directly to calculate $d$, the difference in rankings, for each student:

| Student: | Ann | Ben | Chris | Don | Eric | Faye | Gill | Harry | Ian | Joy | Ken | Liz |
|---|---|---|---|---|---|---|---|---|---|---|---|---|
| $d$: | 1 | 1 | −2 | 1 | 3 | −2 | 1 | −3 | 2 | 2 | −2 | −2 |

Note that the sum of the $d$ values is zero. This must always be the case, so confirming that they do add to zero is an important check!
Hence

$$\sum d^2 = 1 + 1 + 4 + 1 + 9 + 4 + 1 + 9 + 4 + 4 + 4 + 4 = 46$$

So the rank correlation coefficient is

$$r' = 1 - \frac{6 \times 46}{12 \times (12^2 - 1)}$$

$$= 1 - 0.1608 = 0.8392$$

This is a value which looks quite close to $+1$, showing that the two variables increase together. What this means is that a student with a high written rank is likely to also achieve a high verbal rank, and vice versa.

## Example 10.3.2

As part of the market research relating to a new chocolate bar, you and a friend were each given six unidentified bars and asked to assign each a score in the range 1 to 10. You and your friend scored the bars as follows:

| Bar | A | B | C | D | E | F |
|---|---|---|---|---|---|---|
| Your score | 9 | 6 | 7 | 4 | 5 | 8 |
| Your friend's score | 8 | 7 | 5 | 3 | 6 | 9 |

Assess the level of association between scores given by the two of you.

## *Solution to Example 10.3.2*

In this problem we are not given ranks, but only scores. So as a first step we need to rank the assigned scores.

You gave bar A a score of 9 which was the highest score awarded, so give A rank 1. The next highest score you gave was 8 for bar F so give bar F rank 2. Your next highest score was 7 for bar C so give this rank 3. Continue in this way until you reach the lowest score. This is 4 for bar D so bar D receives rank 6. The same process is then applied to the scores awarded by your friend.

| Bar | A | B | C | D | E | F |
|---|---|---|---|---|---|---|
| Your rank | 1 | 4 | 3 | 6 | 5 | 2 |
| Your friend's rank | 2 | 3 | 5 | 6 | 4 | 1 |
| Difference, $d$ | $-1$ | 1 | $-2$ | 0 | 1 | 1 |
| $d^2$ : | 1 | 1 | 4 | 0 | 1 | 1 |

Hence

$$\sum d^2 = 8 \text{ and so } r' = 1 - \frac{6 \sum d^2}{n(n^2 - 1)} = 1 - \frac{6 \times 8}{6 \times 35}$$

$$= 1 - 0.2286 = 0.7714$$

This is not too far from $+1$, so there is a positive association between scores.

In the answer to Example 10.3.2 the bar receiving the highest score was ranked 1 and that receiving the lowest score was ranked 6. It would have been equally acceptable to have ranked the lowest score 1 and the highest 6. If we had done this for both you and your friend, the answer for $r'$ would have been unchanged. It would even have been acceptable (if somewhat perverse) to have used rank 1 for the highest score for you and rank 1 for the lowest score for your friend. This, though, would have led to an answer of $-0.7714$, but the conclusion about the association would have been the same.

In general, when carrying out the ranking process it does not matter whether rank 1 is used to denote the 'best' or the 'worst' item. What matters is that you interpret the coefficient value in a manner that is consistent with whatever way the ranking has been carried out.

When dealing with ranked data we often find that there are one or more **ties** in the ranks. A tie occurs when two or more items achieve the same rank. If the data values are given in ranked form, as in Example 10.3.1 above, then ties are indicated by equals signs. For example, we could have twelve items shown ranked like this:

$$1 \quad 2= \quad 2= \quad 4 \quad 5 \quad 6= \quad 6= \quad 6= \quad 9 \quad 10= \quad 10= \quad 12$$

If we are given data in the form of a set of scores to be ranked, as in Example 10.3.2, a tie will arise if two or more items have equal scores and so need to be assigned the same rank. Suppose twelve chocolate bars received these scores:

$$9 \quad 8 \quad 8 \quad 7 \quad 6 \quad 5 \quad 5 \quad 5 \quad 4 \quad 3 \quad 3 \quad 2$$

If these are ranked, giving rank 1 to the bar with the highest score, we obtain the same set of ranks as in the previous case:

$$1 \quad 2= \quad 2= \quad 4 \quad 5 \quad 6= \quad 6= \quad 6= \quad 9 \quad 10= \quad 10= \quad 12$$

What you have to do with tied ranks before you can calculate the $d$ values, and hence find $r'$, is to give each of the tied items the *mean* of the ranks they would have had if they had been different. Thus, the two items ranked $2=$ would have had ranks 2 and 3 if they had been different. So, for the purpose of calculating d values, each of them should be given rank

$$\frac{2+3}{2} = 2.5$$

Similarly, the two items ranked 10 = would have had ranks 10 and 11 if they had been different, so each of them needs to receive a rank of:

$$\frac{10+11}{2} = 10.5$$

So when an *even* number of items are tied, the ranks assigned will include a 0.5. What about three tied items? Suppose you came across three items ranked 6 =. These would have been ranked 6, 7 and 8 if they had been different. So, for the purpose of calculating $d$ values, they would each have rank:

$$\frac{6+7+8}{3} = 7$$

When an *odd* number of items are tied, the ranks assigned for the purpose of calculating $d$ values will all be whole numbers.

## Example 10.3.3

Eleven brands of paint were tested by a consumer watchdog and ranked according to quality, with the highest quality paint being awarded rank 1. The results were as follows:

| Paint | A | B | C | D | E | F | G | H | I | J | K |
|---|---|---|---|---|---|---|---|---|---|---|---|
| Quality | 2 = | 1 | 6 | 9 = | 9 = | 7 | 2 = | 8 | 5 | 2 = | 11 |
| Price per litre (£) | 5.99 | 5.99 | 4.99 | 3.99 | 4.49 | 4.49 | 5.49 | 3.99 | 4.99 | 6.49 | 3.99 |

Is the consumer being given value for money?

## Solution to Example 10.3.3

We have here a not uncommon type of problem in which one set of values is given in ranked form, and the other is a set of figures which could in themselves be treated as numeric data. If one set of values is ranked, then the other set must be ranked as well, and the rank correlation coefficient used.

The following table repeats the ranks given for quality and shows the price figures in ranked form, using rank 1 for the highest price:

| Paint | A | B | C | D | E | F | G | H | I | J | K |
|---|---|---|---|---|---|---|---|---|---|---|---|
| Quality rank | 2 = | 1 | 6 | 9 = | 9 = | 7 | 2 = | 8 | 5 | 2 = | 11 |
| Price rank | 2 = | 2 = | 5 = | 9 = | 7 = | 7 = | 4 | 9 = | 5 = | 1 | 9 = |

Before we can calculate $d$ values, the three $2 =$ on quality must all become 3 and the two $9 =$ must both become 9.5.

Likewise for the price ranks, the two $2 =$ must become 2.5, the two $5 =$ must become 5.5, the two $7 =$ must become 7.5 and the three $9 =$ must all become 10.

Hence the calculation of the rank correlation coefficient is as follows:

| Paint | A | B | C | D | E | F | G | H | I | J | K |
|---|---|---|---|---|---|---|---|---|---|---|---|
| Quality rank | 3 | 1 | 6 | 9.5 | 9.5 | 7 | 3 | 8 | 5 | 3 | 11 |
| Price rank | 2.5 | 2.5 | 5.5 | 10 | 7.5 | 7.5 | 4 | 10 | 5.5 | 1 | 10 |
| Difference, $d$ | 0.5 | −1.5 | 0.5 | −0.5 | 2 | −0.5 | −1 | −2 | −0.5 | 2 | 1 |
| $d^2$ | 0.25 | 2.25 | 0.25 | 0.25 | 4 | 0.25 | 1 | 4 | 0.25 | 4 | 1 |

Hence $\Sigma d^2 = 17.5$ and so $r' = 1 - \dfrac{6\,\Sigma d^2}{n(n^2 - 1)} = 1 - \dfrac{6 \times 17.5}{11 \times 120}$

$$= 1 - 0.08 = 0.92$$

This is close to $+1$ and indicates a strong positive association between price and quality. On this evidence, the consumer seems to be getting value for money.

**Exercises 10.3**

1 A firm is considering assessing applicants using a new profiling procedure instead of interviews. To find out how well the new procedure predicts candidates who would have been selected by interview, eight applicants were subjected to both methods. Each method led to a score in the range 1 to 10 as follows:

| Applicant: | A | B | C | D | E | F | G | H |
|---|---|---|---|---|---|---|---|---|
| Test score | 9 | 8 | 7 | 6 | 6 | 4 | 3 | 2 |
| Interview score | 8 | 9 | 8 | 7 | 7 | 7 | 3 | 4 |

a Rank each of the two sets of scores using rank 1 for the highest score.
b Calculate the rank correlation coefficient.
c Interpret the result in terms of the comparability of the two selection methods.

2 Ten factories were ranked according to their safety consciousness. The number of accidents which each factory had suffered over the last five years per 1000 people employed was recorded. The results were as follows:

| Factory | A | B | C | D | E | F | G | H | I | J |
|---|---|---|---|---|---|---|---|---|---|---|
| Safety rank | 1 | 2 | 3 | 4 | 5 | 6 | 6 | 8 | 9 | 10 |
| Accidents | 3 | 11 | 17 | 27 | 37 | 32 | 21 | 21 | 45 | 40 |

Rank the accident figures, calculate the rank correlation coefficient and comment on your results.

## Further Exercises

1   The product–moment correlation coefficient has been calculated for data relating to two variables $x$ and $y$. The value found was $-0.95$. What does this indicate?

   A. That the two variables increase together
   B. That $y$ decreases as $x$ increases
   C. That $x$ and $y$ are independent
   D. None of the above

2   The product–moment correlation coefficient has been calculated for data relating to two variables $x$ and $y$. The value found was 0.05. What does this indicate?

   A. That the two variables increase together
   B. That $y$ decreases as $x$ increases
   C. That $x$ and $y$ are independent
   D. None of the above

3   The product–moment correlation coefficient for two variables $x$ and $y$ is 0.9. What proportion of the variation in variable $y$ can be regarded as being explained by its relationship with the variable $x$?

   A. 0.90        B. 0.10        C. 0.81        D. 0.45

4   The percentage of the variation in a variable $y$ that is explained by its relationship with variable $x$ is 64%. Which of the following is a possible value for the product–moment correlation coefficient between $x$ and $y$?

   A. $-0.64$        B. $-0.80$        C. 0.41        D. 0.90

5    Which of the following *could* be true ?

   A. The product–moment correlation coefficient is −0.87.
   B. The coefficient of determination is −0.87.
   C. The coefficient of determination is 1.2.
   D. The rank correlation coefficient is 1.2.

6    Twelve brands of baked beans have been ranked in order of preference from 1 to 12, with the favourite brand being ranked 1. Three of the brands have been ranked equal fifth. If a rank correlation coefficient is to be calculated, what ranks will need to be assigned to the three brands ranked fifth equal for the purposes of the calculation?

   A. 4, 5, 6        B. 5, 5, 5        C. 6, 6, 6        D. 7, 7, 7

7    Five CD-players have been ranked according to quality, with the highest quality being ranked 1, and according to price, with the highest price being ranked 1.

| CD-player | A | B | C | D | E |
|---|---|---|---|---|---|
| Quality rank | 3 | 4 | 5 | 2 | 1 |
| Price rank | 5 | 4 | 3 | 2 | 1 |

   What is the value of the rank correlation coefficient?

   A. 0.4        B. 1.0        C. 0.6        D. 0.8

8    If two variables are measured on ordinal scales, which of the following can be used to assess the level of association between them?

   A. The product–moment correlation coefficient
   B. The coefficient of determination
   C. The rank correlation coefficient
   D. None of the above can be used

9    The weekly output, in tonnes, from a quarry and the weekly wages costs, in thousands of pounds, over an eight week period were as follows:

| Week | 1 | 2 | 3 | 4 | 5 | 6 | 7 | 8 |
|---|---|---|---|---|---|---|---|---|
| Output, $x$ | 44 | 50 | 52 | 46 | 54 | 60 | 58 | 64 |
| Costs, $y$ | 75 | 72 | 90 | 78 | 96 | 112 | 114 | 102 |

   Find the product–moment correlation coefficient between output and costs, and explain the meaning of your result.

10  Ten petrol stations in areas of similar traffic density are ranked according to size of forecourt and according to price charged for petrol. Shown below are these two sets of rankings and also the average weekly petrol sales in hundreds of litres.

| Petrol station | A | B | C | D | E | F | G | H | I | J |
|---|---|---|---|---|---|---|---|---|---|---|
| Size rank | 8 | 4 | 10 | 2 | 1 | 3 | 9 | 6 | 4 | 7 |
| Price rank | 2 | 9 | 8 | 1 | 4 | 5 | 7 | 10 | 3 | 6 |
| Sales (000s of litres) | 214 | 91 | 105 | 164 | 164 | 141 | 150 | 127 | 191 | 109 |

Decide by carrying out appropriate rank correlation coefficient calculations whether forecourt size or price of petrol is the more closely associated with total sales of petrol.

## Chapter Eleven

# Regression

## 11.1 Line of Best Fit

In Chapter 10 we saw how to measure the degree of association of two specific types between two variables. These types of association were:

1   Where the two variables increase together
2   Where one variable decreases as the other increases

We also saw in Chapter 10 how to plot a scatter diagram by plotting values of one variable against values of the other. We noted that variables increasing together corresponded to the plotted points lying close to an upward-sloping straight line while one variable decreasing as the other increases corresponded to the points lying close to a downward-sloping straight line. The essence of **regression** is to go a step further and find the equation of the straight line concerned. This is useful because it enables us to make predictions, as we shall see in Sec. 11.2.

Suppose that two variables have an association and suppose further that we can believe changes in one variable to be responsible for changes in the other. In other words, there is a **causal** relationship between them. The variable causing the changes is called the **independent variable** (usually called $x$) and the one being changed is called the **dependent variable** (usually called $y$). Regression enables us to find the equation $y = a + bx$ (see Chapter 3 for a discussion on the equation of a straight line) of the line to which the points on the scatter diagram lie closest. This line is what is meant by the **line of best fit**.

Figure 11.1 shows what a line of best fit might look like in a case where both variables increase together.

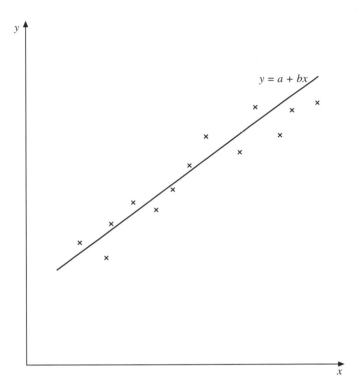

**Figure 11.1** Line of best fit for variables *x* and *y* which increase together

When dealing with regression it is very important to know which variable is independent and which is dependent. In Example 10.1.1 the number of insurance policies issued is the independent variable and the number of hours of overtime is dependent on this. In Example 10.1.2 the number of units of output is the independent variable and the cost per unit is dependent on this.

When we come to use the line of best fit to make predictions in Sec. 11.2, it is valid only to predict the dependent variable for values of the independent variable, and not vice versa. Thus, for the data in Example 10.1.1 regression would only be used to predict the overtime hours needed for a stated number of policies issued. Likewise, for the data in Example 10.1.2, regression would only be used to predict the cost per unit for a specified number of units of output.

Let's go back to the data used in Examples 10.1.1 and 10.1.2 and find the line of best fit in each case, first using EXCEL and then by manual calculation.

## Example 11.1.1

An insurance company recorded the number, $x$, of policies issued during each of six months and the total hours, $y$, of overtime worked each month in the issuing department:

| Policies, $x$ | 150 | 300 | 100 | 400 | 350 | 500 |
|---|---|---|---|---|---|---|
| Overtime hrs, $y$ | 10 | 20 | 10 | 40 | 30 | 35 |

a   Plot this set of data on a scatter diagram and draw on your diagram the straight line you believe passes closest to the points.
b   Find the equation $y = a + bx$ of the line of best fit using EXCEL.
c   Find the equation $y = a + bx$ of the line of best fit by means of manual calculation.
d   Draw the line of best fit on the scatter diagram for this data set in EXCEL.
e   Draw the line of best fit on the manually plotted scatter diagram for this data set.

### Solution to Example 11.1.1

a   Figure 11.2 shows the scatter diagram for the data set with a line drawn on it which the author thought looked closest to the points.

It is important that you carry out this plot yourself and draw your own line. It will almost certainly be different to the one the author has drawn. This shows the approach to be unacceptable and why we must go about things in a more scientific way so that everybody finishes up with the same line.

b   Enter the $x$ values into cells A1 to A6.
Enter the $y$ values into cells B1 to B6.
In cell A8 type the textual expression $b =$
In cell B8 enter the formula =INDEX(LINEST(B1:B6,A1:A6),1)
In cell A9 type the textual expression $a =$
In cell B9 enter the formula =INDEX(LINEST(B1:B6,A1:A6),2)

This will result in the value 0.078261 appearing in cell B8 and the value 0.688406 appearing in cell B9, showing that the line of best fit has equation:

$$y = 0.688406 + 0.078261x.$$

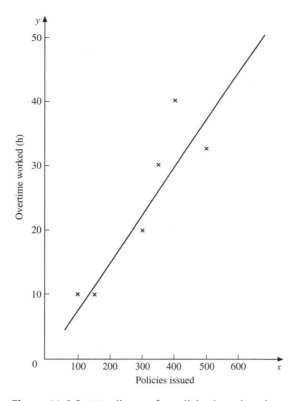

**Figure 11.2** Scatter diagram for policies issued against overtime worked with author's idea of the best fitting line

**c**     The formula needed for calculating $b$ is as follows:

$$b = \frac{n\Sigma xy - (\Sigma x)(\Sigma y)}{n\Sigma x^2 - (\Sigma x)^2}$$

where $n$ is the number of pairs of values being used.

Having found $b$ it is then possible to calculate $a$ using the formula

$$a = \frac{\Sigma y - b\,\Sigma x}{n}$$

As in the correlation coefficient calculation considered in Chapter 10, you must be absolutely clear about what these various summation expressions mean. If you are in any doubt at all, please refer back to the solution to Example 10.2.1 where there is a full explanation of all the summations for this set of data.

For the purpose of evaluating $b$ here we shall use a tabular layout like the one used in the answer to Example 10.2.2.

| $x$ | $y$ | $xy$ | $x^2$ |
|------|------|--------|---------|
| 150 | 10 | 1500 | 22 500 |
| 300 | 20 | 6000 | 90 000 |
| 100 | 10 | 1000 | 10 000 |
| 400 | 40 | 16 000 | 160 000 |
| 350 | 30 | 10 500 | 122 500 |
| 500 | 35 | 17 500 | 250 000 |
| 1800 | 145 | 52 500 | 655 000 |

Hence

$$b = \frac{6 \times 52\,500 - 1800 \times 145}{6 \times 655\,000 - 1800^2}$$

$$= \frac{315\,000 - 261\,000}{3\,930\,000 - 3\,240\,000} = \frac{54\,000}{690\,000} = 0.078261$$

Then

$$a = \frac{145 - 0.078261 \times 1800}{6} = \frac{145 - 140.8698}{6} = \frac{4.1302}{6} = 0.6884$$

So, the equation of the line of best fit is:

$$y = 0.6884 + 0.078261x$$

Did you notice the similarities between the formula for $b$ above and the formula we saw for $r$ in Chapter 10?

The numerator of $b$ is exactly the same as the numerator of $r$, and the denominator of $b$ is the first of the two terms in the square root in the denominator of $r$. So, if $r$ has already been calculated you don't need to embark on a whole new calculation to find $b$.

In this example the 54 000 numerator for $b$ could have been quoted from the numerator for $r$ in the answer to Example 10.2.1, and the 690 000 denominator could also have been quoted from that answer. Then the whole $b$ calculation is just:

$$b = \frac{54\,000}{690\,000} = 0.078261.$$

All the calculator steps needed for finding both the numerator and the denominator in a problem like this are set out in the answer to Example 10.2.2. The final step is considerably simpler than in the correlation case. It is just:

[54000] [÷] [690000] [=]

**d**   To plot the scatter diagram with the regression line on it using EXCEL for this set of data we can proceed by first plotting the scatter diagram as we did in Chapter 10.

Ensure that the $x$ values are in cells A1 to A6 and the $y$ values in cells B1 to B6, and use the Chart Wizard with the $xy$-scatter plot option to obtain the diagram.

Next double click on the graph and click on one of the plotted points in order to select the points. Then go to the Insert menu.

*Within the Insert menu choose Trendline.*

A click on OK here will put the line on the graph. However, if you click on the Options tab first and choose the

Display Equation on Chart

option, the regression line equation will appear alongside the line. Choosing the

Display $R$-squared Value on Chart

option will also give the $R$-squared value on the diagram.

Figure 11.3 shows the diagram with the line drawn on it and both options selected.

**e**   To plot the line manually we need first to calculate $y$ for some values of $x$. Then plot the resulting pairs of values and join them with a ruler. For this purpose it is sensible to use three $x$ values, one near each end of the range of $x$ values in the data and one near to the middle of the range. Two points are strictly enough, but if three are used and they all lie on a line you have a check that you have found the right line.

For this example we could use:

| $x$ | 100 | 300 | 500 |
|---|---|---|---|
| $0.078261x$ | 7.8261 | 23.4783 | 39.1305 |
| 0.6884 | 0.6884 | 0.6884 | 0.6884 |
| $y$ | 8.5145 | 24.1667 | 39.8189 |

Figure 11.4 shows the scatter diagram for this set of data with the line $y = 0.6884 + 0.078261x$ plotted on it using these three points.

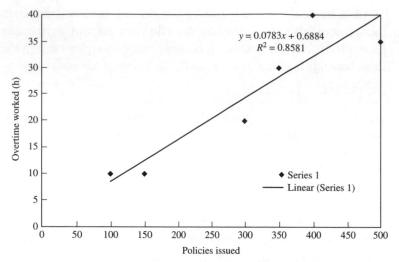

**Figure 11.3** Regression line on scatter diagram in EXCEL for policies issued and overtime worked

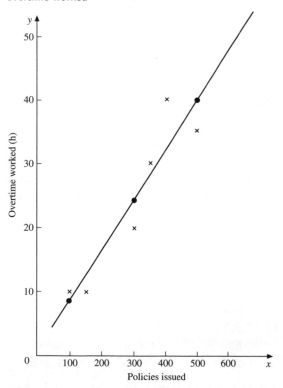

**Figure 11.4** Scatter diagram for policies issued against overtime worked with the calculated regression line plotted

Draw this line on your own graph plotted in answer to part (a) and note how close or otherwise it is to the line you thought would be best at that stage.

Before leaving this example we shall use it to explain the meaning of the values found for $a$ and $b$.

Having $a = 0.6884$ means that $y = 0.6884$ when $x = 0$. In terms of the variables involved in this question, $0.6884$ is the number of hours of over-time which would be needed even when no policies were issued. Graphically this is the value of $y$ at the point where the line crosses the $y$ axis.

Having $b = 0.078261$ means that $y$ gets larger by amount $0.078261$ when $x$ increases by 1. In terms of the variables involved in the question this is telling us that each additional policy issued causes the number of hours of overtime worked to go up by $0.078261$ hours. Graphically it is the gradient of the graph, which is the amount by which we move up vertically as we go one unit to the right while staying on the line.

## Example 11.1.2

You have collected figures over a 10 week period on levels of output and cost per unit of output of radio/cassette players:

| Output, $x$ (in 000s of units) | 10 | 18 | 25 | 20 | 16 | 30 | 32 | 34 | 5 | 24 |
|---|---|---|---|---|---|---|---|---|---|---|
| Cost per unit, $y$ (£) | 20 | 14 | 12 | 14 | 15 | 9 | 9 | 8 | 25 | 11 |

a   Find the equation $y = a + bx$ of the line of best fit using EXCEL.
b   Find the equation $y = a + bx$ of the line of best fit by means of manu-
    al calculation.
c   Draw the line of best fit on the scatter diagram for this data set in
    EXCEL.
d   Plot manually a scatter diagram for this data set and draw the line of
    best fit on it.

## Solution to Example 11.1.2

a   Enter the $x$ values into cells A1 to A10
    Enter the $y$ values into cells B1 to B10
    In cell A12 type the textual expression b =
    In cell B12 enter the formula =INDEX(LINEST(B1:B10,A1:A10),1)
    In cell A13 type the textual expression a =
    In cell B13 enter the formula =INDEX(LINEST(B1:B10,A1:A10),2)

This will result in the value $-0.54663$ appearing in cell B12 and the value 25.39782 appearing in cell B13, indicating a line of best fit which has the equation

$$y = 25.39782 - 0.54663x.$$

**b**   The formulae for the calculation of $b$ and $a$ are set out in the answer to Example 11.1.1 and we haven't repeated them here. We go on immediately to the calculation of the values by substitution into the formulae.

| $x$ | $y$ | $xy$ | $x^2$ |
|---|---|---|---|
| 10 | 20 | 200 | 100 |
| 18 | 14 | 252 | 324 |
| 25 | 12 | 300 | 625 |
| 20 | 14 | 280 | 400 |
| 16 | 15 | 240 | 256 |
| 30 | 9 | 270 | 900 |
| 32 | 9 | 288 | 1024 |
| 34 | 8 | 272 | 1156 |
| 5 | 25 | 125 | 25 |
| 24 | 11 | 264 | 576 |
| 214 | 137 | 2491 | 5386 |

The value of $n$ in this case is 10 as there are 10 pairs of values. So, the formula given for $b$ leads to the following calculation:

$$b = \frac{10 \times 2491 - 214 \times 137}{10 \times 5386 - 214 \times 214}$$

$$= \frac{24\,910 - 29\,318}{53\,860 - 45\,796} = \frac{-4408}{8064} = -0.54663$$

Then

$$a = \frac{137 - (-0.54663 \times 214)}{10} = \frac{137 + 116.978}{10} = \frac{253.978}{10} = 25.3978$$

So, the equation of the line of best fit is:

$$y = 25.3978 - 0.54663x$$

As in Example 11.1.1, the $-4408$ numerator for $b$ here could have been quoted from the numerator for $r$ in the answer to Example 10.2.2 and the 8064 denominator could also have been quoted from that answer. Then the whole $b$ calculation is just

$$b = \frac{-4408}{8064} = -0.54663$$

c   To plot the scatter diagram with the regression line on it using EXCEL for this set of data we can proceed by first plotting the scatter diagram as we did in Chapter 10. Ensure that the $x$ values are in cells A1 to A10 and the $y$ values in cells B1 to B10, and use the Chart Wizard with the $xy$-scatter plot option to obtain the diagram.

Next double click on the graph and click on one of the plotted points in order to select the points. Then go to the Insert menu.
Within the Insert menu choose Trendline.
Click on the Options tab within Trendline and choose the

Display Equation on Chart

option. The regression line equation will appear alongside the line. Choose also the

Display $R$-squared Value on Chart

to obtain the $R$-squared value on the diagram.

Figure 11.5 shows the diagram with the line drawn on it and both options selected.

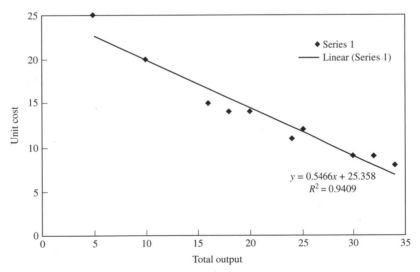

**Figure 11.5** Regression line on scatter diagram in EXCEL for total output and unit cost

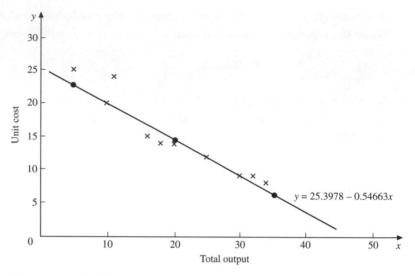

**Figure 11.6** Calculated regression line on scatter diagram for total output and unit cost

**d**   Calculate $y$ values for three suitable values of $x$ as follows:

| $x$ | 5 | 20 | 35 |
|---|---|---|---|
| $-0.54663x$ | $-2.73315$ | $-10.93260$ | $-19.13205$ |
| $25.39782$ | $25.39782$ | $25.39782$ | $25.39782$ |
| $y$ | $22.66467$ | $14.46522$ | $6.26577$ |

Figure 11.6 shows the scatter diagram for this set of data with the line $y = 25.39782 - 0.54663x$ plotted on it using these three points.

**Exercises 11.1**   1   The figures in the table below show the time it takes to do different clerical tasks (A–H) and the cost of doing each of them.

| Task | A | B | C | D | E | F | G | H |
|---|---|---|---|---|---|---|---|---|
| Time needed, $x$ (mins) | 7 | 8 | 10 | 12 | 14 | 16 | 20 | 24 |
| Cost, $y$ (£) | 4 | 7 | 8 | 9 | 10 | 14 | 17 | 18 |

**a**   Find the equation $y = a + bx$ of the line of best fit using EXCEL.
**b**   Find the equation $y = a + bx$ of the line of best fit by means of manual calculation.
**c**   Draw the line of best fit on the scatter diagram for this data set in EXCEL.
**d**   Draw the line of best fit on the manually plotted scatter diagram for this data set.

2   The following table shows, for a group of 12 production workers, the number of months experience each of them had and the numbers of defective items they produced during a particular week.

| Worker | 1 | 2 | 3 | 4 | 5 | 6 | 7 | 8 | 9 | 10 | 11 | 12 |
|---|---|---|---|---|---|---|---|---|---|---|---|---|
| Rejects, $y$ | 26 | 20 | 28 | 16 | 23 | 18 | 24 | 26 | 38 | 22 | 32 | 25 |
| Exp'nce, $x$ (mths) | 7 | 9 | 6 | 14 | 8 | 12 | 10 | 4 | 2 | 11 | 1 | 8 |

a   Find the equation $y = a + bx$ of the line of best fit using EXCEL.
b   Find the equation $y = a + bx$ of the line of best fit by means of manual calculation.
c   Draw the line of best fit on the scatter diagram for this data set in EXCEL.
d   Draw the line of best fit on the manually plotted scatter diagram for this data set.

## 11.2 Prediction

So far in this chapter we have seen how to find the equation of the line of best fit relating a dependent variable, $y$, to an independent variable, $x$. When this equation has been found, it can be used to predict the values of $y$ corresponding to given values of $x$.

There are two basic reasons for wanting to make this sort of prediction.

The first one is where the independent variable $x$ is uncontrollable and you need to **forecast** what value $y$ will take for different possible values of $x$. A particular case of this is where $x$ is time and you want to forecast what values $y$ will take at future points in time. Other examples are prediction of how many umbrellas will be sold per month in an area subject to different possible quantities of rainfall, or daily ice cream sales for different maximum daily temperatures.

The second use of prediction from the equation of a line of best fit is when $x$ is a variable which can be controlled and you want to work out what values for $y$ can be expected in response to different possible settings for $x$. This information can then be used to exercise some measure of control over the $y$ values produced.

The line of best fit has been found only for $x$ values in the range covered by the data. It may not be a valid relationship for values of $x$ outside this range. So predicting $y$ values for $x$ outside the data range must be done with care. You may need to make such predictions, but when you do so you must always ask yourself whether the prediction that emerges makes sense. Also remember that the further your $x$ value is from the centre of the original data the more chance there is of making a seriously inaccurate prediction.

Prediction of $y$ values for $x$ values inside the original data range is an altogether safer process.

However, the accuracy of *any* valid predictions made will depend on how well the line of best fit actually fits the data points, as measured by the correlation coefficient, or coefficient of determination, considered in Chapter 10. The closer the data points are to the line, the more accurate the predictions will be.

The steps involved in actually making predictions are very simple. One possibility would be to go to the graph showing the line of best fit and read off the $y$ value on the vertical axis corresponding to the specified $x$ value on the horizontal axis. Calculation of a prediction could be done using computer software or manually by simply inserting the appropriate $x$ value into the expression $a + bx$ in order to find $y$. We have already seen a number of such calculations, carried out by computer or manually, in Examples 11.1.1 and 11.1.2 where $y$ values were found in order to plot graphs of regression lines. We shall look again at the data in these examples for the purpose of illustrating the prediction process.

Note that you should never state a predicted value to a greater degree of accuracy than that of the original data.

## Example 11.2.1

An insurance company recorded the number, $x$, of policies issued during each of six months and the total hours, $y$, of overtime worked each month in the issuing department:

| Policies, $x$ | 150 | 300 | 100 | 400 | 350 | 500 |
|---|---|---|---|---|---|---|
| Overtime hrs, $y$ | 10 | 20 | 10 | 40 | 30 | 35 |

a    Estimate using the graph in Figure 11.2 the numbers of hours of overtime that would need to be worked in a month when
  • 250 policies are issued
  • 550 policies were issued.
b    Use EXCEL to predict the numbers of hours of overtime that would need to be worked in a month when
  • 250 policies are issued
  • 550 policies are issued.
c    Given that the line of best fit has equation $y = 0.6884 + 0.078261x$ (see Example 11.1.1) use manual calculations to predict the numbers of

hours of overtime that would need to be worked in a month when
- 250 policies are issued
- 550 policies are issued.

**d**    Comment on the predictions made in parts **a**, **b** and **c** above.

## Solution to Example 11.2.1

**a**    • If we go to the point $x = 250$ on the horizontal axis in Fig. 11.4, draw a line up to the line of best fit and then across to the vertical axis, we read off the expected number of hours of overtime to be worked as $y = 20$.

    • If we go to the point $x = 550$ on the horizontal axis in Fig. 11.4, draw a line up to the line of best fit and then across to the vertical axis, we read off the expected number of hours of overtime to be worked as $y = 44$.

These predictions are illustrated in Fig. 11.7.

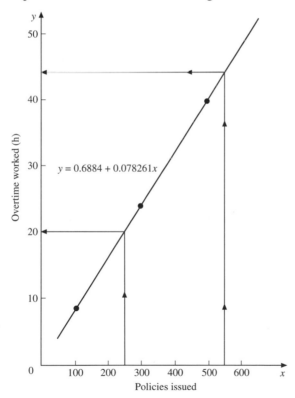

**Figure 11.7** Using the calculated regression line to predict overtime hours needed when 250 and 550 policies issued

**b**    Ensure that the $x$ values are in cells A1 to A6 and the $y$ values in cells B1 to B6.

- We can obtain the required forecast of $y$ when $x = 250$ by putting the cursor in cell C1 and proceeding as follows:

> Click on the Function Wizard icon
> Choose Statistical as the Function Category in the left-hand column of the dialogue box
> Choose FORECAST as the Function Name in the right-hand column of the dialogue box
> Click on Next
> Enter 250 as the $x$ value for which a forecast is required
> Enter B$1:B$6 as the known_$y$'s
> Enter A$1:A$6 as the known_$x$'s

This will result in the value 20.25362 appearing in the top right-hand corner of the dialogue box.

> Click on Finish.
> The value 20.25362 will appear in cell C1.

- We can obtain the required forecast of $y$ when $x = 550$ by putting the cursor in cell C2 and proceeding as follows:

> Click on the Function Wizard icon
> Choose Statistical as the Function Category in the left-hand column of the dialogue box
> Choose FORECAST as the Function Name in the right-hand column of the dialogue box
> Click on Next
> Enter 550 as the $x$ value for which a forecast is required
> Enter B$1:B$6 as the known_$y$'s
> Enter A$1:A$6 as the known_x's

This will result in the value 43.73188 appearing in the top right-hand corner of the dialogue box.

> Click on Finish
> The value 43.73188 will appear in cell C2

**c**    • The predicted number of overtime hours required when 250 policies are issued can be calculated manually as

$$y = 0.6884 + 0.078261 \times 250 = 0.6884 + 19.56525 = 20$$

The calculator steps needed to carry out this operation are

$[0.078261] [\times] [250] [=] [+] [0.6884] [=]$

- The predicted number of overtime hours required when 550 policies are issued can be calculated manually as

$y = 0.6884 + 0.078261 \times 550 = 0.6884 + 43.04355 = 44$

The calculator steps needed to carry out this operation are

$[0.078261] [\times] [550] [=] [+] [0.6884] [=]$

**d**   We saw in Chapter 10 that the correlation coefficient between $x$ and $y$ in this problem was 0.926331, giving a coefficient of determination of 0.858. This showed that 85.8% of the variation in the overtime hours can be explained by the relationship of this variable to the number of policies issued. These figures suggest that the line of best fit is a good fit to the data set and that the regression relationship is capable of producing accurate predictions.

- Specifically, the prediction when $x = 250$ is a prediction of $y$ using an $x$ value for which the regression relationship has been established. We have, therefore, good grounds for confidence in the prediction of $y = 20$ when $x = 250$.
- The prediction when $x = 550$ is a prediction of $y$ using an $x$ value beyond the range for which the regression relationship has been established. We cannot therefore be as certain of ourselves in making the prediction of $y = 44$ as we were in making the prediction when $x = 250$. However, the value 550 is not a long way outside the original range and the resulting prediction would seem a perfectly sensible suggestion for the value of $y$.

## Example 11.2.2

You have collected figures over a 10 week period on levels of output and cost per unit of output of radio/cassette players:

| Output, $x$ (in 000s of units) | 10 | 18 | 25 | 20 | 16 | 30 | 32 | 34 | 5 | 24 |
|---|---|---|---|---|---|---|---|---|---|---|
| Cost per unit, $y$ (£) | 20 | 14 | 12 | 14 | 15 | 9 | 9 | 8 | 25 | 11 |

**a**   Estimate using the graph in Fig. 11.6 the unit cost in a week when
- 15 units are output
- 41 units are output.

**b**    Use EXCEL to predict the unit cost in a week when
- 15 units are output
- 41 units are output.

**c**    Given that the line of best fit has equation $y = 25.3978 - 0.54663x$ (see Example 11.1.2) use manual calculations to predict the unit cost in a week when
- 15 units are output
- 41 units are output.

**d**    Comment on the predictions made in parts **a**, **b** and **c** above.

## Solution to Example 11.2.2

**a**    • If we go to the point $x = 15$ on the horizontal axis in Fig. 11.6, draw a line up to the line of best fit and then across to the vertical axis, we read off the predicted unit cost as $y = 17$
- If we go to the point $x = 41$ on the horizontal axis in Fig. 11.6, draw a line up to the line of best fit and then across to the vertical axis, we read off the predicted unit cost as $y = 3$

These predictions are illustrated in Fig. 11.8.

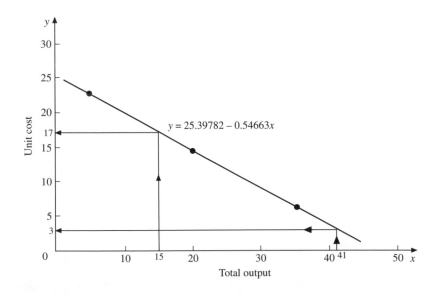

**Figure 11.8** Using the calculated regression line to predict unit cost when total output is 15 units and 41 units

**b**  Ensure that the *x* values are in cells A1 to A10 and the *y* values in cells B1 to B10.

• We can obtain the required forecast of *y* when $x = 15$ by putting the cursor in cell C1 and proceeding as follows:

> Click on the Function Wizard icon
> Choose Statistical as the Function Category in the left-hand column of the dialogue box
> Choose FORECAST as the Function Name in the right-hand column of the dialogue box
> Click on Next
> Enter 15 as the *x* value for which a forecast is required
> Enter B$1:B$10 as the known_*y*'s
> Enter A$1:A$10 as the known_*x*'s

This will result in the value 17.1984127 appearing in the top right-hand corner of the dialogue box.

> Click on Finish.
> The value 17.19841 will appear in cell C1

• We can obtain the required forecast of *y* when $x = 41$ by putting the cursor in cell C2 and proceeding as follows:

> Click on the Function Wizard icon
> Choose Statistical as the Function Category in the left-hand column of the dialogue box
> Choose FORECAST as the Function Name in the right-hand column of the dialogue box
> Click on Next
> Enter 41 as the *x* value for which a forecast is required
> Enter B$1:B$10 as the known_*y*'s
> Enter A$1:A$10 as the known_*x*'s

This will result in the value 2.986111111 appearing in the top right-hand corner of the dialogue box.

> Click on Finish.
> The value 2.986111 will appear in cell C2

**c**  • The predicted unit cost when 15 items are output can be calculated manually as

$$y = 25.39782 - 0.54663 \times 15 = 25.39782 - 8.19945 = 17$$

The calculator steps needed to carry out this operation are

[0.54663] [×] [15] [=] [+] [25.39782] [=]

- The predicted number of overtime hours required when 41 policies are issued can be calculated manually as

$$y = 25.39782 - 0.54663 \times 41 = 25.39782 - 22.41183 = 3$$

The calculator steps needed to carry out this operation are

[0.54663] [×] [41] [=] [+] [25.39782] [=]

**d**  We saw in Chapter 10 that the correlation coefficient between $x$ and $y$ in this problem was 0.96998, giving a coefficient of determination of 0.941, indicating 94.1% of the variation in the overtime hours to be explained by the relationship of this variable to the number of policies issued. These figures suggest that the calculated regression line is a good fit to the data set and that the regression relationship is capable of producing accurate predictions.

- Specifically, the prediction when $x = 15$ is a prediction of $y$ using an $x$ value for which the regression relationship has been established. We have, therefore, good grounds for confidence in the prediction of $y = 17$ when $x = 15$.
- The prediction when $x = 41$ is a prediction of $y$ using an $x$ value beyond the range for which the regression relationship has been established. It is by no means certain that the relationship holds for $x$ values this large. If we tried to use the relationship to predict for $x$ values even a little bit larger than 41, the result would be a negative predicted cost per unit, which would be nonsensical.

**Exercises 11.2**

1  The figures in the table below show the time it takes to do different clerical tasks (A–H) and the cost of doing each of them.

| Task | A | B | C | D | E | F | G | H |
|---|---|---|---|---|---|---|---|---|
| Time needed, $x$ (mins) | 7 | 8 | 10 | 12 | 14 | 16 | 20 | 24 |
| Cost, $y$ (£) | 4 | 7 | 8 | 9 | 10 | 14 | 17 | 18 |

**a**  Predict using your graph drawn in answer to Exercise 11.1.1 the cost of completing a task requiring
- 15 minutes
- 30 minutes.

  **b**  Use EXCEL to predict the cost of completing a task requiring:
- 15 minutes
- 30 minutes.

  **c**  Using the equation found for the line of best fit in your answer to Exercise 11.1.1 carry out manual calculations to predict the cost of completing a task requiring:
- 15 minutes
- 30 minutes.

  **d**  Comment on the predictions made in parts **a**, **b** and **c** above.

2   The following table shows, for a group of 12 production workers, the number of months of experience each of them had and the numbers of defective items they produced during a particular week.

| Worker | 1 | 2 | 3 | 4 | 5 | 6 | 7 | 8 | 9 | 10 | 11 | 12 |
|---|---|---|---|---|---|---|---|---|---|---|---|---|
| Rejects, $y$ | 26 | 20 | 28 | 16 | 23 | 18 | 24 | 26 | 38 | 22 | 32 | 25 |
| Exp'nce, $x$ (mths) | 7 | 9 | 6 | 14 | 8 | 12 | 10 | 4 | 2 | 11 | 1 | 8 |

  **a**  Predict using your graph drawn in answer to Exercise 11.1.2 the number of rejects that will be produced in a week by a worker having
- 5 months of experience
- 20 months of experience.

  **b**  Use EXCEL to predict the number of rejects that will be produced in a week by a worker having
- 5 months of experience
- 20 months of experience.

  **c**  Using the equation found for the line of best fit in your answer to Exercise 11.1.2 carry out manual calculations to predict the number of rejects that will be produced in a week by a worker having
- 5 months of experience
- 20 months of experience.

  **d**  Comment on the predictions made in parts **a**, **b** and **c** above.

## Further Exercises

1.  A company's monthly costs, $y$, were recorded along with the numbers of units, $x$, produced in the month for the last 30 months and a line of best fit was calculated as $y = 12\,000 + 600x$. Which of the following statements about monthly costs is true?

    A. The average cost per month is $400 + 20x$

B. Fixed costs are 400 and variable costs are 20 per unit produced
C. Fixed costs are 600 and variable costs are 12 000
D. Fixed costs are 12 000 and variable costs are 600

2    The line of best fit for two variables $x$ and $y$ has been found as

$$y = 24 + 4x$$

The following five statements are made about the relationship between the two variables:

I    The value of $y$ is always greater than the value of $x$ by 24 units
II   When $x = 0$, then $y = 24$
III  As $x$ increases $y$ also increases
IV  As $x$ increases $y$ decreases
V   The $x$ value cannot equal the $y$ value

Which of the following is true?

    A. II and III      B. III and V      C. I and II      D. II and V

3    The line of best fit equation $y = a + bx$ is to be found for the regression of variable $y$ on variable $x$. Fifteen data pairs have been obtained and the following summations have been calculated

$$\Sigma x = 63 \qquad \Sigma y = 150 \qquad \Sigma x^2 = 712.6 \qquad \Sigma xy = 1974$$

What is the value of $b$?

    A. 2.3          B. 2.5          C. 2.8          D. 3.0

4    The line of best fit for two variables $x$ and $y$ has been found as

$$y = -50 + 17.5x$$

What is the predicted value for $y$ when $x = 15$ ?

    A. 312.5      B. 212.5      C. 67.5      D. 32.5

5    A regression line of $y$ on $x$ has been calculated as $y = 8.5 + 8.5x$ using the following data values

| $x$ | 1 | 2 | 3 | 4 | 5 |
|-----|----|----|----|----|----|
| $y$ | 10 | 30 | 40 | 45 | 45 |

Suppose you are asked to predict $y$ when $x = 3$ using the regression line given. Which of the following is true?

A. $y = 34$ is the predicted value
B. $y = 40$ is the predicted value
C. $y = 45$ is the predicted value
D. The prediction sought cannot be made validly using the regression line given.

6   A regression line of $y$ on $x$ has been calculated as $y = 8.5 + 8.5x$ using the following data values

| $x$ | 1 | 2 | 3 | 4 | 5 |
|-----|----|----|----|----|----|
| $y$ | 10 | 30 | 40 | 45 | 45 |

Suppose you are asked to predict $x$ when $y = 42.5$ using the regression line given. Which of the following is true?

A. $x = 4$ is the predicted value
B. $x = 8.5$ is the predicted value
C. $x = 42.5$ is the predicted value
D. The prediction sought cannot be made validly using the regression line given.

7   A road haulage company wants to analyse its costs into a fixed part and a variable part. It has data for 10 years as follows:

| Year | 1 | 2 | 3 | 4 | 5 | 6 | 7 | 8 | 9 | 10 |
|------|-----|-----|-----|-----|-----|-----|-----|-----|-----|-----|
| Tonne-miles in 000s, $x$ | 330 | 240 | 270 | 270 | 450 | 420 | 360 | 420 | 375 | 330 |
| Costs in £000s, $y$ | 81 | 60 | 75 | 72 | 96 | 90 | 83 | 93 | 82 | 76 |

a   Plot a scatter graph showing cost on the vertical axis and tonne-miles on the horizontal axis.
b   Find the equation of the line of best fit $y = a + bx$ and hence state the company's monthly fixed cost and its variable cost per tonne-mile.
c   Plot the line of best fit on the scatter graph drawn in answer to part **a**.

8   The table below shows the numbers of faulty items in batches of equal size produced by ten production operatives, and the mean time in minutes taken to produce each item.

| Operative | | 1 | 2 | 3 | 4 | 5 | 6 | 7 | 8 | 9 | 10 |
|---|---|---|---|---|---|---|---|---|---|---|---|
| Faulty items, $y$ | | 30 | 16 | 21 | 23 | 21 | 26 | 28 | 20 | 25 | 22 |
| Mean time per item (mins), $x$: | | 16 | 24 | 23 | 20 | 20 | 19 | 22 | 25 | 18 | 17 |

**a** Use EXCEL to plot a scatter graph of number of faulty items against mean time per item.

**b** Use EXCEL to find the line of best fit $y = a + bx$ and to draw it on the scatter graph.

**c** A new employee takes an average of 27 minutes to produce an item. Use EXCEL to obtain a prediction of the number of faulty items there will be in a standard-sized batch produced by this operative and to obtain any other information you need in order to comment on the quality of the prediction made.

9 A study has been carried out to attempt to relate the productivity of production workers to their scores on the aptitude test used in the process of appointing them. Pairs of scores for productivity and aptitude test score are shown below for six randomly chosen employees.

| Employee | 1 | 2 | 3 | 4 | 5 | 6 |
|---|---|---|---|---|---|---|
| Aptitude score, $x$ | 23 | 17 | 20 | 19 | 20 | 9 |
| Productivity, $y$ | 32 | 35 | 29 | 33 | 43 | 23 |

**a** Plot a scatter graph showing productivity on the vertical axis and aptitude score on the horizontal axis, and comment on the relationship between these variables in the light of your graph.

**b** Calculate the equation of the line of best fit $y = a + bx$.

**c** Predict the productivity figure for an employee with an aptitude score of 16 and comment on the likely quality of this prediction.

**d** Predict the productivity figure for an employee with an aptitude score of 30 and comment on the likely quality of this prediction.

10 The time taken to word process a document is believed to consist of an element proportional to the number of words in the document plus a fixed time needed for such activities as arranging the papers, setting up the computer file and printing. The data shown below have been gathered for a sample of 12 documents.

| Document | 1 | 2 | 3 | 4 | 5 | 6 | 7 | 8 | 9 | 10 | 11 | 12 |
|---|---|---|---|---|---|---|---|---|---|---|---|---|
| Words, $x$ | 800 | 1300 | 600 | 900 | 1400 | 1100 | 700 | 1200 | 500 | 1500 | 400 | 1600 |
| Time (mins) $y$ | 14.2 | 19.4 | 11.8 | 14.4 | 20.4 | 17.2 | 12.6 | 17.8 | 11.5 | 20.6 | 10.2 | 22.6 |

a   Use EXCEL to plot a scatter graph of word processing time against number of words in the document.

b   Use EXCEL to find the line of best fit $y = a + bx$ and to draw it on the scatter graph.

c   State the average number of words processed per minute and state also the fixed time needed per document for indirect activities such as those described in the question.

d   A new document consisting of 1000 words is to be word processed. Use EXCEL to obtain a prediction of the time that will be required to deal with this document and to obtain any other information you need in order to comment on the quality of the prediction made.

## Chapter Twelve

# *Probability*

## 12.1 Elementary Ideas of Probability

Probability is about trying to measure whether things are likely to happen or not. Statisticians measure probabilities in the range 0 to 1 where:

the value 0 means that the thing definitely won't happen and
the value 1 means that the thing definitely will happen.

It's the bit in between that we're most interested in.

We use probabilities every day, though we rarely put a value to them. You might say, 'It will probably rain today', but it is very unlikely that you would say, 'There is a 0.85 probability that it will rain today'.

These **subjective probabilities**, as they are called, are very important to those in the gambling industry, who make an excellent living out of offering punters a range of odds against this or that event happening.

Although subjective probabilities are important, we are going to focus here on viewing the probability of an event happening as the proportion of times it happens out of a whole lot of occasions when it might or might not happen.

Imagine rolling a die with four red faces and two white faces hundreds and hundreds of times. What is the likelihood of a red face coming up ? Four out of six you will say (we hope !).

Statisticians put the answer in a slightly different way. They write a capital *P* and, in brackets after it, the event whose likelihood is being measured. So, in this case they would write

$P(\text{red face}) = 2/3 = 0.67$

Four times out of six is two-thirds or, as a decimal, 0.67. Using a decimal is a good idea as it means we all write the answer in the same way.

Thus whenever all outcomes are equally likely, as with the faces of the die in this example, the probability of an event can be calculated as

$$\frac{\text{Number of outcomes which mean the event has occurred}}{\text{Total possible number of outcomes}}$$

The die example is a particular instance of this where the 6 faces are 6 equally likely outcomes. As 4 of the 6 faces are red,

$$P(\text{red face}) = \frac{\text{Number of red faces}}{\text{Total number of faces}} = \frac{4}{6} = \frac{2}{3} = 0.67 \quad \text{as before}$$

An important special case to note is that where the event we are interested in consists of ALL possible outcomes. In this situation we have

$$\frac{\text{Number of outcomes which mean the event has occurred}}{\text{Total possible number of outcomes}}$$

$$= \frac{\text{Total possible number of outcomes}}{\text{Total possible number of outcomes}} = 1$$

that is, total probability $= 1$.

In the case of the die we would have $P(\text{face is red or white}) = \frac{6}{6} = 1$

The fact that total probability is *always* 1 is of great importance and usefulness when working with probabilities.

## Example 12.1.1

A firm has a mixture of large and small customer companies, some of whom are prompt payers for goods received and some of whom are slow payers. The breakdown by size and by speed of payment is shown in the table below:

|  | Prompt payers | Slow payers |
| --- | --- | --- |
| Large customers | 10 | 45 |
| Small customers | 25 | 20 |

The firm intends to select customers at random to investigate more fully the history of its dealings with them.

a   What is the probability that a customer company chosen at random will be both large and a slow payer? (This is called the **joint probability** of the two. It is the probability of both conditions being met together.)

**b**  What is the probability that a company chosen at random will be a prompt payer? (This would be referred to as the **marginal probability** of being a prompt payer. It covers all categories together of the other criterion—size of company.)

**c**  What is the probability that a randomly chosen company will be a large customer? (This is the marginal probability of being a large customer.)

**d**  Draw up an expanded table showing the probability of every combination of customer size and speed of payment and all the marginal probabilities.

### Solution to Example 12.1.1

We begin with a table showing the row and column totals and the grand total.

|                 | Prompt payers | Slow payers | Total |
|-----------------|---------------|-------------|-------|
| Large customers | 10            | 45          | 55    |
| Small customers | 25            | 20          | 45    |
| Total           | 35            | 65          | 100   |

**a**  Out of 100 companies there are 45 who are large and also slow payers, so the joint probability is:

$P$(large and a slow payer) = 45/100 = 0.45

**b**  Out of 100 companies there are 35 prompt payers, so the marginal probability of a prompt payer is:

$P$(prompt payer) = 35/100 = 0.35

**c**  Out of 100 companies there are 55 large customers, so the marginal probability of a large customer is:

$P$(large customer) = 55/100 = 0.55

**d**  From the answers to parts **a**, **b** and **c** we see that all the figures in the table can be converted to the probabilities required if we divide by 100. This leads to the following table of probabilities:

|                 | Prompt payers | Slow payers | Total |
|-----------------|---------------|-------------|-------|
| Large customers | 0.10          | 0.45        | 0.55  |
| Small customers | 0.25          | 0.20        | 0.45  |
| Total           | 0.35          | 0.65        | 1.00  |

## Example 12.1.2

The table below shows the numbers of defective items found in batches of 100 items from each of three production lines making the item concerned.

| | Number of defective items in batches of 100 items | | | |
|---|---|---|---|---|
| | 0 | 1 | 2 | 3 or more |
| Line X | 250 | 100 | 100 | 50 |
| Line Y | 210 | 80 | 40 | 20 |
| Line Z | 300 | 50 | 25 | 25 |

a   What is the probability that a batch chosen at random both contains no defectives and is from line X?  _0.2_
b   What is the probability that a batch chosen at random is from line Y?  _0.28_
c   What is the probability that a batch chosen at random contains 2 defectives?   _0.132_
d   Construct a revised table showing the joint probability of occurrence of every possible combination of production line and number of defectives. Show also the marginal probabilities of the different lines and numbers of defectives.

## Solution to Example 12.1.2

For all the probability calculations required here it is necessary to know the row and column totals and the grand total for the table.

| | Number of defective items in batches of 100 items | | | | |
|---|---|---|---|---|---|
| | 0 | 1 | 2 | 3 or more | Total |
| Line X | 250 | 100 | 100 | 50 | 500 |
| Line Y | 210 | 80 | 40 | 20 | 350 |
| Line Z | 300 | 50 | 25 | 25 | 400 |
| Total | 760 | 230 | 165 | 95 | 1250 |

**a**    Out of a total of 1250 batches there are 250 which meet the conditions stated, so

$$P(\text{no defectives and from line } X) = \frac{250}{1250} = 0.2.$$

**b**    Out of a total of 1250 batches there are 350 from line $Y$. Hence

$$P(\text{batch is from line } Y) = \frac{350}{1250} = 0.28$$

**c**    Out of a total of 1250 batches there are 165 which contain 2 defectives, so

$$P(\text{batch contains 2 defectives}) = \frac{165}{1250} = 0.132$$

**d**    From the answers to parts **a**, **b** and **c** we see that all the figures in the table can be converted to the probabilities required if we divide by 1250. This leads to the following table of probabilities:

| | Number of defective items in batches of 100 items | | | | |
| --- | --- | --- | --- | --- | --- |
| | 0 | 1 | 2 | 3 or more | Total |
| Line X | .200 | .080 | .080 | .040 | .400 |
| Line Y | .168 | .064 | .032 | .016 | .280 |
| Line Z | .240 | .040 | .020 | .020 | .320 |
| | .608 | .184 | .132 | .076 | |

**Exercises 12.1**

1    If a card is drawn at random from a well shuffled standard pack of 52 playing cards, write down the probability of each of the following being chosen:

    **a**    an ace    0.0769

    **b**    a diamond    0.25

    **c**    a red ace    0.0385

    **d**    the ace of diamonds.    0.019

2    The table below shows the method of travel to work of people employed in two neighbouring small firms. Construct a table showing the joint probability of each combination of firm and method of travel, and showing also all the marginal probabilities.

|        | Method of travel   |        |            |         |
|--------|--------------------|--------|------------|---------|
|        | Public transport   | By car | By bicycle | On foot |
| Firm 1 | 20                 | 15     | 10         | 5       |
| Firm 2 | 35                 | 5      | 5          | 5       |

## 12.2 Probability Rules

In order to explain the rules which govern probabilities it is useful to introduce the concept of the **Venn diagram**. This is a device in which events are represented by shapes within (usually) a rectangle. The rectangle represents the collection of all possible outcomes of the experiment being considered. The technical name for the collection of all possible outcomes is the **sample space**. In a Venn diagram the magnitude of the area of a shape is used to represent its probability, so the area of the whole rectangle is 1 (see Fig. 12.1). (There is, however, no requirement to actually draw to scale, so the physical size of shapes drawn in Venn diagrams is irrelevant. All areas are notional and the purpose is only to enable visualization of the probability rules.)

Events consisting of subsets of the whole sample space are drawn as blobs within the rectangle. The (notional) areas of these blobs represent the probabilities of the events. Probability as a number between 0 and 1 is well represented by a Venn diagram as no blob can have a negative area and no blob can contain more outcomes than the whole sample space and so have an area larger than 1 (see Fig. 12.2).

**Figure 12.1** A Venn diagram representing a sample space

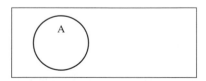

**Figure 12.2** A Venn diagram showing a single event, A

**Mutually exclusive events** are events which have no outcomes in common. Thus if we are told that one of the events in a mutually exclusive set of events has happened, then none of the others can possibly happen. In Venn diagram terms mutually exclusive events are represented by blobs which do not overlap (Fig. 12.3).

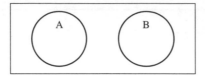

**Figure 12.3** A Venn diagram showing mutually exclusive events, A and B

We see from Fig. 12.3 that if we were asked for the probability that either $A$ or $B$ will occur (noting that both cannot occur together) then this probability will be the sum of the areas of the two blobs. Thus when two events $A$ and $B$ are mutually exclusive, then

$$P(A \textbf{ or } B) = P(A) + P(B)$$

This is called the **addition rule for mutually exclusive events**.

The addition rule can be extended to events which are not mutually exclusive, and the Venn diagram is again helpful in showing how this can be done (see Fig. 12.4). In this case we are looking at events $A$ and $B$ which have some outcomes in common. If we were to suggest $P(A) + P(B)$ as the probability of $A$ or $B$ occurring, we should be wrong to the extent of the double count of the overlap area which represents the probability of $A$ and $B$ occurring together. Thus we need to take away one of the 'copies' of this area to reveal the rule:

$$P(A \textbf{ or } B) = P(A) + P(B) - P(A \textbf{ and } B)$$

This is called the **generalized addition rule**.

We see that the rule for mutually exclusive events is a special case of this generalized rule because if events $A$ and $B$ are mutually exclusive there is no overlap area, so that $P(A \text{ and } B) = 0$ and we are back to the rule as first stated.

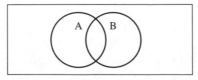

**Figure 12.4** A Venn diagram showing events A and B which are not mutually exclusive

## Example 12.2.1

The table below relates to numbers of defective items found in batches of 100 items from each of three production lines making the item concerned. The table shows the joint probability of occurrence of every possible combination of production line and number of defectives. It also shows the marginal probabilities of the different lines and numbers of defectives.

| | Number of defective items in batches of 100 items | | | | |
| | 0 | 1 | 2 | 3 or more | Total |
| --- | --- | --- | --- | --- | --- |
| Line X | .200 | .080 | .080 | .040 | .400 |
| Line Y | .168 | .064 | .032 | .016 | .280 |
| Line Z | .240 | .040 | .020 | .020 | .320 |
| | .608 | .184 | .132 | .076 | |

a   Use the addition rule for mutually exclusive events to find the probability of a batch chosen at random being from line $X$ or line $Y$.

b   Use the generalized addition rule to find the probability that a batch chosen at random is from line $X$ or contains 0 defectives.

## Solution to Example 12.2.1

a   We first note that the two events being considered here are certainly mutually exclusive as a batch can come from only one line.

Thus $P(\text{line } X \text{ or line } Y) = P(\text{line } X) + P(\text{line } Y) = 0.40 + 0.28 = 0.68$

b   The two events being considered in this part are not mutually exclusive as there are some batches which are both from line X and contain 0 defectives. So

$P(\text{line } X \text{ or } 0 \text{ defectives})$
$= P(\text{line } X) + P(0 \text{ defectives}) - P(\text{line } X \text{ and } 0 \text{ defectives})$
$= 0.400 + 0.608 - 0.200$
$= 0.808$

In order to appreciate the concept of conditional probability, consider again Fig. 12.4. Suppose now that we are told that event $A$ has occurred and asked to find the probability, in the light of this information, that event

$B$ will occur. What is being asked for here is the **conditional probability** of event $B$ given event $A$, and it is denoted $P(B|A)$. This is read as 'the probability of $B$ given $A$'.

In terms of the areas in the Venn diagram, we know that we are in the $A$ area and we want to know the probability of also being in the $B$ area. The only way this can happen is for us to be in the area $A$ **and** $B$. Thus we can think about the required probability as being the $A$ **and** $B$ area as a proportion of the whole $A$ area. This leads us to the definition of the conditional probability $P(B|A)$ as

$$P(B|A) = \frac{P(A \text{ and } B)}{P(A)}$$

If we multiply both sides of this by $P(A)$, we obtain:

$$P(A \text{ and } B) = P(B|A)P(A)$$

This is called the **generalized multiplication rule** for probabilities.

Events are **independent** if the fact that one of them has happened has no influence on the probability of any of the others happening. Thus if $A$ and $B$ are two independent events, knowing that $A$ has happened adds nothing to our knowledge about the probability of $B$ happening. That is to say,

$$P(B|A) = P(B).$$

So from the conditional probability definition we have

$$P(B) = \frac{P(A \text{ and } B)}{P(A)}$$

(To see what this means in terms of a Venn diagram consider again Fig. 12.4. If $A$ and $B$ are independent events, the overlap area as a proportion of the $A$ area would be equal to the full B area.)

Multiplying both sides of the last equation by $P(A)$ we obtain

$$P(A \text{ and } B) = P(A)P(B)$$

This is the **multiplication rule for independent events**.

## Example 12.2.2

The table below shows the numbers of defective items found in batches of 100 items from each of three production lines making the item concerned. The table has been expanded to show the row and column totals and the grand total of batches considered.

| | Number of defective items in batches of 100 items | | | | |
|---|---|---|---|---|---|
| | 0 | 1 | 2 | 3 or more | Total |
| Line X | 250 | 100 | 100 | 50 | 500 |
| Line Y | 210 | 80 | 40 | 20 | 350 |
| Line Z | 300 | 50 | 25 | 25 | 400 |
| | 760 | 230 | 165 | 95 | 1250 |

From this table a further table has been derived showing the joint probability of occurrence of every possible combination of production line and number of defectives. This table also shows the marginal probabilities of the different lines and numbers of defectives.

| | Number of defective items in batches of 100 items | | | | |
|---|---|---|---|---|---|
| | 0 | 1 | 2 | 3 or more | Total |
| Line X | .200 | .080 | .080 | .040 | .400 |
| Line Y | .168 | .064 | .032 | .016 | .280 |
| Line Z | .240 | .040 | .020 | .020 | .320 |
| | .608 | .184 | .132 | .076 | |

**a**  Find the probability that a batch known to have come from line $X$ contains 2 defectives.

**b**  Find the probability that a batch known to contain 2 defectives was produced on line $X$.

**c**  Are the probabilities structured in such a way as to suggest that numbers of defective items in a batch is independent of the line on which it was produced?

## Solution to Example 12.2.2

**a**  $P(2 \text{ defectives} \mid \text{line } X) = \dfrac{P(2 \text{ defectives and line } X)}{P(\text{line } X)}$

$$= \frac{0.080}{0.400} = 0.200$$

(This part of the question could have been answered directly from the initial table showing the numbers of batches. Our attention is being restricted to the line $X$ batches, of which there are 500, and there are 100 of these which contain 2 defectives. Hence

$$P(2 \text{ defectives} \mid \text{line } X) = \frac{100}{500} = 0.200 \quad )$$

**b**   $P(\text{line } X \mid 2 \text{ defectives}) = \dfrac{P(\text{line } X \textbf{ and } 2 \text{ defectives})}{P(2 \text{ defectives})}$

$$= \frac{0.080}{0.132} = 0.606$$

(This part of the question also could be answered from the initial table. Our attention is being restricted to the batches containing 2 defectives of which there are 165. Of these there are 100 which are from line $X$. Hence

$$P(\text{line } X \mid 2 \text{ defectives}) = \frac{100}{165} = 0.606. \quad )$$

**c**   In order for the structure of probabilities to suggest independence we would need a situation where **every** product of marginal probabilities was equal to the joint probability in the cell concerned. In this case

$$P(\text{line } X)P(0 \text{ defectives}) = 0.400 \times 0.608 = 0.2432$$

Since this is not equal to the value 0.200 in the cell for the joint probability of line $X$ and 0 defectives, it follows that the probability structure of this table does *not* suggest that the number of defectives produced is independent of production line.

**Exercises 12.2**   1   An item produced by a company can suffer two kinds of defect, $X$ and $Y$. The probability of an $X$ defect is 0.125 and the probability of a $Y$ defect is 0.167, independent of whether there is an $X$ defect. Find the probability that an item has:

**a**   both $X$ and $Y$ defects
**b**   exactly one defect
**c**   no defect

What relationship is there between your answers to **a**, **b** and **c**?

2   Two salespersons, Mr X and Ms Y, go out on a particular day to each

pursue three contacts which have been made through a telephone sales campaign. On the basis of past performances, the joint probability distribution for the numbers of sales made by the two is believed to be as follows:

| Number of sales | Mr X | | | |
|---|---|---|---|---|
| | 0 | 1 | 2 | 3 |
| Ms Y  0 | .216000 | .216000 | .072000 | .008000 |
| 1 | .162000 | .162000 | .054000 | .006000 |
| 2 | .040500 | .040500 | .013500 | .001500 |
| 3 | .003375 | .003375 | .001125 | .000125 |

**a**  Find the marginal probability distribution for Mr X.
**b**  Find the marginal probability distribution for Ms Y.
**c**  State, with reasons, whether the probabilities given suggest that numbers of sales made by Mr X and Ms Y are independent of each other.

## 12.3 Expected Values of Random Variables

To illustrate the idea of a **random variable** let us think about rolling a die and observing the number of dots on the uppermost face each time it is rolled. This is a variable because it will in principle take a different value each time the die is rolled and it is random because we don't know how many dots are going to appear on any roll.

Thus we have a random variable which can take the values 1, 2, 3, 4, 5 and 6, with each of these six values having probability 1/6 of occurring because each of the six faces is equally likely to finish uppermost on any roll.

We could set out the **probability distribution** for this random variable in the following form:

| Value | 1 | 2 | 3 | 4 | 5 | 6 |
|---|---|---|---|---|---|---|
| Probability | 1/6 | 1/6 | 1/6 | 1/6 | 1/6 | 1/6 |

Every random variable has probabilities associated with the different values it can take in some way, and this is a particularly easy case.

The **expected value** of a random variable is the mean of the values it would take if the experiment were carried out infinitely many times, the value taken by the random variable recorded each time and then the mean of these values calculated. If we imagined our fair die being rolled $n$ times where $n$ is a very large number, then we could expect $n/6$ of the rolls to result in each of the values 1, 2, 3, 4, 5 and 6 of the random variable. Hence the mean would be:

$$\frac{(n/6) \times 1 + (n/6) \times 2 + (n/6) \times 3 + (n/6) \times 4 + (n/6) \times 5 + (n/6) \times 6}{n}$$

The $n$ can be cancelled in the numerator and denominator, leaving us with

$$(1/6) \times 1 + (1/6) \times 2 + (1/6) \times 3 + (1/6) \times 4 + (1/6) \times 5 + (1/6) \times 6$$

$$= 1/6 + 2/6 + 3/6 + 4/6 + 5/6 + 6/6 = 21/6 = 3.5$$

This is in some ways an 'unexpected' number as we would never actually see this many dots on the uppermost face of the die. However, it is the mean of the numbers on the uppermost face over a large number of rolls.

Of most importance in this very simple expected value calculation is the line

$$(1/6) \times 1 + (1/6) \times 2 + (1/6) \times 3 + (1/6) \times 4 + (1/6) \times 5 + (1/6) \times 6$$

because this line can be generalized to *any* such calculation. The way the expected value of any random variable is calculated is to take all the possible values of the random variable, multiply each one by its probability and then add all these products together. This can be conveniently expressed as a formula as follows:

$$\text{Expected value} = \Sigma p V$$

where the $V$'s are the values the random variable can take and the $p$'s are their respective probabilities.

An expected value can be conveniently found on a calculator by accumulating the products $pV$ into the calculator memory.

## Example 12.3.1

A supermarket manager has to make a decision on how many luxury hampers to buy in for the Christmas season. On the basis of trading conditions last Christmas and the current economic climate, the manager estimates the following probability distribution for sales of the hamper:

| Sales (hampers) | 50 | 100 | 150 | 200 | 250 |
|---|---|---|---|---|---|
| Probability | 0.20 | 0.25 | 0.30 | 0.15 | 0.10 |

Find the expected number of hampers to be sold.

### Solution to Example 12.3.1

Expected value =
$$\Sigma pV = 0.20 \times 50 + 0.25 \times 100 + 0.30 \times 150 + 0.15 \times 200 + 0.10 \times 250$$
$$= \quad 10 \quad + \quad 25 \quad + \quad 45 \quad + \quad 30 \quad + \quad 25$$
$$= 135 \text{ hampers}$$

Applications of expected values arise in problems where a number of options are open to a decision maker and the returns to be achieved under each option depend on which of several possible conditions prevail. A probability is associated with each of the conditions, and the random variable is the size of the returns to be made. The procedure is to calculate the expected value of the return for each of the options available and see which one gives the largest expected value. This would constitute grounds for choosing the option concerned.

This approach to decision problems is particularly suitable for situations which are repeated many times over, such as daily decisions on how much of a perishable item should be purchased by a retailer. In cases like this the option with the largest expected value is the one that can be expected to lead to the largest mean return over a large number of repetitions. The following example illustrates the use of the expected value method for dealing with this kind of problem.

## Example 12.3.2

A petrol station sells sandwiches as a side-line. It buys in these sandwiches from a bakery and sells them for 80p each. Experience suggests that, in round figures, the numbers of sandwiches demanded are 80, 100 or 120 with probabilities 0.3, 0.5 and 0.2 respectively. Unsold sandwiches produce no income. If sandwiches cost 45p each, what number ordered every day will produce the largest expected daily profit?

### Solution to Example 12.3.2

The solution to a question like this is best set out in the form of a table where the options available are set down as the headings of columns and the different conditions with their probabilities appear as the rows. In each of the columns we then set out the profits under each of the conditions for each of the policies, multiply these profits by the probabilities of the conditions and add up to find the expected profit. The table for this particular problem is set out below, but before turning to it we shall explain how the profit figures have been calculated. This is fairly straightforward in this case, but in some problems in can be the major part of the solution.

If 80 sandwiches are purchased, then 80 will be sold since this is the minimum demand, and if more are demanded there are only 80 available to sell anyway. So the profit under all conditions if 80 sandwiches are purchased will be:

$$80 \times (80p - 45p) = 80 \times 35p = 2800p$$

If 100 sandwiches are purchased, then if either 100 or 120 are demanded the number actually sold will be 100 and so the profit will be:

$$100 \times (80p - 45p) = 100 \times 35p = 3500p$$

If only 80 sandwiches are demanded, then 20 will be wasted and the profit will be:

$$80 \times (80p - 45p) + 20 \times (-45p) = 2800p - 900p = 1900p$$

If 120 sandwiches are purchased and 120 are demanded, then the profit will be:

$$120 \times (80p - 45p) = 120 \times 35p = 4200p$$

If in this situation 100 sandwiches are demanded, the profit will be:

$$100 \times (80p - 45p) + 20 \times (-45p) = 3500p - 900p = 2600p$$

If 80 sandwiches are demanded when 120 have been purchased, the profit will be:

$$80 \times (80p - 45p) + 40 \times (-45p) = 2800p - 1800p = 1000p$$

Hence we can draw up the table as follows:

| Sandwiches demanded | Probability | Sandwiches bought for sale | | | | | |
| | | 80 Profit | | 100 Profit | | 120 Profit | |
| | $p$ | $V$ | $pV$ | $V$ | $pV$ | $V$ | $pV$ |
| 80 | 0.3 | 2800 | 840 | 1900 | 570 | 1000 | 300 |
| 100 | 0.5 | 2800 | 1400 | 3500 | 1750 | 2600 | 1300 |
| 120 | 0.2 | 2800 | 560 | 3500 | 700 | 4200 | 840 |
| | | | 2800 | | 3020 | | 2440 |

As an example of calculator use in finding an expected value consider the final column of the above table, corresponding to a purchase of 120 sandwiches. The figure 2440 could have been arrived at as follows:

$$[0.3][\times][1000][=][M+][0.5][\times][2600][=][M+][0.2][\times][4200][=][M+][MR]$$

The option having the largest value for expected profit is that of buying 100 sandwiches. If the same number of sandwiches is to be bought each day, the number which will give the largest mean daily profit in the long run is 100 sandwiches each day.

**Exercises 12.3**

1   An investment project is predicted to produce the returns indicated below (in hundreds of thousands of pounds) with the probabilities shown.

| Return | 3 | 4 | 5 | 6 | 7 | 8 | 9 |
|---|---|---|---|---|---|---|---|
| Probability | 0.08 | 0.14 | 0.22 | 0.30 | 0.14 | 0.08 | 0.04 |

Find the expected return from the investment.

2   A football club can obtain its programmes from a printing firm at a cost of 45p per copy so long as it purchases the same number for every game. Records show that, in round figures, the numbers of programmes sold per game are in the following proportions:

| Number of programmes | 2000 | 2500 | 3000 | 3500 | 4000 |
|---|---|---|---|---|---|
| Percentage of games | 15 | 20 | 25 | 25 | 15 |

Programmes are sold at £1.00 each and unsold programmes are sold to a paper recycling company for 2p each.

a   Calculate the football club's expected profit per game under each of the policies of buying 2000, 2500, 3000, 3500 and 4000 copies per game.

b   Identify the policy which gives the highest expected profit per game.

## 12.4 Normal Distribution

We have seen in Sec. 12.3 examples of **discrete probability distributions** where the random variables concerned could take distinct values and it was possible to specify the probability of each of those values occurring. A **continuous probability distribution** is one which relates to a variable which can take *any* value, at least within a specified range. Lengths, weights and times would be examples of random variables which would come into this category. A crucial difference in dealing with continuous as compared with discrete random variables is that we cannot specify the probability of any individual value occurring but must look at the probability of the random variable taking a value in a specified **range**.

The probability distribution for a continuous random variable can be represented by a graph where the areas under different parts of the graph represent the probability of the random variable taking a value in the range concerned. The graph is referred to as the probability density function graph. The **probability density function** graph for a normal distribution has the general shape shown in Fig. 12.5 and is usually described as 'bell shaped'.

The shape is seen to be perfectly symmetrical with a peak in the middle and tails which become narrower the further we move away from the centre. The centre of the bell is actually located at the expected value of the random variable concerned. The mean of the distribution is represented by $\mu$, the lower case version of the Greek letter mu.

The width of the bell is determined by the standard deviation of the distribution. If the standard deviation is small, the bell will be tall and thin while if the standard deviation is large it will have a wider central area with a peak that is less high. The standard deviation is represented by $\sigma$, the lower case version of the Greek letter sigma.

Note that *every* probability density function graph must have a total area of 1 as it is the probability of all possible values which the random variable can take. We shall not be concerned with the mathematical equation of the probability density function graph for the normal distribution. All we need to know is that if the values of the mean and standard deviation are known, then the equation of the graph is completely determined and we can calculate all necessary areas. The way this is done will be explained in the examples which follow.

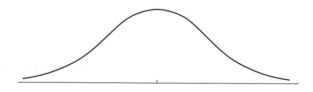

**Figure 12.5** A probability density function graph for a normal distribution

## Example 12.4.1

The durations of telephone calls made by a business executive are normally distributed with mean 10 minutes and standard deviation 1.4 minutes. What is the probability that an individual telephone call selected at random will have a duration longer than 12.1 minutes?

## *Solution to Example 12.4.1*

We have here a normal distribution with mean 10 and standard deviation 1.4, and we require to find the area above 12.1. As the first step in answering any such question about the normal distribution it is best to draw a diagram to represent the situation. This diagram is shown in Fig. 12.6.

The key point to be borne in mind and used for dealing with any problem of this kind is that:

> **The area under a normal distribution probability density function graph beyond a specified number of standard deviations from the mean is always the same, regardless of the particular values of the mean and standard deviation.**

The areas can be looked up in a table which appears in all standard books of statistical tables and in most statistics textbooks. In this book you will find such a table in Appendix 3.

What we have to do is find the number of standard deviations by which the number we are interested in differs from the mean and then look up this number in the normal distribution table to find the tail area beyond that number of standard deviations.

For this example the number of standard deviations by which 12.1 differs from 10 is

$$\frac{12.1 - 10}{1.4} = \frac{2.1}{1.4} = 1.5$$

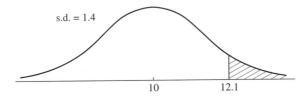

**Figure 12.6**

This calculation could be carried out on a calculator as follows:

$$[1.21]\,[-]\,[10]\,[=]\,[\div]\,[1.4]\,[=]$$

Looking up 1.5 in the table we see that the required tail area is 0.06681. Hence

$$P(\text{Duration of randomly chosen call exceeds } 12.1 \text{ minutes}) = 0.06681.$$

## Example 12.4.2

The lifetimes of super-batteries sold for use with personal stereos are normally distributed with mean 120 hours and standard deviation 20 hours. If a lifetime of 100 hours is guaranteed, what is the probability that an individual super-battery will fail to meet this guaranteed figure?

## *Solution to Example 12.4.2*

We again begin with a diagram to represent the situation. This is shown in Fig. 12.7.

To find the shaded area we need to find the number of standard deviations by which 100 is separated from the mean value of 120. This number is

$$\frac{120 - 100}{20} = \frac{20}{20} = 1$$

Looking up the value 1 in the table we see that the tail area is 0.15866. Hence

$$P(\text{an individual super-battery fails the guarantee}) = 0.15866$$

The answer to Example 12.4.2 has made use of the **symmetry** of the normal distribution probability density function graph to say that the area beyond a value one standard deviation below the mean is equal to the area beyond a value one standard deviation above the mean. It is often neces-

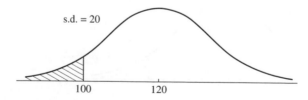

**Figure 12.7**

sary also to use the fact that the total area under the whole graph is 1, as in the following example.

## Example 12.4.3

Incomes in a particular population are believed to be normally distributed with a mean of £25 200 and a standard deviation of £3200. Find the probability that an individual chosen at random has

**a**   an income less than £27 000.
**b**   an income in the range £18 000 to £27 000.

### Solution to Example 12.4.3

**a**   The diagram representing this situation is shown in Fig. 12.8.

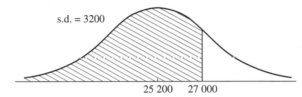

s.d. = 3200

25 200     27 000

**Figure 12.8**

The required probability can be found by obtaining the unshaded area in the tail at the right-hand end of the diagram and then subtracting this from 1.
At the right-hand end we have

$$\frac{27\,000 - 25\,200}{3200} = \frac{1800}{3200} = 0.56$$

So the unshaded area in the right-hand tail is 0.28774. Hence

$$P(\text{an individual earns less than £27\,000}) = 1 - 0.28774 = 0.71226$$

**b**   The diagram representing this situation is shown in Fig. 12.9.
We know from the answer to part **a** that the area in the right-hand

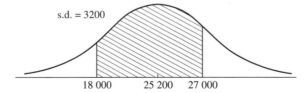

s.d. = 3200

18 000      25 200    27 000

**Figure 12.9**

unshaded tail is 0.28774.

At the left-hand end we have

$$\frac{25\,200 - 18\,000}{3200} = \frac{7200}{3200} = 2.25$$

So the unshaded area in the left-hand tail is 0.01222. Hence

$$P(\text{an individual earns in the range } £18\,000 \text{ to } £27\,000)$$

$$= 1 - 0.28774 - 0.01222 = 0.70004$$

It is sometimes useful to be able to use the normal distribution table in reverse to find the value of the normally distributed variable which cuts off a specified tail area. We present situations in Examples 12.4.4 and 12.4.5 to illustrate the procedure.

## Example 12.4.4

The duration of an executive's telephone calls is normally distributed with mean 10 minutes and standard deviation 1.4 minutes. Above what duration will the longest 1.5% of calls last?

## *Solution to Example 12.4.4*

Let the unknown duration be $D$ minutes. Since 1.5% of calls last longer than $D$ minutes, it follows that a call chosen at random has probability 0.015 of having duration longer than $D$ minutes. So, to answer the question we need to find the value $D$ which has area 0.015 above it.

The diagram representing this situation is shown in Fig. 12.10.

What we need to know initially is the number of standard deviations from the mean of the value which cuts off a tail area of 0.015. By looking up the value 0.015 in the body of the normal distribution table and reading off the figures from the margins of the table we see that this is 2.17.

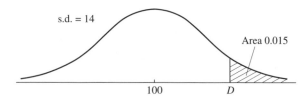

**Figure 12.10**

Hence the duration cutting off the longest 1.5% of calls is 2.17 standard deviations of 1.4 minutes above the mean of 10 minutes. So the required cut off figure is

$$10 + 2.17 \times 1.4 = 10 + 3.038 = 13.038$$

i.e. The longest 1.5% of calls last longer than 13.038 minutes.

## Example 12.4.5

The lifetimes of super-batteries are normally distributed with mean 120 hours and standard deviation 20 hours. At what number of hours would a guarantee on these batteries need to be set in order for no more than 2.5% to fail it?

### Solution to Example 12.4.5

Let the required guaranteed lifetime be $G$ hours. Since only 2.5% of batteries are to have lifetimes less than $G$ hours, it follows that a battery chosen at random will have probability 0.025 of lasting for less than $G$ hours. So, to answer the question we need to find the value $G$ which has area 0.025 below it.

The diagram representing this situation is shown in Fig. 12.11.

What we need to know here is the number of standard deviations from the mean of the value which cuts off tail area 0.025. By looking up the value 0.025 in the body of the normal distribution table and reading off the figures from the margins of the table we see that this is 1.96.

Hence the lifetime cutting off the bottom 2.5% of lifetimes is 1.96 standard deviations of 20 below the mean of 120 hours. So the required guarantee figure is

$$120 - 1.96 \times 20 = 120 - 39.2 = 80.8$$

i.e. The guarantee should be set at 80.8 hours if no more than 2.5% are to fail it.

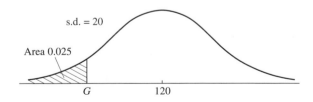

**Figure 12.11**

**Exercises 12.4**   1   In an audit exercise the values of invoices were found to have mean £1175 and standard deviation £50. If the values of invoices are taken to be normally distributed

    **a**   find the probability that an invoice chosen at random will have a value in the range £1100 to £1200.

    **b**   find the figure below which the lowest 1% of invoice values will lie.

2   A management consultant carried out a work study exercise and found the time taken to carry out a routine task to be normally distributed with mean 85.8 minutes and standard deviation 5 minutes.

    **a**   Find the probability that an individual task observed at random will be completed within 90 minutes.

    **b**   Find the time within which the fastest 5% of task completions occur.

    **c**   Find the time exceeded by the slowest 10% of task completions.

## Further Exercises

1   The table below shows the smoking habits of men and women working for a firm.

|       | Smoke | Do not smoke |
|-------|-------|--------------|
| Women | 10    | 30           |
| Men   | 40    | 60           |

What is the probability that a person chosen at random from the firm will be a man who smokes?

    A. 40/140    B. 40/100    C. 100/140    D. 50/140

2   A vote was held on possible rule changes for a professional body, and Associates and Fellows of the body voted as shown below.

|            | For the change | Against the change |
|------------|----------------|--------------------|
| Associates | 800            | 200                |
| Fellows    | 600            | 400                |

What is the probability that a member selected at random would be an Associate in favour of the rule change?

    A. 800/1000    B. 800/1400    C. 1000/2000    D. 800/2000

3  Three companies, Alpha Technologies, Betametrics and Camco are bidding for a contract which will be awarded to one and only one of them. If Alpha Technologies has probability 0.4 of winning the contract and Betametrics has probability 0.5 of winning it, what is the probability that neither of these two companies will win it?

    A. 0.9    B. 0.8    C. 0.1    D. 0.0

4  If one-third of cyclists use battery-powered lamps and two cyclists are chosen at random, what is the probability that neither of them uses battery-powered lamps?

    A. 1/9    B. 2/9    C. 4/9    D. 5/9

5  It is believed that an investment project will produce returns of £10 000, £20 000, £30 000 or £40 000 with probabilities 0.1, 0.2, 0.3 and 0.4 respectively, what is the expected return from the project?

    A. £20 000    B. £25 000    C. £28 000    D. £30 000

6  Telephone bills incurred by individual staff in the marketing department of a large organization in the first quarter of this year were normally distributed with a mean of £270 and a standard deviation of £20.

    What is the probability that an individual staff member chosen at random had a bill in the range £250 to £270?

    A. 0.38201    B. 0.31732    C. 0.35313    D. 0.34134

7  Consider the following statements about the normal distribution.
- The total area under the probability density function graph is 1.
- About 95% of the area under the graph lies within 1 standard deviation either side of the mean.
- The graph has a symmetrical shape.

How many of the above statements are true?

    A. 0    B. 1    C. 2    D. 3

8  A salesperson for a company selling payroll software systems has two appointments for next Monday, one in the morning and one in the afternoon. His experience suggests that the probability of a

Monday morning appointment leading to a sale is 0.3, that the probability of a Monday afternoon appointment leading to a sale is 0.4, and that sales in the afternoon are independent of sales in the morning. Find the following probabilities:

**a**  both next Monday's appointments will lead to sales
**b**  neither of next Monday's appointments will lead to a sale
**c**  only the morning appointment will lead to a sale
**d**  only the afternoon appointment will lead to a sale
**e**  at least one of the two appointments will lead to a sale
**f**  exactly one of the two appointments will lead to a sale

(Hint: You may find a Venn diagram useful in answering this question.)

9    A shop selling women's clothing has an opportunity to buy in summer dresses at the beginning of the summer in batches of 20 at a price of £24 per dress. The normal purchase price is £32 and the dresses sell in the shop at £48 each. If too many dresses are bought in, they will have to be sold off at the end of the summer at £20 each, a price at which it can be assumed all surplus stock will be sold. If demand during the summer exceeds the number initially purchased, then more can be obtained as required at the standard £32 price.

The predicted demand for the dresses over the summer at the £48 price is:

| Number of dresses demanded | 20 | 40 | 60 | 80 |
|---|---|---|---|---|
| Probability | 0.2 | 0.4 | 0.3 | 0.1 |

Find the number of dresses which should be purchased at the special offer price in order to maximize the expected profit on sales of such dresses.

10   The lengths of rods produced by a particular process are normally distributed with mean 100 cm and standard deviation 1 cm. Rods with lengths outside the range 99.3 cm to 101.7 cm are rejected.

**a**  What is the probability that a rod is rejected?
**b**  What would the rejection probability become if the mean rod length changed to 101 cm?
**c**  What would the rejection probability become if the mean rod length changed to 100.5 cm?

# Solutions to Exercises

## Chapter 1

*Exercises 1.1*

1   $830 + (1240 \times 7)\text{p} = 9510\text{p} = £95.10$
2   £192
3   **a** £54 754 300   **b** 54 754 000   **c** £55 000 000
4   **a** 713 530   **b** 714 000
5   £486.17

*Exercises 1.2*

1   11/48
2   35¾, £152.30
3   Bank £45 375   Building Society £41 250
4   1/50
5   **a** 13/20   **b** 3/20   **c** 1/10   **d** 1⅗

*Exercises 1.3*

1   £41.70
2   372€
3   Abdul £250   Bernadette £294
4   £52.18
5   3 hours
6   **a** £2.35   **b** £82.25   **c** £250.44

*Further Exercises*

1　C
2　A
3　D
4　B
5　A
6　£40.50
7　£542.05　£521.20
8　**a** 200 miles　**b** 30 minutes
9　**a** 56　**b** 68.25
10　**a** 420　**b** (i) 370　(ii) 400　**c** 96　**d** 102.5 (6.5)
11　**a** £35.72　**b** 3420, £285
12　**a** £655.50　**b** £2246.50　**c** 21p

# Chapter 2

*Exercises 2.1*

1　A 16%　B 25%　C 24%　D 35%
2　£38.13
3　A 65%　B 56%
4　**a** £35 308　**b** £55.94
5　£476.07
6　**a** £15　**b** (i) £1320　(ii) £1856　(iii) £1936　(iv) 46.7%
7　£9
8　44%
9　A £1145.63
10　**a** £9.75　**b** $2\frac{1}{2}$ years

*Exercises 2.2*

1　£3000　£4000　£5000
2　**a** 7:6　**b** 195　**c** Lectures 4 hours, labs 2.5 hours, free 2 hours
3　A £567　B £453.60　C £340.20
4　**a** £16 875　**b** £3478.50
5　£40 850
6　John £187.50　Alan £675　Barbara £775　Caroline £662.50

*Exercises 2.3*

1　**a** 432　**b** 1600　**c** 1/9　**d** 4

2    £135.41
3    $2.6153 \times 10^2$
4    **a** $5.8 \times 10^7$    **b** (i) $3.207 \times 10^3$  (ii) $£3.2 \times 10^3$
5    **a** 1024    **b** 390 625    **c** 8975    **d** 65 700
6    25

*Further Exercises*

1    C
2    D
3    A
4    B
5    C
6    98%
7    £2208
8    £455.73    £415.27
9    **a** £21    **b** £9240    **c** 54%
10    **a** £240.82    **b** 36.6%
11    **a** £576    **b** £3.60    **c** £748.80    **d** 56%
12    **a** £1466.25    **b** £642
13    **a** 12:1    **b** 15
14    **a** 0.78125    **b** 5    **c** 1.5
15    $£1.2841 \times 10^{11}$
16    **a** £1875    **b** £43.67

## Chapter 3

*Exercises 3.2*

1    **c** intercept = fixed cost = £170
        gradient = charge per mile = £0.08
2    a = 16    **b**= −2    demand function

*Exercises 3.3*

1    $x = 8$
2    $x = -4.25$
3    $x = 4.5$
4    $x = -6$

*Exercises 3.4*

1    The solutions are $x = 1.5$   $y = 1$

2    **c** $x = 4000$   **d** Total revenue = total cost = £48 000

*Exercises 3.5*

1.  **c** $x = 12$
       Total revenue = total cost = £864
2    **d** $x = 20$
       **e** No, because a positive profit cannot be made

*Further Exercises*

1   B
2   D
3   C
4   B
5   D
6   D
7   C
8   **a** $y = 1000 + 0.09x$   $y = 2000 + 0.08x$   $y = 5000 + 0.06x$
    **d** Change from 1 to 2 when $x$ gets to 100 000   C = £10 000
       Change from 2 to 3 when $x$ gets to 150 000   C = £14 000
9   (iii) $y = 120 + 14x$
    (v) $x = 3$
10    (b) $-5x^2 + 100x - 375$
    (c) $x = 5$ or $x = 15$

## Chapter 4

*Exercises 4.1*

1    £12 000
2    £66 485
3    8.45%
4    9 years
5    £13 387

*Exercises 4.2*

1    19.4%
2.    **a** £70 800   **b** £71 551   **c** £71 737   **d** £71 811   **e** £71 830

*Exercises 4.3*

1    £25 667

2   **a** £1639 for project 1    −£8835 for project 2
     **b** Project 1 is viable but not project 2
     **c** Project 1 is to be preferred

*Exercises 4.4*

1   9.5%

*Exercises 4.5*

1.  £9496
2   **b** (i) £48 426  (ii) £46 695  (iii) £44 790

*Further Exercises*

1   £6600
2   £27 531
3   D
4   C
5   B
6   C
7   Use hire method (a) for which the net present value is £1051.
    The purchase method has NPV £1073 and the other hire method has
    NPV £1218
8   **a** 12.6%
    **b** The criterion is met.
9   **a** 9.3%  **b** 8.3%
    **c** Project 1 is better and the 9.3% can be compared with other possible
    returns.
10  **a** £5548
    **b** (i) £16 852  (ii) £13 326  (iii) £9377

# Chapter 5

*Exercises 5.3*

1   **b** Renumber the batch to 00 to 99 (with 1853 = 00, ..., 1952 = 99) and
    use pairs of random digits to select ten of these numbers.
2   **b** (i)    Company payroll
       (ii)   Student registration list
       (iii)  School registers

*Further Exercises*

1   D
2   B
3   D
4   B
5   D

## Chapter 6

*Exercises 6.1*

1   **a**

| Times (mins) | Frequency |
|:---:|:---:|
| 6–10 | 2 |
| 11–15 | 6 |
| 16–20 | 23 |
| 21–25 | 9 |
| 26–30 | 13 |
| 31–35 | 7 |

**b**

| Times (mins) | Frequency |
|---|:---:|
| Less than 10.5 | 2 |
| Less than 15.5 | 8 |
| Less than 20.5 | 31 |
| Less than 25.5 | 40 |
| Less than 30.5 | 53 |
| Less than 35.5 | 60 |

2   **a** Categorical (nominal)
      **b** Numeric (continuous)
      **c** Numeric (continuous)
      **d** Categorical (ordinal)
      **e** Numeric (discrete)

3

| Salary (£000) | Cumulative frequency |
|---|---|
| <10 | 35 |
| <15 | 110 |
| <20 | 206 |
| <25 | 248 |
| <35 | 300 |

4    Numeric (continuous)

| Heights (metres) | Frequency |
|---|---|
| 1.20–1.29 | 3 |
| 1.30–1.39 | 3 |
| 1.40–1.49 | 2 |
| 1.50–1.59 | 3 |
| 1.60–1.69 | 9 |

| Heights (metres) | Cumulative frequency |
|---|---|
| Less than 1.295 | 3 |
| Less than 1.395 | 6 |
| Less than 1.495 | 8 |
| Less than 1.595 | 11 |
| Less than 1.695 | 20 |

*Exercises 6.2*

1    **a**

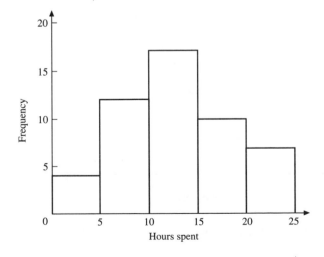

**b**

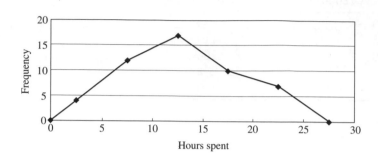

2

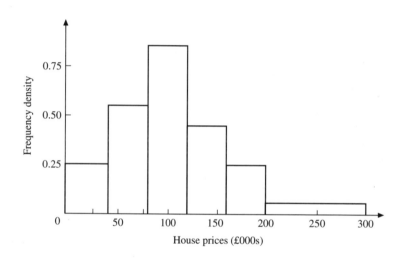

3    **a**

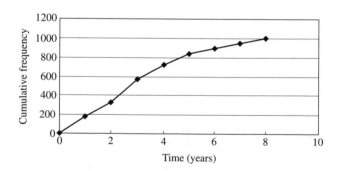

**b** (i) 860    (ii) 55%    (iii) 4.3 years

4   Males have higher salaries.

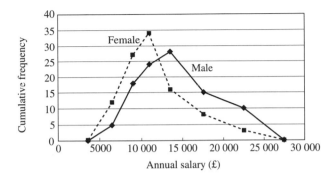

*Exercises 6.3*

1   Number of visitors generally increasing. Below average number of visitors in Q1, and considerably above average in Q3.

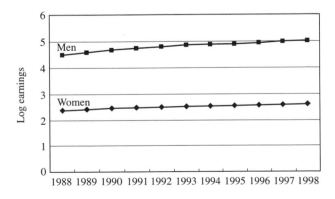

2   Men's earnings are higher. Both sets of earnings are increasing at a similar rate.

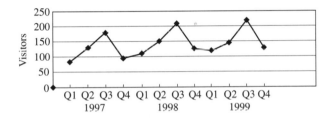

*Exercises 6.4*

1

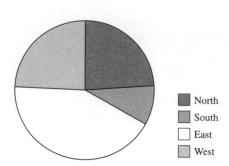

2

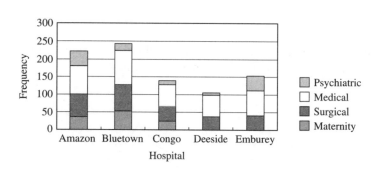

3   Greater percentage of males never married compared with females, but smaller percentage widowed.

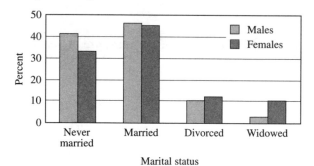

## *Further Exercises*

1   A
2   C
3   D

4   B
5   B
6.

| Group | Frequency |
|---|---|
| £400 up to £420 | 3 |
| £420 up to £440 | 9 |
| £440 up to £460 | 6 |
| £460 up to £480 | 10 |
| £480 up to £500 | 7 |
| £500 up to £520 | 2 |
| £520 up to £540 | 2 |
| £540 up to £560 | 1 |

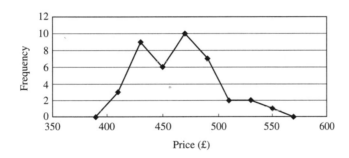

7   The number of disputes is below average in Q1 and above average in Q3. The trend decreases until the end of 1997, and then increases over 1998–99.

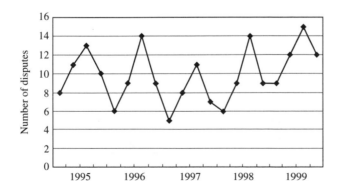

8

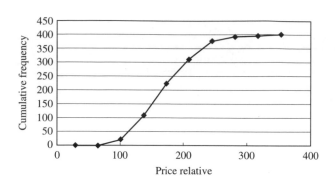

**a** 291   **b** 5%   **c** 235

9

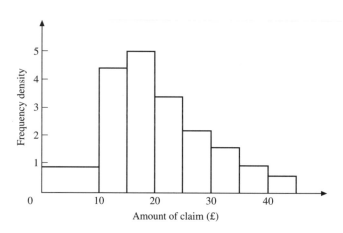

10. A bar chart is not appropriate as it understates the baby battering in the infant class and overstates it at the higher age groups.

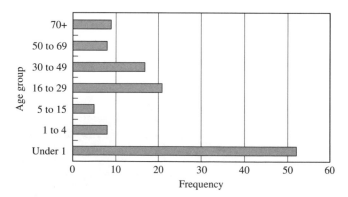

## Chapter 7

*Exercises 7.1*

1   £198; £204
2   Time = 3.5 hours, distance = 95 miles, speed = 27.1 mph
3   £182.87
4   £884

*Exercises 7.2*

1   £18 000; £17 000
2   6
3   9
4   168

*Exercises 7.3*

1   4
2   Red
3   Size 9
4   £167

*Further Exercises*

1   A
2   C
3   C
4   B
5   B
6   D
7   B
8   B
9   C
10   B
11   **a** 67.52   **b** 67.9   **c** 67.9. The median is, perhaps, the most appropriate.
12   **a** £73   **b** £71   **c** £65
13   **a** 7.4   **b** 7   **c** 7
14   £881

## Chapter 8

*Exercises 8.1*

1   **a** 11   **b** 4   **c** 24
2   Monday 41.75, 4
    Tuesday 40.75, 6
    Wednesday 40.75, 4
    Thursday 41, 7
    Friday 39, 7

*Exercises 8.2*

1   $\bar{x} = 260$, $s = 23.90$. Department A has lower wages, less spread out. (However, in relative terms this comment is debatable as $CV_A = 9.2\%$, $CV_B = 7.9\%$.)
2   X 33.3%, Y 75%. Evidence of greater inequality in Y
3   **a** $\bar{x} = £3.01$, $s = £1.56$
    **b** Higher spending on average now, and greater variation. (However, note that the CVs are very close.)
4   $\bar{x} = 8$ , $s = 2.69$

*Exercises 8.3*

1   £11.25
2   Median = £222, Q1 = £163, Q3 = £294, QD = £65.5
3   QD = 8.1 miles

*Further Exercises*

1   C
2   B
3   A
4   D
5   B
6   A $\bar{x} = 90.4$, $s = 6.53$, $CV = 7.2\%$
    B $\bar{x} = 28.2$, $s = 8.35$, $CV = 29.6\%$
7   $\bar{x} = 34.96$, $s = 10.99$, median = 34.7, QD = 6.1

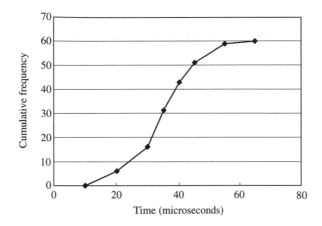

8     **a** =£2594, s=£994

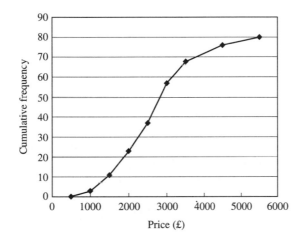

     **b** median = £2575, QD = £631
9     **a** $\bar{x}$ = 17.63, $s$ = 4.20
     **b** median = 18, QD = 3.5
10    **a** $\bar{x}$ = £62.80, s = £23.41
     **b** $CV$ = 37%

## Chapter 9

*Exercises 9.1*

1     **a** 75.5     100.0     121.3     138.3     153.2     183.0     217.0
     **b** 49.3     65.3     79.2     90.3     100.0     119.4     141.7

2　32.5　35.7　39.8　38.9　38.5
In real terms, the revenue has declined over the last two years covered.

*Exercises 9.2*

1　**a** 112.8　**b** 103.2　**c** 113.0　**d** 103.4　**e** 116.6
2　**a** 103.9　**b** 98.4　　**c** 102.2
　　**d** 103.9 × 98.4/100 = 102.2
3　**a** 112.2　**b** 104.4　**c** 104.1

*Further Exercises*

　1　B
　2　C
　3　D
　4　C
　5　C
　6　D
　7　A
　8　A
　9　**a** 104.00,　96.15 and 1/1.04 = 0.9615
　　　**b** 104.73,　This is a Paasche price index
10　**a** 108.1　**b** 100.0
　　　**c** Laspeyres gives more weight to A which has increased in price, while
　　　Paasche gives more weight to C which has gone down in price.

## Chapter 10

*Exercises 10.2*

1　**b** 0.9763　**c** Time and cost increase together
　　**d** 0.9532 so 95.32% of the variation is explained.
2　**b** −0.9085　**c** Rejects decrease as experience increases
　　**d** 0.8253 so 82.53% of the variation is explained

*Exercises 10.3*

1　**b** 0.9167
　　**c** There is close compatibility between the methods.
2　0.8091. There is a strong relationship between safety rank and the
　　number of accidents.

*Further Exercises*

1   B
2   D
3   C
4   B
5   A
6   C
7   C
8   C
9   0.8507. Cost increases as output increases
10  Sales are more closely associated with price than with forecourt size. The rank correlations are $r' = 0.8273$ for price and $r' = 0.2606$ for forecourt size.

## Chapter 11

*Exercises 11.1*

1   **b** $y = -0.507 + 0.8203x$
2   **b** $y = 35.465 - 1.3867x$

*Exercises 11.2*

1   **c** (i) £12   (ii) £24
    $x = 15$ is inside the data range and $x = 30$ is outside the range.
2   **c** (i) 29 rejects  (ii) 8 rejects
    $x = 5$ is inside the data range and $x = 20$ is outside the range.

*Further Exercises*

1   D
2   A
3   D
4   B
5   A
6   D
7   **b** $y = 31.060 + 0.1436x$.
    Monthly fixed cost is £31 060 and variable cost is 14.4p per tonne-mile.

8    **b** $y = 40.976 - 0.8714x$
  **c** When $x = 27$, $y = 17$
  Not very reliable as $x = 27$ is outside the data range and $r = -0.638$ means only 40.7% of the variation is explained.

9    **b** $y = 17.76 + 0.8190x$
  **c** When $x = 16$, $y = 31$
  Having $x = 16$ inside the data range is helpful to reliability of the prediction, but having $r = 0.595$ means that only 35.4% of the variation is explained.
  **e** When $x = 30$, $y = 42$
  The reliability here is not good as we have $x = 30$ outside the data range as well as having only 35.4% of the variation explained.

10   **b** $y = 5.9100 + 0.0101x$
  **c** 99 words per minute, because $1/0.0101 = 99$.
  Fixed time $= 5.9$ mins.
  **d** 15.9 mins
  This is a very reliable prediction as 1000 is within the data range and $r = 0.995$ means that 99.1% of the variation is explained.

## Chapter 12

*Exercises 12.1*

1    **a** 0.0769   **b** 0.2500   **c** 0.0385   **d** 0.0192

2

|  | Public transport | By car | By bicycle | On foot | Marginal Prob |
|---|---|---|---|---|---|
| Firm 1 | 0.20 | 0.15 | 0.10 | 0.05 | 0.50 |
| Firm 2 | 0.35 | 0.05 | 0.05 | 0.05 | 0.50 |
| Marginal Probability | 0.55 | 0.20 | 0.15 | 0.10 |  |

Method of travel

*Exercises 12.2*

1    **a** 0.020875   **b** 0.250250   **c** 0.728875
  They add up to 1 because these are all the possibilities.

2    **a** $P(0) = 0.421875$   $P(1) = 0.421875$   $P(2) = 0.140625$   $P(3) = 0.015625$
  **b** $P(0) = 0.512$   $P(1) = 0.384$   $P(2) = 0.096$   $P(3) = 0.008$
  **c** They are independent because every joint probability is the product of the two marginal probabilities.

*Exercises 12.3*

1    £568 000
2    **a** £1100    £1301.50    £1405    £1386    £1244.50
     **b** The best policy is to buy 3000 programmes per game.

*Exercises 12.4*

1    **a** 0.62465
     **b** £1058.50
2    **a** 0.79955
     **b** 77.6 minutes
     **c** 92.2 minutes

*Further Exercises*

1    A
2    D
3    C
4    C
5    D
6    D
7    C
8    **a** 0.12    **b** 0.42    **c** 0.18    **d** 0.28    **e** 0.58    **f** 0.46
9    60 dresses
     (The expected profits are £996 from buying 20 dresses
                              £1080 from buying 40 dresses
                              £1024 from buying 60 dresses
                and £968 from buying 80 dresses.)
10   **a** 0.28653    **b** Unchanged at 0.28653    **c** 0.23014

# Formulae Sheet

## Equations and Graphs

*Straight line*

The general equation of a straight line is

$$y = a + bx$$

where $a$ is the intercept and $b$ is the gradient of the line.

*Quadratic function*

The general form of a quadratic function is $y = ax^2 + bx + c$

The solutions to the equation $\qquad\qquad ax^2 + bx + c = 0$

are found as $\qquad\qquad x = \dfrac{-b \pm \sqrt{\{b^2 - 4ac\}}}{2a}$

## Financial Arithmetic

*Simple Interest*

The simple interest earned on investment $P$ over $n$ periods is

$$niP$$

Where $i = r/100$, and $r$ is the percentage interest rate per period.

*Compound Interest*

The general compound interest formula is

$$P_n = (1 + i)^n \, P_0$$

where $P_0$ is the initial investment,
and $P_n$ is the size of the investment at the end of $n$ periods

*Effective Interest Rate*

The effective annual (proportional) interest rate is

$$(1 + i)^n - 1$$

*Net Present Value*

$$P_0 = \frac{P_n}{(1 + i)^n}$$

where    $P_0$ is the present value of the amount
$P_n$ received at the end of $n$ periods

## Data Collection

*Sampling Fraction*

$$\text{Sampling fraction} = \frac{\text{Sample size}}{\text{Population size}}$$

## Averages

*Mean*

Mean of raw data        $\bar{x} = \dfrac{\Sigma x}{n}$

Mean of grouped data $\bar{x} = \dfrac{\Sigma xf}{\Sigma f}$

where $\Sigma xf$ is the sum of the observed value $\times$ frequency, and $\Sigma f$ is the sum of the frequency.

## Spread

*Standard Deviation*

Standard deviation of raw data     $s = \sqrt{\{\Sigma(x - \bar{x})^2/n\}}$

or, more frequently used,     $s = \sqrt{\{\Sigma x^2/n - \bar{x}^2\}}$

Standard deviation of grouped data     $s = \sqrt{\{\Sigma(x - \bar{x})^2 f/\Sigma f\}}$

or, equivalently,     $s = \sqrt{\{\Sigma x^2 f/\Sigma f - \bar{x}^2\}}$

*Coefficient of Variation*

$$CV = \frac{\text{standard deviation}}{\text{mean}} \times 100\%$$

*Quartile deviation*

$$\text{Quartile deviation} = \frac{Q3 - Q1}{2}$$

where $Q1$ is the lower quartile and $Q3$ is the upper quartile.

## Index Numbers

*Price relative*

$$\text{Price relative} = \frac{\text{Price at given time}}{\text{Price at base time}}$$

*Laspeyres Price index*

$$= \frac{\text{What the base time quantities would have cost at given time prices}}{\text{What the base time quantities actually cost at base time prices}} \times 100$$

*Paasche Price Index*

$$= \frac{\text{What the given time quantities actually cost at given time prices}}{\text{What the given time quantities would have cost at base time prices}} \times 100$$

*Laspeyres Quantity Index*

$$= \frac{\text{What the given time quantities would have cost at base time prices}}{\text{What the base time quantities actually cost at base time prices}} \times 100$$

*Paasche Quantity Index*

$$= \frac{\text{What the given time quantities actually cost at given time prices}}{\text{What the base time quantities would have cost at given time prices}} \times 100$$

*Value Index*

$$= \frac{\text{What the given time quantities actually cost at given time prices}}{\text{What the base time quantities actually cost at base time prices}} \times 100$$

## Correlation

*Correlation Coefficient*

$$r = \frac{n \sum xy - (\sum x)(\sum y)}{\sqrt{\{(n\sum x^2 - (\sum x)^2)(n\sum y^2 - (\sum y)^2)\}}}$$

*Coefficient of determination*

$$100r^2\%$$

*Spearman's rank correlation coefficient*

$$r' = 1 - \frac{6 \sum d^2}{n(n^2 - 1)}$$

## Regression

*The Equation of the Line of Best Fit*

$$y = a + bx$$

where

$$b = \frac{n\sum xy - (\sum x)(\sum y)}{n\sum x^2 - (\sum x)^2}$$

and

$$a = \frac{\sum y - b \sum x}{n}$$

## Probability

*The Generalized Addition Rule*

$$P(A \text{ or } B) = P(A) + P(B) - P(A \text{ and } B)$$

but $P(A \text{ and } B) = 0$ when $A$ and $B$ are mutually exclusive.

*Conditional Probability*

$$P(B|A) = \frac{P(A \text{ and } B)}{P(A)}$$

*The Generalized Multiplication Rule for Probabilities*

$$P(A \text{ and } B) = P(B|A)P(A)$$

but if $A$ and $B$ are independent $P(B|A) = P(B)$ giving the multiplication rule for independent events

$$P(A \text{ and } B) = P(A)P(B)$$

*Expected Value*

$$\text{Expected value} = \sum pV$$

where the $V$'s are the values the random variable can take and the $p$'s are their respective probabilities.

# Tables

# Table of compound interest factors (1)

Interest Rate (%)

| Years | 1 | 2 | 3 | 4 | 5 | 6 | 7 | 8 | 9 | 10 | 11 | 12 | 13 |
|---|---|---|---|---|---|---|---|---|---|---|---|---|---|
| 1 | 1.0100 | 1.0200 | 1.0300 | 1.0400 | 1.0500 | 1.0600 | 1.0700 | 1.0800 | 1.0900 | 1.1000 | 1.1100 | 1.1200 | 1.1300 |
| 2 | 1.0201 | 1.0404 | 1.0609 | 1.0816 | 1.1025 | 1.1236 | 1.1449 | 1.1664 | 1.1881 | 1.2100 | 1.2321 | 1.2544 | 1.2769 |
| 3 | 1.0303 | 1.0612 | 1.0927 | 1.1249 | 1.1576 | 1.1910 | 1.2250 | 1.2597 | 1.2950 | 1.3310 | 1.3676 | 1.4049 | 1.4429 |
| 4 | 1.0406 | 1.0824 | 1.1255 | 1.1699 | 1.2155 | 1.2625 | 1.3108 | 1.3605 | 1.4116 | 1.4641 | 1.5181 | 1.5735 | 1.6305 |
| 5 | 1.0510 | 1.1041 | 1.1593 | 1.2167 | 1.2763 | 1.3382 | 1.4026 | 1.4693 | 1.5386 | 1.6105 | 1.6851 | 1.7623 | 1.8424 |
| 6 | 1.0615 | 1.1262 | 1.1941 | 1.2653 | 1.3401 | 1.4185 | 1.5007 | 1.5869 | 1.6771 | 1.7716 | 1.8704 | 1.9738 | 2.0820 |
| 7 | 1.0721 | 1.1487 | 1.2299 | 1.3159 | 1.4071 | 1.5036 | 1.6058 | 1.7138 | 1.8280 | 1.9487 | 2.0762 | 2.2107 | 2.3526 |
| 8 | 1.0829 | 1.1717 | 1.2668 | 1.3686 | 1.4775 | 1.5938 | 1.7182 | 1.8509 | 1.9926 | 2.1436 | 2.3045 | 2.4760 | 2.6584 |
| 9 | 1.0937 | 1.1951 | 1.3048 | 1.4233 | 1.5513 | 1.6895 | 1.8385 | 1.9990 | 2.1719 | 2.3579 | 2.5580 | 2.7731 | 3.0040 |
| 10 | 1.1046 | 1.2190 | 1.3439 | 1.4802 | 1.6289 | 1.7908 | 1.9672 | 2.1589 | 2.3674 | 2.5937 | 2.8394 | 3.1058 | 3.3946 |
| 11 | 1.1157 | 1.2434 | 1.3842 | 1.5395 | 1.7103 | 1.8983 | 2.1049 | 2.3316 | 2.5804 | 2.8531 | 3.1518 | 3.4785 | 3.8359 |
| 12 | 1.1268 | 1.2682 | 1.4258 | 1.6010 | 1.7959 | 2.0122 | 2.2522 | 2.5182 | 2.8127 | 3.1384 | 3.4985 | 3.8960 | 4.3345 |
| 13 | 1.1381 | 1.2936 | 1.4685 | 1.6651 | 1.8856 | 2.1329 | 2.4098 | 2.7196 | 3.0658 | 3.4523 | 3.8833 | 4.3635 | 4.8980 |
| 14 | 1.1495 | 1.3195 | 1.5126 | 1.7317 | 1.9799 | 2.2609 | 2.5785 | 2.9372 | 3.3417 | 3.7975 | 4.3104 | 4.8871 | 5.5348 |
| 15 | 1.1610 | 1.3459 | 1.5580 | 1.8009 | 2.0789 | 2.3966 | 2.7590 | 3.1722 | 3.6425 | 4.1772 | 4.7846 | 5.4736 | 6.2543 |
| 16 | 1.1726 | 1.3728 | 1.6047 | 1.8730 | 2.1829 | 2.5404 | 2.9522 | 3.4259 | 3.9703 | 4.5950 | 5.3109 | 6.1304 | 7.0673 |
| 17 | 1.1843 | 1.4002 | 1.6528 | 1.9479 | 2.2920 | 2.6928 | 3.1588 | 3.7000 | 4.3276 | 5.0545 | 5.8951 | 6.8660 | 7.9861 |
| 18 | 1.1961 | 1.4282 | 1.7024 | 2.0258 | 2.4066 | 2.8543 | 3.3799 | 3.9960 | 4.7171 | 5.5599 | 6.5436 | 7.6900 | 9.0243 |
| 19 | 1.2081 | 1.4568 | 1.7535 | 2.1068 | 2.5270 | 3.0256 | 3.6165 | 4.3157 | 5.1417 | 6.1159 | 7.2633 | 8.6128 | 10.1974 |
| 20 | 1.2202 | 1.4859 | 1.8061 | 2.1911 | 2.6533 | 3.2071 | 3.8697 | 4.6610 | 5.6044 | 6.7275 | 8.0623 | 9.6463 | 11.5231 |
| 21 | 1.2324 | 1.5157 | 1.8603 | 2.2788 | 2.7860 | 3.3996 | 4.1406 | 5.0338 | 6.1088 | 7.4002 | 8.9492 | 10.8038 | 13.0211 |
| 22 | 1.2447 | 1.5460 | 1.9161 | 2.3699 | 2.9253 | 3.6035 | 4.4304 | 5.4365 | 6.6586 | 8.1403 | 9.9336 | 12.1003 | 14.7138 |
| 23 | 1.2572 | 1.5769 | 1.9736 | 2.4647 | 3.0715 | 3.8197 | 4.7405 | 5.8715 | 7.2579 | 8.9543 | 11.0263 | 13.5523 | 16.6266 |
| 24 | 1.2697 | 1.6084 | 2.0328 | 2.5633 | 3.2251 | 4.0489 | 5.0724 | 6.3412 | 7.9111 | 9.8497 | 12.2392 | 15.1786 | 18.7881 |
| 25 | 1.2824 | 1.6406 | 2.0938 | 2.6658 | 3.3864 | 4.2919 | 5.4274 | 6.8485 | 8.6231 | 10.8347 | 13.5855 | 17.0001 | 21.2305 |
| 26 | 1.2953 | 1.6734 | 2.1566 | 2.7725 | 3.5557 | 4.5494 | 5.8074 | 7.3964 | 9.3992 | 11.9182 | 15.0799 | 19.0401 | 23.9905 |
| 27 | 1.3082 | 1.7069 | 2.2213 | 2.8834 | 3.7335 | 4.8223 | 6.2139 | 7.9881 | 10.2451 | 13.1100 | 16.7386 | 21.3249 | 27.1093 |
| 28 | 1.3213 | 1.7410 | 2.2879 | 2.9987 | 3.9201 | 5.1117 | 6.6488 | 8.6271 | 11.1671 | 14.4210 | 18.5799 | 23.8839 | 30.6335 |
| 29 | 1.3345 | 1.7758 | 2.3566 | 3.1187 | 4.1161 | 5.4184 | 7.1143 | 9.3173 | 12.1722 | 15.8631 | 20.6237 | 26.7499 | 34.6158 |
| 30 | 1.3478 | 1.8114 | 2.4273 | 3.2434 | 4.3219 | 5.7435 | 7.6123 | 10.0627 | 13.2677 | 17.4494 | 22.8923 | 29.9599 | 39.1159 |
| 31 | 1.3613 | 1.8476 | 2.5001 | 3.3731 | 4.5380 | 6.0881 | 8.1451 | 10.8677 | 14.4618 | 19.1943 | 25.4104 | 33.5551 | 44.2010 |
| 32 | 1.3749 | 1.8845 | 2.5751 | 3.5081 | 4.7649 | 6.4534 | 8.7153 | 11.7371 | 15.7633 | 21.1138 | 28.2056 | 37.5817 | 49.9471 |
| 33 | 1.3887 | 1.9222 | 2.6523 | 3.6484 | 5.0032 | 6.8406 | 9.3253 | 12.6760 | 17.1820 | 23.2252 | 31.3082 | 42.0915 | 56.4402 |

# Table of compound interest factors (2)

**Interest Rate (%)**

| Years | 14 | 15 | 16 | 17 | 18 | 19 | 20 | 21 | 22 | 23 | 24 | 25 | 26 |
|---|---|---|---|---|---|---|---|---|---|---|---|---|---|
| 1 | 1.1400 | 1.1500 | 1.1600 | 1.1700 | 1.1800 | 1.1900 | 1.2000 | 1.2100 | 1.2200 | 1.2300 | 1.2400 | 1.2500 | 1.2600 |
| 2 | 1.2996 | 1.3225 | 1.3456 | 1.3689 | 1.3924 | 1.4161 | 1.4400 | 1.4641 | 1.4884 | 1.5129 | 1.5376 | 1.5625 | 1.5876 |
| 3 | 1.4815 | 1.5209 | 1.5609 | 1.6016 | 1.6430 | 1.6852 | 1.7280 | 1.7716 | 1.8158 | 1.8609 | 1.9066 | 1.9531 | 2.0004 |
| 4 | 1.6890 | 1.7490 | 1.8106 | 1.8739 | 1.9388 | 2.0053 | 2.0736 | 2.1436 | 2.2153 | 2.2889 | 2.3642 | 2.4414 | 2.5205 |
| 5 | 1.9254 | 2.0114 | 2.1003 | 2.1924 | 2.2878 | 2.3864 | 2.4883 | 2.5937 | 2.7027 | 2.8153 | 2.9316 | 3.0518 | 3.1758 |
| 6 | 2.1950 | 2.3131 | 2.4364 | 2.5652 | 2.6996 | 2.8398 | 2.9860 | 3.1384 | 3.2973 | 3.4628 | 3.6352 | 3.8147 | 4.0015 |
| 7 | 2.5023 | 2.6600 | 2.8262 | 3.0012 | 3.1855 | 3.3793 | 3.5832 | 3.7975 | 4.0227 | 4.2593 | 4.5077 | 4.7684 | 5.0419 |
| 8 | 2.8526 | 3.0590 | 3.2784 | 3.5115 | 3.7589 | 4.0214 | 4.2998 | 4.5950 | 4.9077 | 5.2389 | 5.5895 | 5.9605 | 6.3528 |
| 9 | 3.2519 | 3.5179 | 3.8030 | 4.1084 | 4.4355 | 4.7854 | 5.1598 | 5.5599 | 5.9874 | 6.4439 | 6.9310 | 7.4506 | 8.0045 |
| 10 | 3.7072 | 4.0456 | 4.4114 | 4.8068 | 5.2338 | 5.6947 | 6.1917 | 6.7275 | 7.3046 | 7.9259 | 8.5944 | 9.3132 | 10.0857 |
| 11 | 4.2262 | 4.6524 | 5.1173 | 5.6240 | 6.1759 | 6.7767 | 7.4301 | 8.1403 | 8.9117 | 9.7489 | 10.6571 | 11.6415 | 12.7080 |
| 12 | 4.8179 | 5.3503 | 5.9360 | 6.5801 | 7.2876 | 8.0642 | 8.9161 | 9.8497 | 10.8722 | 11.9912 | 13.2148 | 14.5519 | 16.0120 |
| 13 | 5.4924 | 6.1528 | 6.8858 | 7.6987 | 8.5994 | 9.5964 | 10.6993 | 11.9182 | 13.2641 | 14.7491 | 16.3863 | 18.1899 | 20.1752 |
| 14 | 6.2613 | 7.0757 | 7.9875 | 9.0075 | 10.1472 | 11.4198 | 12.8392 | 14.4210 | 16.1822 | 18.1414 | 20.3191 | 22.7374 | 25.4207 |
| 15 | 7.1379 | 8.1371 | 9.2655 | 10.5387 | 11.9737 | 13.5895 | 15.4070 | 17.4494 | 19.7423 | 22.3140 | 25.1956 | 28.4217 | 32.0301 |
| 16 | 8.1372 | 9.3576 | 10.7480 | 12.3303 | 14.1290 | 16.1715 | 18.4884 | 21.1138 | 24.0856 | 27.4462 | 31.2426 | 35.5271 | 40.3579 |
| 17 | 9.2765 | 10.7613 | 12.4677 | 14.4265 | 16.6722 | 19.2441 | 22.1861 | 25.5477 | 29.3844 | 33.7588 | 38.7408 | 44.4089 | 50.8510 |
| 18 | 10.5752 | 12.3755 | 14.4625 | 16.8790 | 19.6733 | 22.9005 | 26.6233 | 30.9127 | 35.8490 | 41.5233 | 48.0386 | 55.5112 | 64.0722 |
| 19 | 12.0557 | 14.2318 | 16.7765 | 19.7484 | 23.2144 | 27.2516 | 31.9480 | 37.4043 | 43.7358 | 51.0737 | 59.5679 | 69.3889 | 80.7310 |
| 20 | 13.7435 | 16.3665 | 19.4608 | 23.1056 | 27.3930 | 32.4294 | 38.3376 | 45.2593 | 53.3576 | 62.8206 | 73.8641 | 86.7362 | 101.7211 |
| 21 | 15.6676 | 18.8215 | 22.5745 | 27.0336 | 32.3238 | 38.5910 | 46.0051 | 54.7637 | 65.0963 | 77.2694 | 91.5915 | 108.4202 | 128.1685 |
| 22 | 17.8610 | 21.6447 | 26.1864 | 31.6293 | 38.1421 | 45.9233 | 55.2061 | 66.2641 | 79.4175 | 95.0413 | 113.5735 | 135.5253 | 161.4924 |
| 23 | 20.3616 | 24.8915 | 30.3762 | 37.0062 | 45.0076 | 54.6487 | 66.2474 | 80.1795 | 96.8894 | 116.9008 | 140.8312 | 169.4066 | 203.4804 |
| 24 | 23.2122 | 28.6252 | 35.2364 | 43.2973 | 53.1090 | 65.0320 | 79.4968 | 97.0172 | 118.2050 | 143.7880 | 174.6306 | 211.7582 | 256.3853 |
| 25 | 26.4619 | 32.9190 | 40.8742 | 50.6578 | 62.6686 | 77.3881 | 95.3962 | 117.3909 | 144.2101 | 176.8593 | 216.5420 | 264.6978 | 323.0454 |
| 26 | 30.1666 | 37.8568 | 47.4141 | 59.2697 | 73.9490 | 92.0918 | 114.4755 | 142.0429 | 175.9364 | 217.5369 | 268.5121 | 330.8722 | 407.0373 |
| 27 | 34.3899 | 43.5353 | 55.0004 | 69.3455 | 87.2598 | 109.5893 | 137.3706 | 171.8719 | 214.6424 | 267.5704 | 332.9550 | 413.5903 | 512.8670 |
| 28 | 39.2045 | 50.0656 | 63.8004 | 81.1342 | 102.9666 | 130.4112 | 164.8447 | 207.9651 | 261.8637 | 329.1115 | 412.8642 | 516.9879 | 646.2124 |
| 29 | 44.6931 | 57.5755 | 74.0085 | 94.9271 | 121.5005 | 155.1893 | 197.8136 | 251.6377 | 319.4737 | 404.8072 | 511.9516 | 646.2349 | 814.2276 |
| 30 | 50.9502 | 66.2118 | 85.8499 | 111.0647 | 143.3706 | 184.6753 | 237.3763 | 304.4816 | 389.7579 | 497.9129 | 634.8199 | 807.7936 | 1025.927 |
| 31 | 58.0832 | 76.1435 | 99.5859 | 129.9456 | 169.1774 | 219.7636 | 284.8516 | 368.4228 | 475.5046 | 612.4328 | 787.1767 | 1009.742 | 1292.668 |
| 32 | 66.2148 | 87.5651 | 115.5196 | 152.0364 | 199.6293 | 261.5187 | 341.8219 | 445.7916 | 580.1156 | 753.2924 | 976.0991 | 1262.177 | 1628.761 |
| 33 | 75.4849 | 100.6998 | 134.0027 | 177.8826 | 235.5625 | 311.2073 | 410.1863 | 539.4078 | 707.7411 | 926.5496 | 1210.363 | 1577.722 | 2052.239 |

# Table of depreciation factors (1)

| Years | Interest Rate (%) | | | | | | | | | | | | |
|---|---|---|---|---|---|---|---|---|---|---|---|---|---|
| | 1 | 2 | 3 | 4 | 5 | 6 | 7 | 8 | 9 | 10 | 11 | 12 | 13 |
| 1 | 0.9900 | 0.9800 | 0.9700 | 0.9600 | 0.9500 | 0.9400 | 0.9300 | 0.9200 | 0.9100 | 0.9000 | 0.8900 | 0.8800 | 0.8700 |
| 2 | 0.9801 | 0.9604 | 0.9409 | 0.9216 | 0.9025 | 0.8836 | 0.8649 | 0.8464 | 0.8281 | 0.8100 | 0.7921 | 0.7744 | 0.7569 |
| 3 | 0.9703 | 0.9412 | 0.9127 | 0.8847 | 0.8574 | 0.8306 | 0.8044 | 0.7787 | 0.7536 | 0.7290 | 0.7050 | 0.6815 | 0.6585 |
| 4 | 0.9606 | 0.9224 | 0.8853 | 0.8493 | 0.8145 | 0.7807 | 0.7481 | 0.7164 | 0.6857 | 0.6561 | 0.6274 | 0.5997 | 0.5729 |
| 5 | 0.9510 | 0.9039 | 0.8587 | 0.8154 | 0.7738 | 0.7339 | 0.6957 | 0.6591 | 0.6240 | 0.5905 | 0.5584 | 0.5277 | 0.4984 |
| 6 | 0.9415 | 0.8858 | 0.8330 | 0.7828 | 0.7351 | 0.6899 | 0.6470 | 0.6064 | 0.5679 | 0.5314 | 0.4970 | 0.4644 | 0.4336 |
| 7 | 0.9321 | 0.8681 | 0.8080 | 0.7514 | 0.6983 | 0.6485 | 0.6017 | 0.5578 | 0.5168 | 0.4783 | 0.4423 | 0.4087 | 0.3773 |
| 8 | 0.9227 | 0.8508 | 0.7837 | 0.7214 | 0.6634 | 0.6096 | 0.5596 | 0.5132 | 0.4703 | 0.4305 | 0.3937 | 0.3596 | 0.3282 |
| 9 | 0.9135 | 0.8337 | 0.7602 | 0.6925 | 0.6302 | 0.5730 | 0.5204 | 0.4722 | 0.4279 | 0.3874 | 0.3504 | 0.3165 | 0.2855 |
| 10 | 0.9044 | 0.8171 | 0.7374 | 0.6648 | 0.5987 | 0.5386 | 0.4840 | 0.4344 | 0.3894 | 0.3487 | 0.3118 | 0.2785 | 0.2484 |
| 11 | 0.8953 | 0.8007 | 0.7153 | 0.6382 | 0.5688 | 0.5063 | 0.4501 | 0.3996 | 0.3544 | 0.3138 | 0.2775 | 0.2451 | 0.2161 |
| 12 | 0.8864 | 0.7847 | 0.6938 | 0.6127 | 0.5404 | 0.4759 | 0.4186 | 0.3677 | 0.3225 | 0.2824 | 0.2470 | 0.2157 | 0.1880 |
| 13 | 0.8775 | 0.7690 | 0.6730 | 0.5882 | 0.5133 | 0.4474 | 0.3893 | 0.3383 | 0.2935 | 0.2542 | 0.2198 | 0.1898 | 0.1636 |
| 14 | 0.8687 | 0.7536 | 0.6528 | 0.5647 | 0.4877 | 0.4205 | 0.3620 | 0.3112 | 0.2670 | 0.2288 | 0.1956 | 0.1670 | 0.1423 |
| 15 | 0.8601 | 0.7386 | 0.6333 | 0.5421 | 0.4633 | 0.3953 | 0.3367 | 0.2863 | 0.2430 | 0.2059 | 0.1741 | 0.1470 | 0.1238 |
| 16 | 0.8515 | 0.7238 | 0.6143 | 0.5204 | 0.4401 | 0.3716 | 0.3131 | 0.2634 | 0.2211 | 0.1853 | 0.1550 | 0.1293 | 0.1077 |
| 17 | 0.8429 | 0.7093 | 0.5958 | 0.4996 | 0.4181 | 0.3493 | 0.2912 | 0.2423 | 0.2012 | 0.1668 | 0.1379 | 0.1138 | 0.0937 |
| 18 | 0.8345 | 0.6951 | 0.5780 | 0.4796 | 0.3972 | 0.3283 | 0.2708 | 0.2229 | 0.1831 | 0.1501 | 0.1227 | 0.1002 | 0.0815 |
| 19 | 0.8262 | 0.6812 | 0.5606 | 0.4604 | 0.3774 | 0.3086 | 0.2519 | 0.2051 | 0.1666 | 0.1351 | 0.1092 | 0.0881 | 0.0709 |
| 20 | 0.8179 | 0.6676 | 0.5438 | 0.4420 | 0.3585 | 0.2901 | 0.2342 | 0.1887 | 0.1516 | 0.1216 | 0.0972 | 0.0776 | 0.0617 |
| 21 | 0.8097 | 0.6543 | 0.5275 | 0.4243 | 0.3406 | 0.2727 | 0.2178 | 0.1736 | 0.1380 | 0.1094 | 0.0865 | 0.0683 | 0.0537 |
| 22 | 0.8016 | 0.6412 | 0.5117 | 0.4073 | 0.3235 | 0.2563 | 0.2026 | 0.1597 | 0.1256 | 0.0985 | 0.0770 | 0.0601 | 0.0467 |
| 23 | 0.7936 | 0.6283 | 0.4963 | 0.3911 | 0.3074 | 0.2410 | 0.1884 | 0.1469 | 0.1143 | 0.0886 | 0.0685 | 0.0529 | 0.0406 |
| 24 | 0.7857 | 0.6158 | 0.4814 | 0.3754 | 0.2920 | 0.2265 | 0.1752 | 0.1352 | 0.1040 | 0.0798 | 0.0610 | 0.0465 | 0.0354 |
| 25 | 0.7778 | 0.6035 | 0.4670 | 0.3604 | 0.2774 | 0.2129 | 0.1630 | 0.1244 | 0.0946 | 0.0718 | 0.0543 | 0.0409 | 0.0308 |
| 26 | 0.7700 | 0.5914 | 0.4530 | 0.3460 | 0.2635 | 0.2001 | 0.1516 | 0.1144 | 0.0861 | 0.0646 | 0.0483 | 0.0360 | 0.0268 |
| 27 | 0.7623 | 0.5796 | 0.4394 | 0.3321 | 0.2503 | 0.1881 | 0.1409 | 0.1053 | 0.0784 | 0.0581 | 0.0430 | 0.0317 | 0.0233 |
| 28 | 0.7547 | 0.5680 | 0.4262 | 0.3189 | 0.2378 | 0.1768 | 0.1311 | 0.0968 | 0.0713 | 0.0523 | 0.0383 | 0.0279 | 0.0203 |
| 29 | 0.7472 | 0.5566 | 0.4134 | 0.3061 | 0.2259 | 0.1662 | 0.1219 | 0.0891 | 0.0649 | 0.0471 | 0.0341 | 0.0245 | 0.0176 |
| 30 | 0.7397 | 0.5455 | 0.4010 | 0.2939 | 0.2146 | 0.1563 | 0.1134 | 0.0820 | 0.0591 | 0.0424 | 0.0303 | 0.0216 | 0.0153 |
| 31 | 0.7323 | 0.5346 | 0.3890 | 0.2821 | 0.2039 | 0.1469 | 0.1054 | 0.0754 | 0.0537 | 0.0382 | 0.0270 | 0.0190 | 0.0133 |
| 32 | 0.7250 | 0.5239 | 0.3773 | 0.2708 | 0.1937 | 0.1381 | 0.0981 | 0.0694 | 0.0489 | 0.0343 | 0.0240 | 0.0167 | 0.0116 |
| 33 | 0.7177 | 0.5134 | 0.3660 | 0.2600 | 0.1840 | 0.1298 | 0.0912 | 0.0638 | 0.0445 | 0.0309 | 0.0214 | 0.0147 | 0.0101 |

# Table of depreciation factors (2)

Interest Rate (%)

| Years | 14 | 15 | 16 | 17 | 18 | 19 | 20 | 21 | 22 | 23 | 24 | 25 | 26 |
|---|---|---|---|---|---|---|---|---|---|---|---|---|---|
| 1 | 0.8600 | 0.8500 | 0.8400 | 0.8300 | 0.8200 | 0.8100 | 0.8000 | 0.7900 | 0.7800 | 0.7700 | 0.7600 | 0.7500 | 0.7400 |
| 2 | 0.7396 | 0.7225 | 0.7056 | 0.6889 | 0.6724 | 0.6561 | 0.6400 | 0.6241 | 0.6084 | 0.5929 | 0.5776 | 0.5625 | 0.5476 |
| 3 | 0.6361 | 0.6141 | 0.5927 | 0.5718 | 0.5514 | 0.5314 | 0.5120 | 0.4930 | 0.4746 | 0.4565 | 0.4390 | 0.4219 | 0.4052 |
| 4 | 0.5470 | 0.5220 | 0.4979 | 0.4746 | 0.4521 | 0.4305 | 0.4096 | 0.3895 | 0.3702 | 0.3515 | 0.3336 | 0.3164 | 0.2999 |
| 5 | 0.4704 | 0.4437 | 0.4182 | 0.3939 | 0.3707 | 0.3487 | 0.3277 | 0.3077 | 0.2887 | 0.2707 | 0.2536 | 0.2373 | 0.2219 |
| 6 | 0.4046 | 0.3771 | 0.3513 | 0.3269 | 0.3040 | 0.2824 | 0.2621 | 0.2431 | 0.2252 | 0.2084 | 0.1927 | 0.1780 | 0.1642 |
| 7 | 0.3479 | 0.3206 | 0.2951 | 0.2714 | 0.2493 | 0.2288 | 0.2097 | 0.1920 | 0.1757 | 0.1605 | 0.1465 | 0.1335 | 0.1215 |
| 8 | 0.2992 | 0.2725 | 0.2479 | 0.2252 | 0.2044 | 0.1853 | 0.1678 | 0.1517 | 0.1370 | 0.1236 | 0.1113 | 0.1001 | 0.0899 |
| 9 | 0.2573 | 0.2316 | 0.2082 | 0.1869 | 0.1676 | 0.1501 | 0.1342 | 0.1199 | 0.1069 | 0.0952 | 0.0846 | 0.0751 | 0.0665 |
| 10 | 0.2213 | 0.1969 | 0.1749 | 0.1552 | 0.1374 | 0.1216 | 0.1074 | 0.0947 | 0.0834 | 0.0733 | 0.0643 | 0.0563 | 0.0492 |
| 11 | 0.1903 | 0.1673 | 0.1469 | 0.1288 | 0.1127 | 0.0985 | 0.0859 | 0.0748 | 0.0650 | 0.0564 | 0.0489 | 0.0422 | 0.0364 |
| 12 | 0.1637 | 0.1422 | 0.1234 | 0.1069 | 0.0924 | 0.0798 | 0.0687 | 0.0591 | 0.0507 | 0.0434 | 0.0371 | 0.0317 | 0.0270 |
| 13 | 0.1408 | 0.1209 | 0.1037 | 0.0887 | 0.0758 | 0.0646 | 0.0550 | 0.0467 | 0.0396 | 0.0334 | 0.0282 | 0.0238 | 0.0200 |
| 14 | 0.1211 | 0.1028 | 0.0871 | 0.0736 | 0.0621 | 0.0523 | 0.0440 | 0.0369 | 0.0309 | 0.0258 | 0.0214 | 0.0178 | 0.0148 |
| 15 | 0.1041 | 0.0874 | 0.0731 | 0.0611 | 0.0510 | 0.0424 | 0.0352 | 0.0291 | 0.0241 | 0.0198 | 0.0163 | 0.0134 | 0.0109 |
| 16 | 0.0895 | 0.0743 | 0.0614 | 0.0507 | 0.0418 | 0.0343 | 0.0281 | 0.0230 | 0.0188 | 0.0153 | 0.0124 | 0.0100 | 0.0081 |
| 17 | 0.0770 | 0.0631 | 0.0516 | 0.0421 | 0.0343 | 0.0278 | 0.0225 | 0.0182 | 0.0146 | 0.0118 | 0.0094 | 0.0075 | 0.0060 |
| 18 | 0.0662 | 0.0536 | 0.0434 | 0.0349 | 0.0281 | 0.0225 | 0.0180 | 0.0144 | 0.0114 | 0.0091 | 0.0072 | 0.0056 | 0.0044 |
| 19 | 0.0569 | 0.0456 | 0.0364 | 0.0290 | 0.0230 | 0.0182 | 0.0144 | 0.0113 | 0.0089 | 0.0070 | 0.0054 | 0.0042 | 0.0033 |
| 20 | 0.0490 | 0.0388 | 0.0306 | 0.0241 | 0.0189 | 0.0148 | 0.0115 | 0.0090 | 0.0069 | 0.0054 | 0.0041 | 0.0032 | 0.0024 |
| 21 | 0.0421 | 0.0329 | 0.0257 | 0.0200 | 0.0155 | 0.0120 | 0.0092 | 0.0071 | 0.0054 | 0.0041 | 0.0031 | 0.0024 | 0.0018 |
| 22 | 0.0362 | 0.0280 | 0.0216 | 0.0166 | 0.0127 | 0.0097 | 0.0074 | 0.0056 | 0.0042 | 0.0032 | 0.0024 | 0.0018 | 0.0013 |
| 23 | 0.0312 | 0.0238 | 0.0181 | 0.0138 | 0.0104 | 0.0079 | 0.0059 | 0.0044 | 0.0033 | 0.0025 | 0.0018 | 0.0013 | 0.0010 |
| 24 | 0.0268 | 0.0202 | 0.0152 | 0.0114 | 0.0085 | 0.0064 | 0.0047 | 0.0035 | 0.0026 | 0.0019 | 0.0014 | 0.0010 | 0.0007 |
| 25 | 0.0230 | 0.0172 | 0.0128 | 0.0095 | 0.0070 | 0.0052 | 0.0038 | 0.0028 | 0.0020 | 0.0015 | 0.0010 | 0.0008 | 0.0005 |
| 26 | 0.0198 | 0.0146 | 0.0107 | 0.0079 | 0.0057 | 0.0042 | 0.0030 | 0.0022 | 0.0016 | 0.0011 | 0.0008 | 0.0006 | 0.0004 |
| 27 | 0.0170 | 0.0124 | 0.0090 | 0.0065 | 0.0047 | 0.0034 | 0.0024 | 0.0017 | 0.0012 | 0.0009 | 0.0006 | 0.0004 | 0.0003 |
| 28 | 0.0147 | 0.0106 | 0.0076 | 0.0054 | 0.0039 | 0.0027 | 0.0019 | 0.0014 | 0.0010 | 0.0007 | 0.0005 | 0.0003 | 0.0002 |
| 29 | 0.0126 | 0.0090 | 0.0064 | 0.0045 | 0.0032 | 0.0022 | 0.0015 | 0.0011 | 0.0007 | 0.0005 | 0.0003 | 0.0002 | 0.0002 |
| 30 | 0.0108 | 0.0076 | 0.0054 | 0.0037 | 0.0026 | 0.0018 | 0.0012 | 0.0008 | 0.0006 | 0.0004 | 0.0003 | 0.0002 | 0.0001 |
| 31 | 0.0093 | 0.0065 | 0.0045 | 0.0031 | 0.0021 | 0.0015 | 0.0010 | 0.0007 | 0.0005 | 0.0003 | 0.0002 | 0.0001 | 0.0001 |
| 32 | 0.0080 | 0.0055 | 0.0038 | 0.0026 | 0.0017 | 0.0012 | 0.0008 | 0.0005 | 0.0004 | 0.0002 | 0.0002 | 0.0001 | 0.0001 |
| 33 | 0.0069 | 0.0047 | 0.0032 | 0.0021 | 0.0014 | 0.0010 | 0.0006 | 0.0004 | 0.0003 | 0.0002 | 0.0001 | 0.0001 | 0.0000 |

# Table of present value factors (1)

| Years | | | | | | | | | | | | | |
| --- | --- | --- | --- | --- | --- | --- | --- | --- | --- | --- | --- | --- | --- |
| | **1** | **2** | **3** | **4** | **5** | **6** | **7** | **8** | **9** | **10** | **11** | **12** | **13** |
| 1 | 0.9901 | 0.9804 | 0.9709 | 0.9615 | 0.9524 | 0.9434 | 0.9346 | 0.9259 | 0.9174 | 0.9091 | 0.9009 | 0.8929 | 0.8850 |
| 2 | 0.9803 | 0.9612 | 0.9426 | 0.9246 | 0.9070 | 0.8900 | 0.8734 | 0.8573 | 0.8417 | 0.8264 | 0.8116 | 0.7972 | 0.7831 |
| 3 | 0.9706 | 0.9423 | 0.9151 | 0.8890 | 0.8638 | 0.8396 | 0.8163 | 0.7938 | 0.7722 | 0.7513 | 0.7312 | 0.7118 | 0.6931 |
| 4 | 0.9610 | 0.9238 | 0.8885 | 0.8548 | 0.8227 | 0.7921 | 0.7629 | 0.7350 | 0.7084 | 0.6830 | 0.6587 | 0.6355 | 0.6133 |
| 5 | 0.9515 | 0.9057 | 0.8626 | 0.8219 | 0.7835 | 0.7473 | 0.7130 | 0.6806 | 0.6499 | 0.6209 | 0.5935 | 0.5674 | 0.5428 |
| 6 | 0.9420 | 0.8880 | 0.8375 | 0.7903 | 0.7462 | 0.7050 | 0.6663 | 0.6302 | 0.5963 | 0.5645 | 0.5346 | 0.5066 | 0.4803 |
| 7 | 0.9327 | 0.8706 | 0.8131 | 0.7599 | 0.7107 | 0.6651 | 0.6227 | 0.5835 | 0.5470 | 0.5132 | 0.4817 | 0.4523 | 0.4251 |
| 8 | 0.9235 | 0.8535 | 0.7894 | 0.7307 | 0.6768 | 0.6274 | 0.5820 | 0.5403 | 0.5019 | 0.4665 | 0.4339 | 0.4039 | 0.3762 |
| 9 | 0.9143 | 0.8368 | 0.7664 | 0.7026 | 0.6446 | 0.5919 | 0.5439 | 0.5002 | 0.4604 | 0.4241 | 0.3909 | 0.3606 | 0.3329 |
| 10 | 0.9053 | 0.8203 | 0.7441 | 0.6756 | 0.6139 | 0.5584 | 0.5083 | 0.4632 | 0.4224 | 0.3855 | 0.3522 | 0.3220 | 0.2946 |
| 11 | 0.8963 | 0.8043 | 0.7224 | 0.6496 | 0.5847 | 0.5268 | 0.4751 | 0.4289 | 0.3875 | 0.3505 | 0.3173 | 0.2875 | 0.2607 |
| 12 | 0.8874 | 0.7885 | 0.7014 | 0.6246 | 0.5568 | 0.4970 | 0.4440 | 0.3971 | 0.3555 | 0.3186 | 0.2858 | 0.2567 | 0.2307 |
| 13 | 0.8787 | 0.7730 | 0.6810 | 0.6006 | 0.5303 | 0.4688 | 0.4150 | 0.3677 | 0.3262 | 0.2897 | 0.2575 | 0.2292 | 0.2042 |
| 14 | 0.8700 | 0.7579 | 0.6611 | 0.5775 | 0.5051 | 0.4423 | 0.3878 | 0.3405 | 0.2992 | 0.2633 | 0.2320 | 0.2046 | 0.1807 |
| 15 | 0.8613 | 0.7430 | 0.6419 | 0.5553 | 0.4810 | 0.4173 | 0.3624 | 0.3152 | 0.2745 | 0.2394 | 0.2090 | 0.1827 | 0.1599 |
| 16 | 0.8528 | 0.7284 | 0.6232 | 0.5339 | 0.4581 | 0.3936 | 0.3387 | 0.2919 | 0.2519 | 0.2176 | 0.1883 | 0.1631 | 0.1415 |
| 17 | 0.8444 | 0.7142 | 0.6050 | 0.5134 | 0.4363 | 0.3714 | 0.3166 | 0.2703 | 0.2311 | 0.1978 | 0.1696 | 0.1456 | 0.1252 |
| 18 | 0.8360 | 0.7002 | 0.5874 | 0.4936 | 0.4155 | 0.3503 | 0.2959 | 0.2502 | 0.2120 | 0.1799 | 0.1528 | 0.1300 | 0.1108 |
| 19 | 0.8277 | 0.6864 | 0.5703 | 0.4746 | 0.3957 | 0.3305 | 0.2765 | 0.2317 | 0.1945 | 0.1635 | 0.1377 | 0.1161 | 0.0981 |
| 20 | 0.8195 | 0.6730 | 0.5537 | 0.4564 | 0.3769 | 0.3118 | 0.2584 | 0.2145 | 0.1784 | 0.1486 | 0.1240 | 0.1037 | 0.0868 |
| 21 | 0.8114 | 0.6598 | 0.5375 | 0.4388 | 0.3589 | 0.2942 | 0.2415 | 0.1987 | 0.1637 | 0.1351 | 0.1117 | 0.0926 | 0.0768 |
| 22 | 0.8034 | 0.6468 | 0.5219 | 0.4220 | 0.3418 | 0.2775 | 0.2257 | 0.1839 | 0.1502 | 0.1228 | 0.1007 | 0.0826 | 0.0680 |
| 23 | 0.7954 | 0.6342 | 0.5067 | 0.4057 | 0.3256 | 0.2618 | 0.2109 | 0.1703 | 0.1378 | 0.1117 | 0.0907 | 0.0738 | 0.0601 |
| 24 | 0.7876 | 0.6217 | 0.4919 | 0.3901 | 0.3101 | 0.2470 | 0.1971 | 0.1577 | 0.1264 | 0.1015 | 0.0817 | 0.0659 | 0.0532 |
| 25 | 0.7798 | 0.6095 | 0.4776 | 0.3751 | 0.2953 | 0.2330 | 0.1842 | 0.1460 | 0.1160 | 0.0923 | 0.0736 | 0.0588 | 0.0471 |
| 26 | 0.7720 | 0.5976 | 0.4637 | 0.3607 | 0.2812 | 0.2198 | 0.1722 | 0.1352 | 0.1064 | 0.0839 | 0.0663 | 0.0525 | 0.0417 |
| 27 | 0.7644 | 0.5859 | 0.4502 | 0.3468 | 0.2678 | 0.2074 | 0.1609 | 0.1252 | 0.0976 | 0.0763 | 0.0597 | 0.0469 | 0.0369 |
| 28 | 0.7568 | 0.5744 | 0.4371 | 0.3335 | 0.2551 | 0.1956 | 0.1504 | 0.1159 | 0.0895 | 0.0693 | 0.0538 | 0.0419 | 0.0326 |
| 29 | 0.7493 | 0.5631 | 0.4243 | 0.3207 | 0.2429 | 0.1846 | 0.1406 | 0.1073 | 0.0822 | 0.0630 | 0.0485 | 0.0374 | 0.0289 |
| 30 | 0.7419 | 0.5521 | 0.4120 | 0.3083 | 0.2314 | 0.1741 | 0.1314 | 0.0994 | 0.0754 | 0.0573 | 0.0437 | 0.0334 | 0.0256 |
| 31 | 0.7346 | 0.5412 | 0.4000 | 0.2965 | 0.2204 | 0.1643 | 0.1228 | 0.0920 | 0.0691 | 0.0521 | 0.0394 | 0.0298 | 0.0226 |
| 32 | 0.7273 | 0.5306 | 0.3883 | 0.2851 | 0.2099 | 0.1550 | 0.1147 | 0.0852 | 0.0634 | 0.0474 | 0.0355 | 0.0266 | 0.0200 |
| 33 | 0.7201 | 0.5202 | 0.3770 | 0.2741 | 0.1999 | 0.1462 | 0.1072 | 0.0789 | 0.0582 | 0.0431 | 0.0319 | 0.0238 | 0.0177 |

Interest Rate (%)

# Table of present factors (2)

**Interest Rate (%)**

| Years | 14 | 15 | 16 | 17 | 18 | 19 | 20 | 21 | 22 | 23 | 24 | 25 | 26 |
|---|---|---|---|---|---|---|---|---|---|---|---|---|---|
| 1 | 0.8772 | 0.8696 | 0.8621 | 0.8547 | 0.8475 | 0.8403 | 0.8333 | 0.8264 | 0.8197 | 0.8130 | 0.8065 | 0.8000 | 0.7937 |
| 2 | 0.7695 | 0.7561 | 0.7432 | 0.7305 | 0.7182 | 0.7062 | 0.6944 | 0.6830 | 0.6719 | 0.6610 | 0.6504 | 0.6400 | 0.6299 |
| 3 | 0.6750 | 0.6575 | 0.6407 | 0.6244 | 0.6086 | 0.5934 | 0.5787 | 0.5645 | 0.5507 | 0.5374 | 0.5245 | 0.5120 | 0.4999 |
| 4 | 0.5921 | 0.5718 | 0.5523 | 0.5337 | 0.5158 | 0.4987 | 0.4823 | 0.4665 | 0.4514 | 0.4369 | 0.4230 | 0.4096 | 0.3968 |
| 5 | 0.5194 | 0.4972 | 0.4761 | 0.4561 | 0.4371 | 0.4190 | 0.4019 | 0.3855 | 0.3700 | 0.3552 | 0.3411 | 0.3277 | 0.3149 |
| 6 | 0.4556 | 0.4323 | 0.4104 | 0.3898 | 0.3704 | 0.3521 | 0.3349 | 0.3186 | 0.3033 | 0.2888 | 0.2751 | 0.2621 | 0.2499 |
| 7 | 0.3996 | 0.3759 | 0.3538 | 0.3332 | 0.3139 | 0.2959 | 0.2791 | 0.2633 | 0.2486 | 0.2348 | 0.2218 | 0.2097 | 0.1983 |
| 8 | 0.3506 | 0.3269 | 0.3050 | 0.2848 | 0.2660 | 0.2487 | 0.2326 | 0.2176 | 0.2038 | 0.1909 | 0.1789 | 0.1678 | 0.1574 |
| 9 | 0.3075 | 0.2843 | 0.2630 | 0.2434 | 0.2255 | 0.2090 | 0.1938 | 0.1799 | 0.1670 | 0.1552 | 0.1443 | 0.1342 | 0.1249 |
| 10 | 0.2697 | 0.2472 | 0.2267 | 0.2080 | 0.1911 | 0.1756 | 0.1615 | 0.1486 | 0.1369 | 0.1262 | 0.1164 | 0.1074 | 0.0992 |
| 11 | 0.2366 | 0.2149 | 0.1954 | 0.1778 | 0.1619 | 0.1476 | 0.1346 | 0.1228 | 0.1122 | 0.1026 | 0.0938 | 0.0859 | 0.0787 |
| 12 | 0.2076 | 0.1869 | 0.1685 | 0.1520 | 0.1372 | 0.1240 | 0.1122 | 0.1015 | 0.0920 | 0.0834 | 0.0757 | 0.0687 | 0.0625 |
| 13 | 0.1821 | 0.1625 | 0.1452 | 0.1299 | 0.1163 | 0.1042 | 0.0935 | 0.0839 | 0.0754 | 0.0678 | 0.0610 | 0.0550 | 0.0496 |
| 14 | 0.1597 | 0.1413 | 0.1252 | 0.1110 | 0.0985 | 0.0876 | 0.0779 | 0.0693 | 0.0618 | 0.0551 | 0.0492 | 0.0440 | 0.0393 |
| 15 | 0.1401 | 0.1229 | 0.1079 | 0.0949 | 0.0835 | 0.0736 | 0.0649 | 0.0573 | 0.0507 | 0.0448 | 0.0397 | 0.0352 | 0.0312 |
| 16 | 0.1229 | 0.1069 | 0.0930 | 0.0811 | 0.0708 | 0.0618 | 0.0541 | 0.0474 | 0.0415 | 0.0364 | 0.0320 | 0.0281 | 0.0248 |
| 17 | 0.1078 | 0.0929 | 0.0802 | 0.0693 | 0.0600 | 0.0520 | 0.0451 | 0.0391 | 0.0340 | 0.0296 | 0.0258 | 0.0225 | 0.0197 |
| 18 | 0.0946 | 0.0808 | 0.0691 | 0.0592 | 0.0508 | 0.0437 | 0.0376 | 0.0323 | 0.0279 | 0.0241 | 0.0208 | 0.0180 | 0.0156 |
| 19 | 0.0829 | 0.0703 | 0.0596 | 0.0506 | 0.0431 | 0.0367 | 0.0313 | 0.0267 | 0.0229 | 0.0196 | 0.0168 | 0.0144 | 0.0124 |
| 20 | 0.0728 | 0.0611 | 0.0514 | 0.0433 | 0.0365 | 0.0308 | 0.0261 | 0.0221 | 0.0187 | 0.0159 | 0.0135 | 0.0115 | 0.0098 |
| 21 | 0.0638 | 0.0531 | 0.0443 | 0.0370 | 0.0309 | 0.0259 | 0.0217 | 0.0183 | 0.0154 | 0.0129 | 0.0109 | 0.0092 | 0.0078 |
| 22 | 0.0560 | 0.0462 | 0.0382 | 0.0316 | 0.0262 | 0.0218 | 0.0181 | 0.0151 | 0.0126 | 0.0105 | 0.0088 | 0.0074 | 0.0062 |
| 23 | 0.0491 | 0.0402 | 0.0329 | 0.0270 | 0.0222 | 0.0183 | 0.0151 | 0.0125 | 0.0103 | 0.0086 | 0.0071 | 0.0059 | 0.0049 |
| 24 | 0.0431 | 0.0349 | 0.0284 | 0.0231 | 0.0188 | 0.0154 | 0.0126 | 0.0103 | 0.0085 | 0.0070 | 0.0057 | 0.0047 | 0.0039 |
| 25 | 0.0378 | 0.0304 | 0.0245 | 0.0197 | 0.0160 | 0.0129 | 0.0105 | 0.0085 | 0.0069 | 0.0057 | 0.0046 | 0.0038 | 0.0031 |
| 26 | 0.0331 | 0.0264 | 0.0211 | 0.0169 | 0.0135 | 0.0109 | 0.0087 | 0.0070 | 0.0057 | 0.0046 | 0.0037 | 0.0030 | 0.0025 |
| 27 | 0.0291 | 0.0230 | 0.0182 | 0.0144 | 0.0115 | 0.0091 | 0.0073 | 0.0058 | 0.0047 | 0.0037 | 0.0030 | 0.0024 | 0.0019 |
| 28 | 0.0255 | 0.0200 | 0.0157 | 0.0123 | 0.0097 | 0.0077 | 0.0061 | 0.0048 | 0.0038 | 0.0030 | 0.0024 | 0.0019 | 0.0015 |
| 29 | 0.0224 | 0.0174 | 0.0135 | 0.0105 | 0.0082 | 0.0064 | 0.0051 | 0.0040 | 0.0031 | 0.0025 | 0.0020 | 0.0015 | 0.0012 |
| 30 | 0.0196 | 0.0151 | 0.0116 | 0.0090 | 0.0070 | 0.0054 | 0.0042 | 0.0033 | 0.0026 | 0.0020 | 0.0016 | 0.0012 | 0.0010 |
| 31 | 0.0172 | 0.0131 | 0.0100 | 0.0077 | 0.0059 | 0.0046 | 0.0035 | 0.0027 | 0.0021 | 0.0016 | 0.0013 | 0.0010 | 0.0008 |
| 32 | 0.0151 | 0.0114 | 0.0087 | 0.0066 | 0.0050 | 0.0038 | 0.0029 | 0.0022 | 0.0017 | 0.0013 | 0.0010 | 0.0008 | 0.0006 |
| 33 | 0.0132 | 0.0099 | 0.0075 | 0.0056 | 0.0042 | 0.0032 | 0.0024 | 0.0019 | 0.0014 | 0.0011 | 0.0008 | 0.0006 | 0.0005 |

# Table of capital recovery factors (1)

Interest Rate (%)

| Years | 1 | 2 | 3 | 4 | 5 | 6 | 7 | 8 | 9 | 10 | 11 | 12 | 13 |
|---|---|---|---|---|---|---|---|---|---|---|---|---|---|
| 1 | 1.0100 | 1.0200 | 1.0300 | 1.0400 | 1.0500 | 1.0600 | 1.0700 | 1.0800 | 1.0900 | 1.1000 | 1.1100 | 1.1200 | 1.1300 |
| 2 | 0.5075 | 0.5150 | 0.5226 | 0.5302 | 0.5378 | 0.5454 | 0.5531 | 0.5608 | 0.5685 | 0.5762 | 0.5839 | 0.5917 | 0.5995 |
| 3 | 0.3400 | 0.3468 | 0.3535 | 0.3603 | 0.3672 | 0.3741 | 0.3811 | 0.3880 | 0.3951 | 0.4021 | 0.4092 | 0.4163 | 0.4235 |
| 4 | 0.2563 | 0.2626 | 0.2690 | 0.2755 | 0.2820 | 0.2886 | 0.2952 | 0.3019 | 0.3087 | 0.3155 | 0.3223 | 0.3292 | 0.3362 |
| 5 | 0.2060 | 0.2122 | 0.2184 | 0.2246 | 0.2310 | 0.2374 | 0.2439 | 0.2505 | 0.2571 | 0.2638 | 0.2706 | 0.2774 | 0.2843 |
| 6 | 0.1725 | 0.1785 | 0.1846 | 0.1908 | 0.1970 | 0.2034 | 0.2098 | 0.2163 | 0.2229 | 0.2296 | 0.2364 | 0.2432 | 0.2502 |
| 7 | 0.1486 | 0.1545 | 0.1605 | 0.1666 | 0.1728 | 0.1791 | 0.1856 | 0.1921 | 0.1987 | 0.2054 | 0.2122 | 0.2191 | 0.2261 |
| 8 | 0.1307 | 0.1365 | 0.1425 | 0.1485 | 0.1547 | 0.1610 | 0.1675 | 0.1740 | 0.1807 | 0.1874 | 0.1943 | 0.2013 | 0.2084 |
| 9 | 0.1167 | 0.1225 | 0.1284 | 0.1345 | 0.1407 | 0.1470 | 0.1535 | 0.1601 | 0.1668 | 0.1736 | 0.1806 | 0.1877 | 0.1949 |
| 10 | 0.1056 | 0.1113 | 0.1172 | 0.1233 | 0.1295 | 0.1359 | 0.1424 | 0.1490 | 0.1558 | 0.1627 | 0.1698 | 0.1770 | 0.1843 |
| 11 | 0.0965 | 0.1022 | 0.1081 | 0.1141 | 0.1204 | 0.1268 | 0.1334 | 0.1401 | 0.1469 | 0.1540 | 0.1611 | 0.1684 | 0.1758 |
| 12 | 0.0888 | 0.0946 | 0.1005 | 0.1066 | 0.1128 | 0.1193 | 0.1259 | 0.1327 | 0.1397 | 0.1468 | 0.1540 | 0.1614 | 0.1690 |
| 13 | 0.0824 | 0.0881 | 0.0940 | 0.1001 | 0.1065 | 0.1130 | 0.1197 | 0.1265 | 0.1336 | 0.1408 | 0.1482 | 0.1557 | 0.1634 |
| 14 | 0.0769 | 0.0826 | 0.0885 | 0.0947 | 0.1010 | 0.1076 | 0.1143 | 0.1213 | 0.1284 | 0.1357 | 0.1432 | 0.1509 | 0.1587 |
| 15 | 0.0721 | 0.0778 | 0.0838 | 0.0899 | 0.0963 | 0.1030 | 0.1098 | 0.1168 | 0.1241 | 0.1315 | 0.1391 | 0.1468 | 0.1547 |
| 16 | 0.0679 | 0.0737 | 0.0796 | 0.0858 | 0.0923 | 0.0990 | 0.1059 | 0.1130 | 0.1203 | 0.1278 | 0.1355 | 0.1434 | 0.1514 |
| 17 | 0.0643 | 0.0700 | 0.0760 | 0.0822 | 0.0887 | 0.0954 | 0.1024 | 0.1096 | 0.1170 | 0.1247 | 0.1325 | 0.1405 | 0.1486 |
| 18 | 0.0610 | 0.0667 | 0.0727 | 0.0790 | 0.0855 | 0.0924 | 0.0994 | 0.1067 | 0.1142 | 0.1219 | 0.1298 | 0.1379 | 0.1462 |
| 19 | 0.0581 | 0.0638 | 0.0698 | 0.0761 | 0.0827 | 0.0896 | 0.0968 | 0.1041 | 0.1117 | 0.1195 | 0.1276 | 0.1358 | 0.1441 |
| 20 | 0.0554 | 0.0612 | 0.0672 | 0.0736 | 0.0802 | 0.0872 | 0.0944 | 0.1019 | 0.1095 | 0.1175 | 0.1256 | 0.1339 | 0.1424 |
| 21 | 0.0530 | 0.0588 | 0.0649 | 0.0713 | 0.0780 | 0.0850 | 0.0923 | 0.0998 | 0.1076 | 0.1156 | 0.1238 | 0.1322 | 0.1408 |
| 22 | 0.0509 | 0.0566 | 0.0627 | 0.0692 | 0.0760 | 0.0830 | 0.0904 | 0.0980 | 0.1059 | 0.1140 | 0.1223 | 0.1308 | 0.1395 |
| 23 | 0.0489 | 0.0547 | 0.0608 | 0.0673 | 0.0741 | 0.0813 | 0.0887 | 0.0964 | 0.1044 | 0.1126 | 0.1210 | 0.1296 | 0.1383 |
| 24 | 0.0471 | 0.0529 | 0.0590 | 0.0656 | 0.0725 | 0.0797 | 0.0872 | 0.0950 | 0.1030 | 0.1113 | 0.1198 | 0.1285 | 0.1373 |
| 25 | 0.0454 | 0.0512 | 0.0574 | 0.0640 | 0.0710 | 0.0782 | 0.0858 | 0.0937 | 0.1018 | 0.1102 | 0.1187 | 0.1275 | 0.1364 |
| 26 | 0.0439 | 0.0497 | 0.0559 | 0.0626 | 0.0696 | 0.0769 | 0.0846 | 0.0925 | 0.1007 | 0.1092 | 0.1178 | 0.1267 | 0.1357 |
| 27 | 0.0424 | 0.0483 | 0.0546 | 0.0612 | 0.0683 | 0.0757 | 0.0834 | 0.0914 | 0.0997 | 0.1083 | 0.1170 | 0.1259 | 0.1350 |
| 28 | 0.0411 | 0.0470 | 0.0533 | 0.0600 | 0.0671 | 0.0746 | 0.0824 | 0.0905 | 0.0989 | 0.1075 | 0.1163 | 0.1252 | 0.1344 |
| 29 | 0.0399 | 0.0458 | 0.0521 | 0.0589 | 0.0660 | 0.0736 | 0.0814 | 0.0896 | 0.0981 | 0.1067 | 0.1156 | 0.1247 | 0.1339 |
| 30 | 0.0387 | 0.0446 | 0.0510 | 0.0578 | 0.0651 | 0.0726 | 0.0806 | 0.0888 | 0.0973 | 0.1061 | 0.1150 | 0.1241 | 0.1334 |
| 31 | 0.0377 | 0.0436 | 0.0500 | 0.0569 | 0.0641 | 0.0718 | 0.0798 | 0.0881 | 0.0967 | 0.1055 | 0.1145 | 0.1237 | 0.1330 |
| 32 | 0.0367 | 0.0426 | 0.0490 | 0.0559 | 0.0633 | 0.0710 | 0.0791 | 0.0875 | 0.0961 | 0.1050 | 0.1140 | 0.1233 | 0.1327 |
| 33 | 0.0357 | 0.0417 | 0.0482 | 0.0551 | 0.0625 | 0.0703 | 0.0784 | 0.0869 | 0.0956 | 0.1045 | 0.1136 | 0.1229 | 0.1323 |

# Table of capital recovery factors (2)

Interest Rate (%)

| Years | 14 | 15 | 16 | 17 | 18 | 19 | 20 | 21 | 22 | 23 | 24 | 25 | 26 |
|---|---|---|---|---|---|---|---|---|---|---|---|---|---|
| 1 | 1.1400 | 1.1500 | 1.1600 | 1.1700 | 1.1800 | 1.1900 | 1.2000 | 1.2100 | 1.2200 | 1.2300 | 1.2400 | 1.2500 | 1.2600 |
| 2 | 0.6073 | 0.6151 | 0.6230 | 0.6308 | 0.6387 | 0.6466 | 0.6545 | 0.6625 | 0.6705 | 0.6784 | 0.6864 | 0.6944 | 0.7025 |
| 3 | 0.4307 | 0.4380 | 0.4453 | 0.4526 | 0.4599 | 0.4673 | 0.4747 | 0.4822 | 0.4897 | 0.4972 | 0.5047 | 0.5123 | 0.5199 |
| 4 | 0.3432 | 0.3503 | 0.3574 | 0.3645 | 0.3717 | 0.3790 | 0.3863 | 0.3936 | 0.4010 | 0.4085 | 0.4159 | 0.4234 | 0.4310 |
| 5 | 0.2913 | 0.2983 | 0.3054 | 0.3126 | 0.3198 | 0.3271 | 0.3344 | 0.3418 | 0.3492 | 0.3567 | 0.3642 | 0.3718 | 0.3795 |
| 6 | 0.2572 | 0.2642 | 0.2714 | 0.2786 | 0.2859 | 0.2933 | 0.3007 | 0.3082 | 0.3158 | 0.3234 | 0.3311 | 0.3388 | 0.3466 |
| 7 | 0.2332 | 0.2404 | 0.2476 | 0.2549 | 0.2624 | 0.2699 | 0.2774 | 0.2851 | 0.2928 | 0.3006 | 0.3084 | 0.3163 | 0.3243 |
| 8 | 0.2156 | 0.2229 | 0.2302 | 0.2377 | 0.2452 | 0.2529 | 0.2606 | 0.2684 | 0.2763 | 0.2843 | 0.2923 | 0.3004 | 0.3086 |
| 9 | 0.2022 | 0.2096 | 0.2171 | 0.2247 | 0.2324 | 0.2402 | 0.2481 | 0.2561 | 0.2641 | 0.2722 | 0.2805 | 0.2888 | 0.2971 |
| 10 | 0.1917 | 0.1993 | 0.2069 | 0.2147 | 0.2225 | 0.2305 | 0.2385 | 0.2467 | 0.2549 | 0.2632 | 0.2716 | 0.2801 | 0.2886 |
| 11 | 0.1834 | 0.1911 | 0.1989 | 0.2068 | 0.2148 | 0.2229 | 0.2311 | 0.2394 | 0.2478 | 0.2563 | 0.2649 | 0.2735 | 0.2822 |
| 12 | 0.1767 | 0.1845 | 0.1924 | 0.2005 | 0.2086 | 0.2169 | 0.2253 | 0.2337 | 0.2423 | 0.2509 | 0.2596 | 0.2684 | 0.2773 |
| 13 | 0.1712 | 0.1791 | 0.1872 | 0.1954 | 0.2037 | 0.2121 | 0.2206 | 0.2292 | 0.2379 | 0.2467 | 0.2556 | 0.2645 | 0.2736 |
| 14 | 0.1666 | 0.1747 | 0.1829 | 0.1912 | 0.1997 | 0.2082 | 0.2169 | 0.2256 | 0.2345 | 0.2434 | 0.2524 | 0.2615 | 0.2706 |
| 15 | 0.1628 | 0.1710 | 0.1794 | 0.1878 | 0.1964 | 0.2051 | 0.2139 | 0.2228 | 0.2317 | 0.2408 | 0.2499 | 0.2591 | 0.2684 |
| 16 | 0.1596 | 0.1679 | 0.1764 | 0.1850 | 0.1937 | 0.2025 | 0.2114 | 0.2204 | 0.2295 | 0.2387 | 0.2479 | 0.2572 | 0.2666 |
| 17 | 0.1569 | 0.1654 | 0.1740 | 0.1827 | 0.1915 | 0.2004 | 0.2094 | 0.2186 | 0.2278 | 0.2370 | 0.2464 | 0.2558 | 0.2652 |
| 18 | 0.1546 | 0.1632 | 0.1719 | 0.1807 | 0.1896 | 0.1987 | 0.2078 | 0.2170 | 0.2263 | 0.2357 | 0.2451 | 0.2546 | 0.2641 |
| 19 | 0.1527 | 0.1613 | 0.1701 | 0.1791 | 0.1881 | 0.1972 | 0.2065 | 0.2158 | 0.2251 | 0.2346 | 0.2441 | 0.2537 | 0.2633 |
| 20 | 0.1510 | 0.1598 | 0.1687 | 0.1777 | 0.1868 | 0.1960 | 0.2054 | 0.2147 | 0.2242 | 0.2337 | 0.2433 | 0.2529 | 0.2626 |
| 21 | 0.1495 | 0.1584 | 0.1674 | 0.1765 | 0.1857 | 0.1951 | 0.2044 | 0.2139 | 0.2234 | 0.2330 | 0.2426 | 0.2523 | 0.2620 |
| 22 | 0.1483 | 0.1573 | 0.1664 | 0.1756 | 0.1848 | 0.1942 | 0.2037 | 0.2132 | 0.2228 | 0.2324 | 0.2421 | 0.2519 | 0.2616 |
| 23 | 0.1472 | 0.1563 | 0.1654 | 0.1747 | 0.1841 | 0.1935 | 0.2031 | 0.2127 | 0.2223 | 0.2320 | 0.2417 | 0.2515 | 0.2613 |
| 24 | 0.1463 | 0.1554 | 0.1647 | 0.1740 | 0.1835 | 0.1930 | 0.2025 | 0.2122 | 0.2219 | 0.2316 | 0.2414 | 0.2512 | 0.2610 |
| 25 | 0.1455 | 0.1547 | 0.1640 | 0.1734 | 0.1829 | 0.1925 | 0.2021 | 0.2118 | 0.2215 | 0.2313 | 0.2411 | 0.2509 | 0.2608 |
| 26 | 0.1448 | 0.1541 | 0.1634 | 0.1729 | 0.1825 | 0.1921 | 0.2018 | 0.2115 | 0.2213 | 0.2311 | 0.2409 | 0.2508 | 0.2606 |
| 27 | 0.1442 | 0.1535 | 0.1630 | 0.1725 | 0.1821 | 0.1917 | 0.2015 | 0.2112 | 0.2210 | 0.2309 | 0.2407 | 0.2506 | 0.2605 |
| 28 | 0.1437 | 0.1531 | 0.1625 | 0.1721 | 0.1818 | 0.1915 | 0.2012 | 0.2110 | 0.2208 | 0.2307 | 0.2406 | 0.2505 | 0.2604 |
| 29 | 0.1432 | 0.1527 | 0.1622 | 0.1718 | 0.1815 | 0.1912 | 0.2010 | 0.2108 | 0.2207 | 0.2306 | 0.2405 | 0.2504 | 0.2603 |
| 30 | 0.1428 | 0.1523 | 0.1619 | 0.1715 | 0.1813 | 0.1910 | 0.2008 | 0.2107 | 0.2206 | 0.2305 | 0.2404 | 0.2503 | 0.2603 |
| 31 | 0.1425 | 0.1520 | 0.1616 | 0.1713 | 0.1811 | 0.1909 | 0.2007 | 0.2106 | 0.2205 | 0.2304 | 0.2403 | 0.2502 | 0.2602 |
| 32 | 0.1421 | 0.1517 | 0.1614 | 0.1711 | 0.1809 | 0.1907 | 0.2006 | 0.2105 | 0.2204 | 0.2303 | 0.2402 | 0.2502 | 0.2602 |
| 33 | 0.1419 | 0.1515 | 0.1612 | 0.1710 | 0.1808 | 0.1906 | 0.2005 | 0.2104 | 0.2203 | 0.2302 | 0.2402 | 0.2502 | 0.2601 |

# Table of annuity factors (1)

Interest Rate (%)

| Years | 1 | 2 | 3 | 4 | 5 | 6 | 7 | 8 | 9 | 10 | 11 | 12 | 13 |
|---|---|---|---|---|---|---|---|---|---|---|---|---|---|
| 1 | 0.9901 | 0.9804 | 0.9709 | 0.9615 | 0.9524 | 0.9434 | 0.9346 | 0.9259 | 0.9174 | 0.9091 | 0.9009 | 0.8929 | 0.8850 |
| 2 | 1.9704 | 1.9416 | 1.9135 | 1.8861 | 1.8594 | 1.8334 | 1.8080 | 1.7833 | 1.7591 | 1.7355 | 1.7125 | 1.6901 | 1.6681 |
| 3 | 2.9410 | 2.8839 | 2.8286 | 2.7751 | 2.7232 | 2.6730 | 2.6243 | 2.5771 | 2.5313 | 2.4869 | 2.4437 | 2.4018 | 2.3612 |
| 4 | 3.9020 | 3.8077 | 3.7171 | 3.6299 | 3.5460 | 3.4651 | 3.3872 | 3.3121 | 3.2397 | 3.1699 | 3.1024 | 3.0373 | 2.9745 |
| 5 | 4.8534 | 4.7135 | 4.5797 | 4.4518 | 4.3295 | 4.2124 | 4.1002 | 3.9927 | 3.8897 | 3.7908 | 3.6959 | 3.6048 | 3.5172 |
| 6 | 5.7955 | 5.6014 | 5.4172 | 5.2421 | 5.0757 | 4.9173 | 4.7665 | 4.6229 | 4.4859 | 4.3553 | 4.2305 | 4.1114 | 3.9975 |
| 7 | 6.7282 | 6.4720 | 6.2303 | 6.0021 | 5.7864 | 5.5824 | 5.3893 | 5.2064 | 5.0330 | 4.8684 | 4.7122 | 4.5638 | 4.4226 |
| 8 | 7.6517 | 7.3255 | 7.0197 | 6.7327 | 6.4632 | 6.2098 | 5.9713 | 5.7466 | 5.5348 | 5.3349 | 5.1461 | 4.9676 | 4.7988 |
| 9 | 8.5660 | 8.1622 | 7.7861 | 7.4353 | 7.1078 | 6.8017 | 6.5152 | 6.2469 | 5.9952 | 5.7590 | 5.5370 | 5.3282 | 5.1317 |
| 10 | 9.4713 | 8.9826 | 8.5302 | 8.1109 | 7.7217 | 7.3601 | 7.0236 | 6.7101 | 6.4177 | 6.1446 | 5.8892 | 5.6502 | 5.4262 |
| 11 | 10.3676 | 9.7868 | 9.2526 | 8.7605 | 8.3064 | 7.8869 | 7.4987 | 7.1390 | 6.8052 | 6.4951 | 6.2065 | 5.9377 | 5.6869 |
| 12 | 11.2551 | 10.5753 | 9.9540 | 9.3851 | 8.8633 | 8.3838 | 7.9427 | 7.5361 | 7.1607 | 6.8137 | 6.4924 | 6.1944 | 5.9176 |
| 13 | 12.1337 | 11.3484 | 10.6350 | 9.9856 | 9.3936 | 8.8527 | 8.3577 | 7.9038 | 7.4869 | 7.1034 | 6.7499 | 6.4235 | 6.1218 |
| 14 | 13.0037 | 12.1062 | 11.2961 | 10.5631 | 9.8986 | 9.2950 | 8.7455 | 8.2442 | 7.7862 | 7.3667 | 6.9819 | 6.6282 | 6.3025 |
| 15 | 13.8651 | 12.8493 | 11.9379 | 11.1184 | 10.3797 | 9.7122 | 9.1079 | 8.5595 | 8.0607 | 7.6061 | 7.1909 | 6.8109 | 6.4624 |
| 16 | 14.7179 | 13.5777 | 12.5611 | 11.6523 | 10.8378 | 10.1059 | 9.4466 | 8.8514 | 8.3126 | 7.8237 | 7.3792 | 6.9740 | 6.6039 |
| 17 | 15.5623 | 14.2919 | 13.1661 | 12.1657 | 11.2741 | 10.4773 | 9.7632 | 9.1216 | 8.5436 | 8.0216 | 7.5488 | 7.1196 | 6.7291 |
| 18 | 16.3983 | 14.9920 | 13.7535 | 12.6593 | 11.6896 | 10.8276 | 10.0591 | 9.3719 | 8.7556 | 8.2014 | 7.7016 | 7.2497 | 6.8399 |
| 19 | 17.2260 | 15.6785 | 14.3238 | 13.1339 | 12.0853 | 11.1581 | 10.3356 | 9.6036 | 8.9501 | 8.3649 | 7.8393 | 7.3658 | 6.9380 |
| 20 | 18.0456 | 16.3514 | 14.8775 | 13.5903 | 12.4622 | 11.4699 | 10.5940 | 9.8181 | 9.1285 | 8.5136 | 7.9633 | 7.4694 | 7.0248 |
| 21 | 18.8570 | 17.0112 | 15.4150 | 14.0292 | 12.8212 | 11.7641 | 10.8355 | 10.0168 | 9.2922 | 8.6487 | 8.0751 | 7.5620 | 7.1016 |
| 22 | 19.6604 | 17.6580 | 15.9369 | 14.4511 | 13.1630 | 12.0416 | 11.0612 | 10.2007 | 9.4424 | 8.7715 | 8.1757 | 7.6446 | 7.1695 |
| 23 | 20.4558 | 18.2922 | 16.4436 | 14.8568 | 13.4886 | 12.3034 | 11.2722 | 10.3711 | 9.5802 | 8.8832 | 8.2664 | 7.7184 | 7.2297 |
| 24 | 21.2434 | 18.9139 | 16.9355 | 15.2470 | 13.7986 | 12.5504 | 11.4693 | 10.5288 | 9.7066 | 8.9847 | 8.3481 | 7.7843 | 7.2829 |
| 25 | 22.0232 | 19.5235 | 17.4131 | 15.6221 | 14.0939 | 12.7834 | 11.6536 | 10.6748 | 9.8226 | 9.0770 | 8.4217 | 7.8431 | 7.3300 |
| 26 | 22.7952 | 20.1210 | 17.8768 | 15.9828 | 14.3752 | 13.0032 | 11.8258 | 10.8100 | 9.9290 | 9.1609 | 8.4881 | 7.8957 | 7.3717 |
| 27 | 23.5596 | 20.7069 | 18.3270 | 16.3296 | 14.6430 | 13.2105 | 11.9867 | 10.9352 | 10.0266 | 9.2372 | 8.5478 | 7.9426 | 7.4086 |
| 28 | 24.3164 | 21.2813 | 18.7641 | 16.6631 | 14.8981 | 13.4062 | 12.1371 | 11.0511 | 10.1161 | 9.3066 | 8.6016 | 7.9844 | 7.4412 |
| 29 | 25.0658 | 21.8444 | 19.1885 | 16.9837 | 15.1411 | 13.5907 | 12.2777 | 11.1584 | 10.1983 | 9.3696 | 8.6501 | 8.0218 | 7.4701 |
| 30 | 25.8077 | 22.3965 | 19.6004 | 17.2920 | 15.3725 | 13.7648 | 12.4090 | 11.2578 | 10.2737 | 9.4269 | 8.6938 | 8.0552 | 7.4957 |
| 31 | 26.5423 | 22.9377 | 20.0004 | 17.5885 | 15.5928 | 13.9291 | 12.5318 | 11.3498 | 10.3428 | 9.4790 | 8.7331 | 8.0850 | 7.5183 |
| 32 | 27.2696 | 23.4683 | 20.3888 | 17.8736 | 15.8027 | 14.0840 | 12.6466 | 11.4350 | 10.4062 | 9.5264 | 8.7686 | 8.1116 | 7.5383 |
| 33 | 27.9897 | 23.9886 | 20.7658 | 18.1476 | 16.0025 | 14.2302 | 12.7538 | 11.5139 | 10.4644 | 9.5694 | 8.8005 | 8.1354 | 7.5560 |

# Table of annuity factors (2)

**Interest Rate (%)**

| Years | 14 | 15 | 16 | 17 | 18 | 19 | 20 | 21 | 22 | 23 | 24 | 25 | 26 |
|---|---|---|---|---|---|---|---|---|---|---|---|---|---|
| 1 | 0.8772 | 0.8696 | 0.8621 | 0.8547 | 0.8475 | 0.8403 | 0.8333 | 0.8264 | 0.8197 | 0.8130 | 0.8065 | 0.8000 | 0.7937 |
| 2 | 1.6467 | 1.6257 | 1.6052 | 1.5852 | 1.5656 | 1.5465 | 1.5278 | 1.5095 | 1.4915 | 1.4740 | 1.4568 | 1.4400 | 1.4235 |
| 3 | 2.3216 | 2.2832 | 2.2459 | 2.2096 | 2.1743 | 2.1399 | 2.1065 | 2.0739 | 2.0422 | 2.0114 | 1.9813 | 1.9520 | 1.9234 |
| 4 | 2.9137 | 2.8550 | 2.7982 | 2.7432 | 2.6901 | 2.6386 | 2.5887 | 2.5404 | 2.4936 | 2.4483 | 2.4043 | 2.3616 | 2.3202 |
| 5 | 3.4331 | 3.3522 | 3.2743 | 3.1993 | 3.1272 | 3.0576 | 2.9906 | 2.9260 | 2.8636 | 2.8035 | 2.7454 | 2.6893 | 2.6351 |
| 6 | 3.8887 | 3.7845 | 3.6847 | 3.5892 | 3.4976 | 3.4098 | 3.3255 | 3.2446 | 3.1669 | 3.0923 | 3.0205 | 2.9514 | 2.8850 |
| 7 | 4.2883 | 4.1604 | 4.0386 | 3.9224 | 3.8115 | 3.7057 | 3.6046 | 3.5079 | 3.4155 | 3.3270 | 3.2423 | 3.1611 | 3.0833 |
| 8 | 4.6389 | 4.4873 | 4.3436 | 4.2072 | 4.0776 | 3.9544 | 3.8372 | 3.7256 | 3.6193 | 3.5179 | 3.4212 | 3.3289 | 3.2407 |
| 9 | 4.9464 | 4.7716 | 4.6065 | 4.4506 | 4.3030 | 4.1633 | 4.0310 | 3.9054 | 3.7863 | 3.6731 | 3.5655 | 3.4631 | 3.3657 |
| 10 | 5.2161 | 5.0188 | 4.8332 | 4.6586 | 4.4941 | 4.3389 | 4.1925 | 4.0541 | 3.9232 | 3.7993 | 3.6819 | 3.5705 | 3.4648 |
| 11 | 5.4527 | 5.2337 | 5.0286 | 4.8364 | 4.6560 | 4.4865 | 4.3271 | 4.1769 | 4.0354 | 3.9018 | 3.7757 | 3.6564 | 3.5435 |
| 12 | 5.6603 | 5.4206 | 5.1971 | 4.9884 | 4.7932 | 4.6105 | 4.4392 | 4.2784 | 4.1274 | 3.9852 | 3.8514 | 3.7251 | 3.6059 |
| 13 | 5.8424 | 5.5831 | 5.3423 | 5.1183 | 4.9095 | 4.7147 | 4.5327 | 4.3624 | 4.2028 | 4.0530 | 3.9124 | 3.7801 | 3.6555 |
| 14 | 6.0021 | 5.7245 | 5.4675 | 5.2293 | 5.0081 | 4.8023 | 4.6106 | 4.4317 | 4.2646 | 4.1082 | 3.9616 | 3.8241 | 3.6949 |
| 15 | 6.1422 | 5.8474 | 5.5755 | 5.3242 | 5.0916 | 4.8759 | 4.6755 | 4.4890 | 4.3152 | 4.1530 | 4.0013 | 3.8593 | 3.7261 |
| 16 | 6.2651 | 5.9542 | 5.6685 | 5.4053 | 5.1624 | 4.9377 | 4.7296 | 4.5364 | 4.3567 | 4.1894 | 4.0333 | 3.8874 | 3.7509 |
| 17 | 6.3729 | 6.0472 | 5.7487 | 5.4746 | 5.2223 | 4.9897 | 4.7746 | 4.5755 | 4.3908 | 4.2190 | 4.0591 | 3.9099 | 3.7705 |
| 18 | 6.4674 | 6.1280 | 5.8178 | 5.5339 | 5.2732 | 5.0333 | 4.8122 | 4.6079 | 4.4187 | 4.2431 | 4.0799 | 3.9279 | 3.7861 |
| 19 | 6.5504 | 6.1982 | 5.8775 | 5.5845 | 5.3162 | 5.0700 | 4.8435 | 4.6346 | 4.4415 | 4.2627 | 4.0967 | 3.9424 | 3.7985 |
| 20 | 6.6231 | 6.2593 | 5.9288 | 5.6278 | 5.3527 | 5.1009 | 4.8696 | 4.6557 | 4.4603 | 4.2786 | 4.1103 | 3.9539 | 3.8083 |
| 21 | 6.6870 | 6.3125 | 5.9731 | 5.6648 | 5.3837 | 5.1268 | 4.8913 | 4.6750 | 4.4756 | 4.2916 | 4.1212 | 3.9631 | 3.8161 |
| 22 | 6.7429 | 6.3587 | 6.0113 | 5.6964 | 5.4099 | 5.1486 | 4.9094 | 4.6900 | 4.4882 | 4.3021 | 4.1300 | 3.9705 | 3.8223 |
| 23 | 6.7921 | 6.3988 | 6.0442 | 5.7234 | 5.4321 | 5.1668 | 4.9245 | 4.7025 | 4.4985 | 4.3106 | 4.1371 | 3.9764 | 3.8273 |
| 24 | 6.8351 | 6.4338 | 6.0726 | 5.7465 | 5.4509 | 5.1822 | 4.9371 | 4.7128 | 4.5070 | 4.3176 | 4.1428 | 3.9811 | 3.8312 |
| 25 | 6.8729 | 6.4641 | 6.0971 | 5.7662 | 5.4669 | 5.1951 | 4.9476 | 4.7213 | 4.5139 | 4.3232 | 4.1474 | 3.9849 | 3.8342 |
| 26 | 6.9061 | 6.4906 | 6.1182 | 5.7831 | 5.4804 | 5.2060 | 4.9563 | 4.7284 | 4.5196 | 4.3278 | 4.1511 | 3.9879 | 3.8367 |
| 27 | 6.9352 | 6.5135 | 6.1364 | 5.7975 | 5.4919 | 5.2151 | 4.9636 | 4.7342 | 4.5243 | 4.3316 | 4.1542 | 3.9903 | 3.8387 |
| 28 | 6.9607 | 6.5335 | 6.1520 | 5.8099 | 5.5016 | 5.2228 | 4.9697 | 4.7390 | 4.5281 | 4.3346 | 4.1566 | 3.9923 | 3.8402 |
| 29 | 6.9830 | 6.5509 | 6.1656 | 5.8204 | 5.5098 | 5.2292 | 4.9747 | 4.7430 | 4.5312 | 4.3371 | 4.1585 | 3.9938 | 3.8414 |
| 30 | 7.0027 | 6.5660 | 6.1772 | 5.8294 | 5.5168 | 5.2347 | 4.9789 | 4.7463 | 4.5338 | 4.3391 | 4.1601 | 3.9950 | 3.8424 |
| 31 | 7.0199 | 6.5791 | 6.1872 | 5.8371 | 5.5227 | 5.2392 | 4.9824 | 4.7490 | 4.5359 | 4.3407 | 4.1614 | 3.9960 | 3.8432 |
| 32 | 7.0350 | 6.5905 | 6.1959 | 5.8437 | 5.5277 | 5.2430 | 4.9854 | 4.7512 | 4.5376 | 4.3421 | 4.1624 | 3.9968 | 3.8438 |
| 33 | 7.0482 | 6.6005 | 6.2034 | 5.8493 | 5.5320 | 5.2462 | 4.9873 | 4.7531 | 4.5390 | 4.3431 | 4.1632 | 3.9975 | 3.8443 |

# Tail Areas of the Normal Distribution

The table shows the area in the tail of the normal distribution beyond the stated number, Z, of standard deviations from the mean.
The first decimal place of Z is given by the row label and the second place by the column heading.

| Z | 0.00 | 0.01 | 0.02 | 0.03 | 0.04 | 0.05 | 0.06 | 0.07 | 0.08 | 0.09 |
|---|---|---|---|---|---|---|---|---|---|---|
| 0.0 | 0.50000 | 0.49601 | 0.49202 | 0.48803 | 0.48405 | 0.48006 | 0.47608 | 0.47210 | 0.46812 | 0.46414 |
| 0.1 | 0.46017 | 0.45621 | 0.45224 | 0.44828 | 0.44433 | 0.44038 | 0.43644 | 0.43251 | 0.42858 | 0.42466 |
| 0.2 | 0.42074 | 0.41683 | 0.41294 | 0.40905 | 0.40517 | 0.40129 | 0.39743 | 0.39358 | 0.38974 | 0.38591 |
| 0.3 | 0.38209 | 0.37828 | 0.37448 | 0.37070 | 0.36693 | 0.36317 | 0.35942 | 0.35569 | 0.35197 | 0.34827 |
| 0.4 | 0.34458 | 0.34090 | 0.33724 | 0.33360 | 0.32997 | 0.32636 | 0.32276 | 0.31918 | 0.31561 | 0.31207 |
| 0.5 | 0.30854 | 0.30503 | 0.30153 | 0.29806 | 0.29460 | 0.29116 | 0.28774 | 0.28434 | 0.28096 | 0.27760 |
| 0.6 | 0.27425 | 0.27093 | 0.26763 | 0.26435 | 0.26109 | 0.25785 | 0.25463 | 0.25143 | 0.24825 | 0.24510 |
| 0.7 | 0.24196 | 0.23885 | 0.23576 | 0.23270 | 0.22965 | 0.22663 | 0.22363 | 0.22065 | 0.21770 | 0.21476 |
| 0.8 | 0.21186 | 0.20897 | 0.20611 | 0.20327 | 0.20045 | 0.19766 | 0.19490 | 0.19215 | 0.18943 | 0.18673 |
| 0.9 | 0.18406 | 0.18141 | 0.17879 | 0.17619 | 0.17361 | 0.17106 | 0.16853 | 0.16602 | 0.16354 | 0.16109 |
| 1.0 | 0.15866 | 0.15625 | 0.15386 | 0.15151 | 0.14917 | 0.14686 | 0.14457 | 0.14231 | 0.14007 | 0.13786 |
| 1.1 | 0.13567 | 0.13350 | 0.13136 | 0.12924 | 0.12714 | 0.12507 | 0.12302 | 0.12100 | 0.11900 | 0.11702 |
| 1.2 | 0.11507 | 0.11314 | 0.11123 | 0.10935 | 0.10749 | 0.10565 | 0.10384 | 0.10204 | 0.10027 | 0.09853 |
| 1.3 | 0.09680 | 0.09510 | 0.09342 | 0.09176 | 0.09012 | 0.08851 | 0.08692 | 0.08534 | 0.08379 | 0.08226 |
| 1.4 | 0.08076 | 0.07927 | 0.07780 | 0.07636 | 0.07493 | 0.07353 | 0.07215 | 0.07078 | 0.06944 | 0.06811 |
| 1.5 | 0.06681 | 0.06552 | 0.06426 | 0.06301 | 0.06178 | 0.06057 | 0.05938 | 0.05821 | 0.05705 | 0.05592 |
| 1.6 | 0.05480 | 0.05370 | 0.05262 | 0.05155 | 0.05050 | 0.04947 | 0.04846 | 0.04746 | 0.04648 | 0.04551 |
| 1.7 | 0.04457 | 0.04363 | 0.04272 | 0.04182 | 0.04093 | 0.04006 | 0.03920 | 0.03836 | 0.03754 | 0.03673 |
| 1.8 | 0.03593 | 0.03515 | 0.03438 | 0.03363 | 0.03288 | 0.03216 | 0.03144 | 0.03074 | 0.03005 | 0.02938 |
| 1.9 | 0.02872 | 0.02807 | 0.02743 | 0.02680 | 0.02619 | 0.02559 | 0.02500 | 0.02442 | 0.02385 | 0.02330 |
| 2.0 | 0.02275 | 0.02222 | 0.02169 | 0.02118 | 0.02068 | 0.02018 | 0.01970 | 0.01923 | 0.01876 | 0.01831 |
| 2.1 | 0.01786 | 0.01743 | 0.01700 | 0.01659 | 0.01618 | 0.01578 | 0.01539 | 0.01500 | 0.01463 | 0.01426 |
| 2.2 | 0.01390 | 0.01355 | 0.01321 | 0.01287 | 0.01255 | 0.01222 | 0.01191 | 0.01160 | 0.01130 | 0.01101 |
| 2.3 | 0.01072 | 0.01044 | 0.01017 | 0.00990 | 0.00964 | 0.00939 | 0.00914 | 0.00889 | 0.00866 | 0.00842 |
| 2.4 | 0.00820 | 0.00798 | 0.00776 | 0.00755 | 0.00734 | 0.00714 | 0.00695 | 0.00676 | 0.00657 | 0.00639 |
| 2.5 | 0.00621 | 0.00604 | 0.00587 | 0.00570 | 0.00554 | 0.00539 | 0.00523 | 0.00509 | 0.00494 | 0.00480 |
| 2.6 | 0.00466 | 0.00453 | 0.00440 | 0.00427 | 0.00415 | 0.00403 | 0.00391 | 0.00379 | 0.00368 | 0.00357 |
| 2.7 | 0.00347 | 0.00336 | 0.00326 | 0.00317 | 0.00307 | 0.00298 | 0.00289 | 0.00280 | 0.00272 | 0.00264 |
| 2.8 | 0.00256 | 0.00248 | 0.00240 | 0.00233 | 0.00226 | 0.00219 | 0.00212 | 0.00205 | 0.00199 | 0.00193 |
| 2.9 | 0.00187 | 0.00181 | 0.00175 | 0.00170 | 0.00164 | 0.00159 | 0.00154 | 0.00149 | 0.00144 | 0.00140 |

**Tail Areas of the Normal Distribution**—*continued*

| Z | 0.00 | 0.01 | 0.02 | 0.03 | 0.04 | 0.05 | 0.06 | 0.07 | 0.08 | 0.09 |
|---|------|------|------|------|------|------|------|------|------|------|
| 3.0 | 0.00135 | 0.00131 | 0.00126 | 0.00122 | 0.00118 | 0.00114 | 0.00111 | 0.00107 | 0.00104 | 0.00100 |
| 3.1 | 0.00097 | 0.00094 | 0.00090 | 0.00087 | 0.00084 | 0.00082 | 0.00079 | 0.00076 | 0.00074 | 0.00071 |
| 3.2 | 0.00069 | 0.00066 | 0.00064 | 0.00062 | 0.00060 | 0.00058 | 0.00056 | 0.00054 | 0.00052 | 0.00050 |
| 3.3 | 0.00048 | 0.00047 | 0.00045 | 0.00043 | 0.00042 | 0.00040 | 0.00039 | 0.00038 | 0.00036 | 0.00035 |
| 3.4 | 0.00034 | 0.00032 | 0.00031 | 0.00030 | 0.00029 | 0.00028 | 0.00027 | 0.00026 | 0.00025 | 0.00024 |
| 3.5 | 0.00023 | 0.00022 | 0.00022 | 0.00021 | 0.00020 | 0.00019 | 0.00019 | 0.00018 | 0.00017 | 0.00017 |
| 3.6 | 0.00016 | 0.00015 | 0.00015 | 0.00014 | 0.00014 | 0.00013 | 0.00013 | 0.00012 | 0.00012 | 0.00011 |
| 3.7 | 0.00011 | 0.00010 | 0.00010 | 0.00010 | 0.00009 | 0.00009 | 0.00009 | 0.00008 | 0.00008 | 0.00008 |
| 3.8 | 0.00007 | 0.00007 | 0.00007 | 0.00006 | 0.00006 | 0.00006 | 0.00006 | 0.00005 | 0.00005 | 0.00005 |
| 3.9 | 0.00005 | 0.00005 | 0.00004 | 0.00004 | 0.00004 | 0.00004 | 0.00004 | 0.00004 | 0.00003 | 0.00003 |

# Index